I0881653

WRITING ARIZONA, 1912–2012

WRITING ARIZONA 1912–2012

A Cultural and Environmental Chronicle

KIM ENGEL-PEARSON

UNIVERSITY OF OKLAHOMA PRESS : NORMAN

Library of Congress Cataloging-in-Publication Data

Names: Engel-Pearson, Kim, author.
Title: Writing Arizona, 1912–2012 : a cultural and environmental chronicle / Kim Engel-Pearson.
Description: Norman : University of Oklahoma Press, 2017. | Includes bibliographical references and index.
Identifiers: LCCN 2016058029 | ISBN 978-0-8061-5738-2 (pbk. : alk. paper)
Subjects: LCSH: American literature—Arizona—History and criticism. | Arizona—In literature.
Classification: LCC PS571.A6 E54 2017 | DDC 810.8/09791—dc23
LC record available at https://lccn.loc.gov/2016058029

The paper in this book meets the guidelines for permanence and durability of the Committee on Production Guidelines for Book Longevity of the Council on Library Resources, Inc. ∞

For my kids. Your stories give me hope.

CONTENTS

ACKNOWLEDGMENTS

About ten years ago in a classroom on the main campus of Arizona State University I took part in a discussion about identity. In response to the questions “Who are you? How do you identify yourself?” participants gave answers like Polish, Hopi, or Italian, or placed themselves within their religious heritage—Irish Catholic, Mormon. One woman replied Honduran. Often the people had brief stories, sometimes just a sentence or two, about why they identified themselves in a particular way; more than the groups that people identified with, those stories seemed to better answer the questions. I nervously waited for my turn, anxious because until that day I had not realized that I do not identify myself by who my people are but rather where my place is, where I come from. “I’m from a small town in southwestern Colorado,” I said, when it came my turn. My answer seemed like a non sequitur; the question hadn’t been “Where are you from?” but “Who are you?” For me they turned out to be the same question, or at least to have the same answer.

As I explored this connection between who and where, and the stories people tell explaining both, I began to see how stories laid down over time contribute to an understanding of both people and places. What started as a non sequitur became an exploration of place in stories and stories in place. My thanks to Peter Iverson, with whom I explored the idea that both roads and stories provide access to places, a short first version of this study, and to the late Noel Stowe, who provided the intellectual space to explore change over time through the lens of words and assured me that though the tool is different, the craft is still history.

My understanding of the relationships between people and places, and the stories people tell about their places, deepened as I worked on a National Park Service project, rewriting interpretive signs for national monuments in central Arizona. My colleagues and I were tasked with updating obsolete information and making cross-monument connections for visitors. With an eye, and mind, already focused on place as a concept, I realized that three landscapes entwine to create our sense of place—the natural landscape, the space that moves and changes beyond humans; the cultural landscape, the space people affect, move, and change; and the intellectual landscape, the way people think about the place, talk about it, sing about it, write it, rhyme it, and draw it. Thank you to Nancy Dallett for introducing me to historians, geographers, geologists, and archaeologists who study various aspects of place, which broadened my understanding of how people perceive place and how to elucidate context—where we are standing—in the place-creating dynamic.

Thank you to Steve Pyne for his careful reading and counsel. He helped me corral the kraken when interesting (but at that moment, for this work, irrelevant) bits of historical information threatened to take me off course. Many thanks to Paul Hirt for his meticulous editing and his questions that kept me focused on detail and made this work more precise. And thank you to Joni Adamson, who made certain that when minority groups' voices were missing from the written record, they were not silent in my narrative. My thanks to the anonymous readers, who provided thoughtful and comprehensive comments and suggestions. My appreciation to David Wrobel, whose thorough assessment of my study helped immeasurably. I am grateful for the time and care that these historians and other scholars gave my project; the changes I made due to their critiques and suggestions make this a stronger work, and any errors of fact or awkward prose within these pages are completely my own. Thanks also to the folks at the University of Oklahoma Press: acquisitions editor Kent Calder for his patience as he shepherded me through this process, and manuscript editor Sarah Smith and copyeditor Leslie Tingle for their work in preparing this manuscript for publication.

I want to give my deepest appreciation to my family. My parents, Jim and Norma Engel, have encouraged my love of words from the time I was small, when, rather than a first word, so the story goes, I uttered a first sentence. They never minded exploring the "why" question, recognizing with me that often the backstory is the best story. Like me, my husband Byron Pearson also describes who he is by where he is from. A southwesterner with roots three generations deep in Arizona's gritty desert dirt and rich mountain soil, he is my soul mate. Byron has been enthusiastic and encouraging about this project from its inception; his insight, and his willingness to converse endlessly about Arizona history, was invaluable. His historian's brain and word-nerd tendencies complement and challenge my own. This book is dedicated to my kids—Cammy and Cass, Nate and Josh—because when my story was in danger of becoming a declension narrative, they reminded me that stories are always new and always changing, and to my grandparents, Jack and Emma Kinkade, because their stories started it all.

WRITING ARIZONA, 1912–2012

PROLOGUE

Points of Entry

> The first word gives origin to the second, the first and second to the third, the first, second, and third to the fourth, and so on. You cannot begin with the second word and tell the story, for the telling of the story is a cumulative process, a chain of becoming, at last of being.
>
> N. SCOTT MOMADAY

I grew up in a small southwestern Colorado town, a community where everyone knew one another, and had for generations, a place where the Anglo, Mexican, Ute, and Navajo kids in my school were the children of the same families my mom and grandma had gone to school with. My brother and I were the fourth generation of my family to reside there. A few miles south of my childhood home, the Montezuma Valley spreads out to meet the Mesa Verdes. A two-hour drive to the west, the red-rock canyon country of Utah and the high desert plateau beckon. To the north, within minutes of my town, the foothills of the San Juan Mountains give way to snowy peaks, and with a hard morning hike, tree line is attainable before lunch.

The town has always been small, but years ago it boasted three car dealerships and a movie theater. That was before I was born, but those places are part of my memories anyway because of the stories attached to the vacant lot where the theater burned down and the big empty building that once housed the Ford garage. My town is situated in a river valley, with the buildings along the north side of the river, the river nestled up against a juniper- and oak-brush-clad mesa. Snowmelt fed, in spring the river runs thick and red, swift and determined. Official measurements during spring runoff calculate depth, but when I was a kid townspeople unofficially measured the river by how many feet, or inches, remained between its surface and the bridge. Several years, the runoff crested across the bridge. But July along the river is wonderful. In places only a foot deep over gravel and stones, it shimmers and whispers beneath cottonwood trees as the zip and whir of fly-fishing reels signify relaxation and recreation.

Small towns have few secrets and many stories, narratives that belong to the place—words that grow out of its rocky soil, fed by mountain streams—and to the people who share them. My grandpa was an outstanding storyteller. He owned the Chevy dealership that housed one of the few gas stations in town, and he seemed to know everyone in Montezuma County. I learned at an early age that every place has more than one story. Depending on what we were doing on any given day, a different story belonged to the place and the activity. Fishing on the Dolores River brought forth the story of my mom's first catch, in later years the story of my first catch, but once Grandpa told a cautionary tale about the boys (one of them my great-uncle) who drowned. Other river stories centered on floods, the day a thunderstorm upriver brought water pouring down the valley and washed out the bridge, or the time the high water decided to take its old route through the barnyard. Sometimes the stories included my grandpa or my family, but more often the narratives involved people my grandpa had known and events that had happened before I was born. The place I grew up in was a varied story landscape, as rich in words as it was in natural places and diverse people.

All of my stories begin as Dolores River Valley stories. Whether or not you have ever been there, it now exists for you because I have told you a story about it. I am a product of that place; growing up there, and hearing the stories of its natural and cultural landscapes, affects in some measure how I view the world. And my story about the place has created it for you; my words have constructed an image of the Dolores River Valley for you to ponder.

Words

I have always seen the world through words. When I hear a story, I see the words as they flow across space, each word as it is articulated, connected to the word preceding and the word following. When I view a landscape, I see the place through words, either as stories I know that are connected to it, as long chains of words laid out on the land, or as inquiries I have about it, question marks punctuating sage-covered hills or empty buildings. I also understand the world through words, comprehending best when I read about places and events.

A lover of words—how they fit together, how a group of words employed in a certain order creates a place or an event for a listener or a reader, how once turned into a story the words exist forever—I have always been interested in the process of story making. I listened as Grandpa would alter a story he had told many times to make it a lesson and as he added or left out details to suit the occasion. The place or event that the story was attached to in these different tellings had not changed, but the narrative did.

Words into Stories

I also noticed that people new to our town had to learn the stories that belonged to the place. A simple statement—"We're taking the horses down to McElmo tomorrow," for example—would mean nothing to a newcomer. To a longtime resident of Montezuma County, McElmo Canyon denoted winter range for cattle and horses; my grandma knew it as a place to gather wild rhubarb along the irrigation ditches and buy cantaloupe from the dryland farmers; area high school kids knew it as a post–football game party location. Embedded in our knowledge of the place McElmo were stories about early ranchers and a vague understanding that the land had once belonged to the Ute tribe, stories we knew existed but were intangible to us. The narrative about McElmo Canyon told to the newcomer depended on who was telling the story. The place would become real in whatever manner the narrative was told. The many layers of stories covering a single place fascinated me.

I have lived most of my adult life in Arizona. When I moved to Flagstaff to attend college, I became the newcomer. Because I had grown up in an environment where the stories were part of what made the place and its people, naturally I wanted to know the narratives that belong to my new home. I became a student of Arizona stories and experienced from the other side the myriad narratives attached to any one place. My own stories of northern Arizona had been formed directionally, from north to south. When I envisioned the San Francisco Peaks, I viewed them from their north side; the Peaks had always been "south" for me. At Northern Arizona University, however, many Arizona stories began south of the mountain; Flagstaff is "north" for many NAU students. For longtime Flagstaff residents the narratives are not directionally oriented at all but are central to their lives, the way Dolores River Valley stories are for me.

How a person mentally processes a narrative depends on where that person is standing.[1] The stories people hear and tell are refracted by their experiences and their perceptions. This is important when looking at narratives about and arising from a place; different experiences beget different narratives, creating different places but anchored to the same place. It is the power in the words of a story, in the variety of narratives about and enabled by Arizona, and how the words are used that interests me. All of the words laid down over time, word by word, as N. Scott Momaday says, story by story, until we stand one hundred years later in an Arizona where the narratives reflect a diverse and multilayered cultural landscape, yet a place where a constitutional amendment declares only English words are "official."

Words on the Land

Once created, both spoken and written narratives have an existence separate from their creator; the story becomes an entity apart from its author or narrator.[2] Narratives about, and generated from, places are no exception. Writers and storytellers bring understanding of a place based on their perceptions and experiences; readers and listeners come with their own perspectives. The written narrative landscape of a place, examined over time, reflects these differing experiences and perspectives.

Words help write a place into being, according to Momaday, the first word giving origin to the second, the first and second to the third, and so on. Momaday's narrative in *The Names* writes his life into being and at the same time creates for his readers the places he has lived and visited and the events he has experienced. He describes this process of creating and becoming in his address and subsequent essay "The Man Made of Words," as he explains how an event central to Kiowa identity, a night of meteor showers in 1833, had to be dealt with in words to be understood.[3] The story had to be told to give the event meaning. Similarly, in an analysis of George R. Stewart's *Names on the Land*, Wallace Stegner explains, "Nothing is comprehended, much less possessed, until it has been given a name."[4] Stories facilitate understanding, words on the land connecting people to their places.

Stories about and grown out of the land have been told for centuries. In "The Sense of Place," Stegner discusses Yeats and the legends that belong to the land in Ireland and suggests that America is too large and new to have this sort of thing. However, places in America and the American West do have legends attached to them, and places are often named and known for these narratives. In *Wisdom Sits in Places*, Keith Basso explores such places and studies the connected nature of Western Apache language, history, and place. The names of the places evoke the stories of the past, centering the people morally and anchoring their identity to the landscape.[5] Marsha Weisiger makes a similar observation about Navajo place-naming practices, every name a description of the place or thing being named, so that "in naming nature, Diné delineated the richness that they saw in a landscape that outsiders often viewed as impoverished wasteland."[6]

But the Navajo names and Western Apache narratives attached to a place could not be imparted to people who did not speak or understand the words. If all people spoke the same language, and if the words meant the same thing in every culture, then the Spanish explorers coming into what would become the American Southwest would have heard the legends and stories attached to the place. Likewise, the British settlers landing on America's Atlantic shore would not have been entering what was for them a blank page of a place but instead a place with stories covering it, narratives they could understand. The creation of a place often occurs in words, spoken and written. When culturally and linguistically different people enter a landscape that is new to them, the place is created anew in their language.

Stegner also describes the contributions words, stories, make in creating a place. "The fact that Daniel Boone killed a bear at a certain spot in Kentucky did not make it a place," Stegner writes. "It began to be one, though, when he remembered the spot as Bear Run, and other people picked up the name and called their settlement by it. . . . The very fact that people remembered Boone's bear-killing, and told about it, added something of placeness. No place is a place until things that have happened in it are remembered in history, ballads, yarns, legends, or monuments."[7] The stories do not have to be true. Novels, poems, and songs contribute to place making as well. If we think about place in this manner, a place does not exist until it is named, until it is created in words, until it is spoken or written into being. Americans have rewritten and overwritten the country's landscape, forcing their own narratives on the places they perceived as blank pages and changing stories as they translated older, non-English narratives.

Equally true, however, a place also contributes to, facilitates, the words written about it or emanating from it. A desert plain populated with saguaro cacti and granite boulders will (probably) inspire a narrative different from a story motivated by a seventh-floor walkup in a city center. But what if that city is at the edge of the Sonoran Desert? As Momaday says, "None of us live apart from the land entirely."[8] The land and the stories about it are cogenerating, each contributing to the creation of the other. Through these stories, in the writing and telling and in the listening and reading, humanity can come to an understanding of the world and our place in it.

William Cronon explores the relationship between the natural world, narratives, and history in "A Place for Stories," using stories written about the Dust Bowl as his lens. He notes that in seeking to comprehend the events that culminated in the Dust Bowl and its aftermath, contemporaries of the catastrophe and historians writing about it later explained and contextualized the issues differently, depending on their own perceptions and experiences. The Dust Bowl narratives, and all place-centered stories, are never complete; they are rewritten as people continue to explain and understand their world. Geographer Tim Ingold describes this as developing a "dwelling perspective," explaining that "telling a story is not like weaving a tapestry to *cover up* the world[;] it is a way of guiding the attention of the listeners or readers *into* it."[9] Examining the written narratives about and brought forth from natural and cultural landscapes reveals this phenomenon: past words about a place and present words about it are met at the current moment, when the reader consumes the words.

Cronon writes, "The importance of the natural world, its objective effects on people, and the concrete ways people affect it in turn," are at the heart of environmental historians' project.[10] Stories not only give meaning to a place, but the stories written about a place also reveal writers' perceptions, views about what is important and useful, what motivates or attracts, perceptions derived from an actual landscape. Those perceptions written down also create an image of the place for a reader. Arizona's natural landscapes, its deserts, forests, mountains, and valleys, affected the lives of the people who visited and occupied them. Arizona also was written into being and, like the Kiowa night of falling stars, had to be dealt with in words to be understood. This study is an exploration of that process, how Arizona's natural and cultural places contribute to the creation of stories and how stories contribute to the creation of Arizona.[11]

Words and Arizona

From before Arizona became a state in 1912 to the day its citizens celebrated one hundred years as a state in 2012, words have played a role in making it the place it is. When we examine the words about Arizona that have been readily available to the English-reading public, the importance of the power of the printed word becomes clear. Arizona became the place it is in the twenty-first century, in part, because people with power—people in the federal and state governments, and boosters and business leaders—wrote about it in such a way as to influence growth and tourism, often at the expense of minority groups and the environment. A lack of access to the means of exercising the power of words meant that the Arizona known and experienced by Native Americans, for example, was absent from the written narrative until the second half of the twentieth century. Those who wrote and published in English, who had access to and control over the means of publishing, had an advantage (one of many) over those whose narratives were told orally and in other languages; the Arizona written into being in English words became the Arizona most well known to the nation and the world.

The narratives about Arizona did change over time, from literature dominated by boosterism and promotion that was written predominately by Anglo men at the time of statehood (an intellectual landscape that obscured narratives not written down or told in English and that neglected stories not told by men) to a body of literature with many layers, many voices. The words of Native Americans, Hispanics, women, and environmentalists created representations of Arizona that earlier stories had not envisioned. Those who control the words control the narrative, which determines the nature of the place written into being. Natural and cultural landscapes entwine with words about and brought forth from them to create a place.

Sampling all of the narratives written about and enabled by Arizona over one hundred years would be unwieldy, if not impossible. Instead, to capture the span of published material contributing to the creation of Arizona in words drawn forth from its natural landscape, I chose dates at twenty-five year intervals, sections of time marking statehood and its twenty-fifth, fiftieth, seventy-fifth, and one-hundredth anniversaries. Rather like guidebooks for stops along a journey, or core samples of geologic formations, these chapters offer a way to delve more deeply into the written intellectual landscape of the place. Short Overlook sections between the chapters provide a view of the intervening twenty-five years, points from which to survey the historical plain. Just as strata maps provide context for the core samples, and similar to the perspective gained from "you are here" maps along roadways, the

Overlooks outline key cultural, political, and economic developments that occurred over time and within which the narrative layers were laid down. The study is arranged chronologically; just as words arranged in a sentence need the first word first, the second next, and so on, to give words meaning, so too narratives about a place are built on each other. What did people know about Arizona at a given moment in time? What types of literature, philosophy, or policy were produced in Arizona at that given moment? And how did the natural landscape influence the words written about it?

I chose sources from several genres, including official state publications, newspapers, novels, poetry, autobiography, journals, federal publications, and *Arizona Highways* magazine, sources that demonstrate a wide readership (award winners and bestsellers, for example) and that would have been available to the English-reading public. Any reader is an active participant in the words-creating-place process. "The 'meaning' does not reside ready-made 'in' the text or 'in' the reader," according to literary theorist and reading educator Louise M. Rosenblatt, "but happens or comes into being during the transaction between reader and text." Rosenblatt recognizes the human ability to "evoke images of things or events not present, and even never experienced."[12] This ability is enacted as an author writes a narrative and is acted out again and again each time the story is consumed, words creating for readers. But readers bring their own contexts—experiences, memories, ideas, biases—to a text, hence the difficulty in assessing the meaning taken from the narrative without conversation with the reader or access to a reader's notes, marginalia, or diary entries.[13] This study, then, is concerned with the words that create place and how those stories are used. Thus my attempt to focus primarily on widely available and heavily read texts, assuring that the narratives I chose would have created, in some form, the place Arizona in the minds of members of the English-reading public.

When we examine the formation of Arizona narratives, themes emerge. Literature boosting the state is present throughout its hundred-year span, but it is especially prevalent at the fifty- and one-hundred-year anniversaries. Descriptions of the state's natural landscapes appear in many forms. In early booster narratives, Arizona is land and resources to be exploited; at mid-twentieth century, land ethic and conservation themes emerge. The dichotomy of "modern miracle" versus "Old West" and the cliché of temporal extremes—the oldest landscape–youngest state, or the oldest natural landscape–youngest cultural landscape (until American Indian narratives in their own words become part of Arizona's written record)—are also prominent characteristics in the narratives.

Arizona has been created in fiction and verse, with inherent contrasts: the romantic westerns of Zane Grey and the stark portrayals of federal Indian policy by Oliver La Farge describe the same places in vastly different ways, and Sharlot Hall's poetry proclaims the dominance of men over the Arizona land while Wendy Rose reveals the Hopi reverence for the place that she cannot fully claim. Memoirs, inhabiting the desert narratives, range from pioneer reminiscences to modern stories of homelessness and include early twentieth-century Native American autobiographies in the as-told-to genre (narratives filtered through Anglo perceptions) and Native American memoirs written in the authors' own words in the 1970s and 1980s. Finally, Arizona's official words, those in the state's constitution and added as right-to-work and English-only amendments and anti-immigration measures, reflect citizens' perceptions. The contrary nature of Arizonans who held the power to affect the words produced a progressive, labor-friendly constitution, but over time the liberal character of the document has been eroded.

Words into Stories in Early Arizona

The place that became the state of Arizona had been inhabited and explored for centuries before Europeans arrived. The early desert and plateau dwellers, whose empty homes had become places of mystery and wonder by the early twentieth century, told stories about the place in which they lived, evoking an image of the place in words for their listeners. The region was spoken into consciousness in the languages of native people long before Euro-Americans immigrated into the land. Those narratives complicated the place when Arizona's Native

Americans wrote and published their own stories and the historic connections between the occupants of the ancient structures and modern people became accessible to English speakers and readers.

Native American traditional knowledge encompasses these places and includes the time when these structures, built by the ancestors of modern tribes, were inhabited. Narratives that were told and performed orally for centuries, the original stories that created the place for listeners, also shaped the listeners' history. The narrative landscape entwined people and place; each did not exist without the other.[14] For example, Hopi (and modern Pueblo) origin narratives connect the tribe to the ancestral Puebloan people who inhabited the Colorado Plateau region. Hopi people refer to the ancient structures as footprints, places marking their ancestors' migration.[15] In southern Arizona the deer songs of the Yaqui people and Tohono O'odham songs to bring the rain have been sung for generations.[16] Navajo origin stories center the people within the four sacred mountains (Mount Humphreys, Mount Taylor, Mount Hesperus, and Mount Blanca), and even the place names of the Western Apaches anchor the people to the land; entire stories are embedded within the name of a hill or canyon.[17] These narratives, spoken rather than written, had already created the place in words long before anyone put pen to paper to give it meaning.

Seventeenth- and eighteenth-century Spanish priests and explorers traveled from the south and east into Arizona's interior and wrote about their journeys. The nineteenth century brought American explorers and settlers, miners, railroad companies, and soldiers entering Arizona from the east and across the Colorado River from the west. Mormon farmers entered from Utah, first occupying the Arizona Strip on the north side of Grand Canyon's natural barrier, then, after establishing a Colorado River crossing at Lee's Ferry, settling along the Mogollon Rim and among the valleys of the Little Colorado, San Francisco, Gila, and Salt Rivers. As settlers and visitors to Arizona, Americans dealt with the place in words in several ways. They brought their own stories and created new ones to explain landscapes markedly different from the ones they had known. They rewrote older stories, translating words from indigenous languages and Spanish into English, and adding to or subtracting from the narratives to conform the stories to their own cultural understanding. They remade the exotic landscapes into forms they could understand and fashioned an imagined future from the wealth of natural resources they encountered.

As a model of how newcomers encountered and translated, consider Elliot Coues's 1900 English translation of Father Francisco Garcés's diaries from his 1776 explorations of Sonora and Arizona. Coues, army surgeon, scientist, and historian, so heavily footnoted Garcés's text that it is as much Coues as Garcés who created the idea of Arizona for readers of the journals. A virtual palimpsest—words written over partly erased words on a manuscript—Garcés translated into Spanish the narratives told in the Hualapai language, which Coues then translated into English. Coues's familiarity with and interest in the journey allowed him to annotate seemingly mile by mile. Whereas Garcés wrote, "June 7. I traveled four leagues east, and arrived at the Jaguallapas [Hualapai]" and described the place simply, "At this rancheria there is an arroyo with running water, plenty of grass, much game, and much seed of *chia*," Coues's version of the story adds to the narrative. "Crossing what remained to him of the Sacramento Valley, Garcés finds the Hualapai or Walapai Indians living in the vicinity of present Kingman, seat of Mojave County," Coues wrote in his translator's notes, in an over five-hundred-word rewriting of Garcés's concise journal entry. Coues built contemporary (circa 1900) images from Garcés's eighteenth-century translations of Hualapai words.[18] His rewriting of Garcés's encounters with indigenous peoples added another layer of words obscuring Native American voices of the time. The Native Americans' own stories in their languages existed first. Then Garcés's stories about these people were written in Spanish and told from his perspective. In Coues's 1900 translation, his perspective about the various tribes in his extensive notes were added.

Americans attempted to comprehend the natural landscapes of Arizona by capturing the place in words. American explorers had been coping with and writing about the unique and awe-inspiring (or plain awful, in some of the descriptions) Arizona landscapes since the mid-nineteenth century. First in reports to Congress, later in articles and books, the descriptions of the land these men explored, the people they met, and the experiences they enjoyed and endured created a place in the minds of their readers.

Commissioned by the U.S. secretary of war, Joseph Ives's 1857 expedition followed the Colorado River to Grand Canyon and traveled east through the northern part of what would become Arizona. Ives's report to Congress, published in 1861, quickly dispensed with the stated purpose of his mission, which was to affirm the river's navigability. He then committed a significant portion of the report to the specifics of a place of remarkable, rugged beauty and interesting people. Ives stated, "The region explored after leaving the navigable portion of the Colorado—though, in a scientific point of view, of the highest interest and presenting natural features whose strange sublimity is perhaps unparalleled in any part of the world—is not of much value. Most of it is uninhabitable, and a great deal of it is impassable." However, rather than submit a brief report writing off the territory as a beautiful yet useless wasteland, Ives composed his expedition journal into nearly three hundred pages detailing the geography, zoology, and ethnography of the northern regions of the territory, creating an Arizona as a region of dualities for the readers of this report, a place of uselessness and possibility, of barrenness and unimaginable beauty, a place uninhabitable and yet inhabited.[19]

No landscape was as remarkable as Grand Canyon, a place that revealed the inadequacy of descriptive language. Readers were challenged by two countervisions, John Wesley Powell's from the river and Clarence Dutton's from the rim. The popular edition of Powell's report to Congress, *Exploration of the Colorado River of the West* (published in 1875, republished and expanded into *Canyons of the Colorado* in 1895), became famous for its visual descriptions and the chronicle of his trip through Grand Canyon. A travel book published by the Atchison, Topeka, and Santa Fe Railway Company between 1902 and 1906, *Titan of Chasms*, included an eleven-page essay by Powell that reiterated much of his previous work for a new audience, travelers on the AT&SF heading west. "It is a region more difficult to traverse than the Alps or the Himalayas, but if strength and courage are sufficient for the task, by a year's toil a concept of sublimity can be obtained never again to be equaled on the hither side of Paradise," he stated.[20] Powell's readers could conclude that this Arizona was mysterious, remarkable, and unreachable except by a few daring souls who explored the hard, rugged terrain and re-created with words its unusual challenges and exceptional landscapes; ensconced safely and comfortably in their railcars, travelers read even as they passed near the very places Powell described.

Dutton's *Tertiary History of the Grand Canyon District* (1882) presented a parallel view from the canyon's rim, the view most visitors would experience. Dutton's is a thick book, dense with information yet eloquently written, which sought to comprehend the vast landscape at geological and literary levels, much as naturalists endeavored to understand Arizona's natural landscapes seventy years later. "The earth suddenly sinks at our feet to illimitable depths," Dutton wrote upon reaching the edge of the great chasm. He described the view from Powell's Point: "A stretch of the river six miles long is in full view, flowing in the dark depths of the granite more than a mile below." Writing the place into being for readers, he portrayed a view that could also be seen by regular folks traveling to the canyon, unlike the descriptions of the sheer rock walls viewed from the river that only a few adventurers would see.[21]

While explorers' journals and reports detailed desolate expanses of wilderness and astonishing scenery, other books and pamphlets disclaimed the rugged wildness, embraced its progress toward "civilization," and extolled the virtues of Arizona's climate and resources. Again this duality—desolation and possibility—created an Arizona in the minds of readers that was at once barren and verdant, harsh and pleasant, uninhabitable and the perfect place for settlements. Writers of the state have produced booster literature for over a century, the narratives employing words about its natural landscapes to promote economic development rather than a scientific, experiential, or moral understanding of the place.

"Arizona is a land of marvels for the scientist and the sightseer," wrote Patrick Hamilton, introducing Arizona to readers in 1881. "The topography of the country in variety, weird beauty, and massive grandeur, is not excelled on the continent."[22] Hamilton was editor of the

Prescott Democrat when the territorial legislators commissioned him to compile a handbook in 1880 to expound on Arizona's resources and entice immigrants to the territory. Several editions of *The Resources of Arizona* were published, each more expansive than the previous. Two separate editions published in 1881 were printed at the territorial capital in Prescott. The third edition grew to 275 pages, a fourth to 414, and the book was sent to A. L. Bancroft and Company in San Francisco for professional publication. Such was the impact of Hamilton's *Resources* on the perception of Arizona that in an 1885 speech to the thirteenth territorial legislature, Territorial Governor Frederick A. Tritle extolled the book's "thoroughly reliable and exhaustive resume of the attractions and resources of the Territory" and claimed "it has had an extensive circulation, not only in the United States, but I have been informed in Great Britain and Canada."[23]

Railroad companies participated in creating Arizona in words as well, as seen by the AT&SF travel book. The railroad travel books added new words to Eastern travelers' vocabularies. *A New Guide to the Pacific Coast, Santa Fe Route* described "buttes, mesas, plateaus, and canyons," desert language naming the natural landscape of the Southwest.[24] The Southern Pacific Railroad Company employed literature to create a place attractive for settlement. The booklet *New Arizona* was a condensed, easy-to-read, forty-page volume distributed at train stations. Published in 1900, its purpose was to attract wealthy men with money to invest. The pamphlet contains "a thoughtful message addressed to thoughtful men. . . . If you have a little money, or, better still, a great deal, there are few countries that have within themselves the power to respond so quickly, surely, and generously to well-directed efforts."[25] Boosters imagined a future Arizona prospering under the influence of wealthy men. Their understanding of the place, the Arizona their words created for readers, left no room for wilderness, minorities, or working-class people.

In *The Desert*, John C. Van Dyke's 1901 book about a two-year wander through the desert Southwest, including Arizona, the art historian and critic wrote poetically and passionately (if sometimes inaccurately) about the natural landscape. Recent scholarship reveals that he did not make the trip in the way he described, but his words built an image of the place for readers whether or not he ever saw it. Through several printings and editions, *The Desert* created the arid landscape for early twentieth-century readers in a way that gave it aesthetic value. "To speak about sparing anything because it is beautiful is to waste one's breath and incur ridicule in the bargain," Van Dyke wrote, presaging the words of naturalists and environmentalists several generations hence. Often sounding like Joseph Wood Krutch, Ann Woodin, Ann Zwinger, and Edward Abbey, Van Dyke decried the extractive industries and their destruction of the land. "Men . . . must have copper if they wreck all the mountains of Montana and Arizona," he lamented. "They have stripped the land of its robes of beauty, and what have they given in its place? Weeds, wire fences, oil-derricks, board shanties and board towns—things that not even a 'practical man' can do less than curse at."[26]

Arizona at the time of statehood was remote and wild, but its narratives already revealed opposing ideas about the landscape. Themes that would mark the literature of Arizona in ensuing decades—desolation, beauty, opportunity, loss—emerged in prestatehood narratives. Those themes would be developed and challenged throughout the state's first one hundred years.

OVERLOOK

Arizona Territory

PRELUDE TO A STATE

"Shut Out from Progress," exclaimed the *Washington Post* headline describing "the isolated conditions of the territory of Arizona." In 1878 the territory was nearly inaccessible. The railroad lines had not yet reached its borders, and its interior contained few roads. "Broken ranges of mountains, swelling occasionally into lofty peaks and pine-covered mesas, and alternating evenly with elevated valleys or mountain basins of greater or less size, represent the face of the country," the newspaper reported.[1] Twenty-five years later the *Los Angeles Times* could report on "the great and growing territory of Arizona," with its thriving copper mines, its increasingly profitable cattle ranching, and its agricultural production poised to yield considerable harvests. The territory was in excellent financial condition, the *Times* reported, its floating debt "wiped out" and "a substantial cash balance on hand."[2] In the intervening years the population of Arizona grew from just over 40,000 in 1880 to 122,931 in 1900, aided by transportation lines in the opening of the railroads and by communication lines that increased exposure through newspaper articles and a concerted effort by boosters, businessmen, and territorial government leaders to promote their territory.[3]

As railroads began to cross the territory, Arizona became less isolated. In the fall of 1877 the Southern Pacific Railroad extended only to Yuma from the west; it reached Tucson on March 20, 1880. In the next year Chinese workers laid track across the territory's southeastern desert and arrived at the New Mexico Territory border in May 1881. In northern Arizona tracklayers for the Atlantic and Pacific Railroad (soon to become the Atchison, Topeka, and Santa Fe Railway) built its road along the thirty-fifth parallel in the spring and summer of 1880 and reached Needles, California, in June 1883. Throughout the territory dozens of regional rail lines connected mining and lumber camps to the small communities where ore and logs could be sent to market and supplies could be brought in.[4]

An issue that had characterized Arizona from its inception as a territory, its ongoing Indian wars, led Territorial Governor John C. Fremont to declare in 1878, "The solution of the Indian question is to be found in placing the Indians under the absolute and plenary control of the army." In 1905 the *LA Times* reported Native Americans were being "civilized" (as defined by the writer), asserting, "The Arizona Indians during the past few years have been advancing most encouragingly toward civilization. . . . No trouble has been had with any of the tribes."[5] The land that became America's Arizona Territory had been the home of Indian peoples for centuries. Hopi farmers built villages on the mesa tops, nomadic Navajo and Apache tribes hunted and raided throughout the region, and O'odham peoples cultivated their crops along the Gila River. As Spanish explorers and priests advanced further north, Native Americans adopted new crops and livestock into their ways of life at the same time they resisted conquest and Catholicism.

In the minds of Euro-Americans, the nomadic, raiding tribes were the least desirable and the most in need of their version of "civilizing." When northern Mexico became part of the United States in 1848, after the Mexican-American War, Anglo settlement was already well underway (further aided by the Gadsden Purchase [1853]). As Anglo colonizers inundated Apache lands, the new settlements, mining communities, and ranches provided opportunities for Apache raiders. These settlers demanded protection, and the U.S. government complied. The Apache wars spanned over twenty years, culminating with Geronimo and his Chiricahua Apache band's surrender in 1886 and subsequent removal to Florida.

Arizona Territory boosters downplayed the threat posed by the conflicts, while newspapers sensationalized the danger. Charles Lummis (of *Out West* magazine fame) believed the coverage of the Apache wars was inaccurate and exaggerated. In March 1886 he traveled to Arizona Territory to cover the surrender of Geronimo's band to Gen. George Crook. The *Los Angeles Times* published Lummis's reports in a series of articles that sought to provide less superficial and more objective coverage. Upon arriving at Fort Bowie, Lummis learned that Geronimo and three dozen members of his tribe had fled their temporary encampment and that the military campaign was resuming. Lummis convinced General Crook that his coverage would be fair, and he was allowed to stay at the fort and follow the troops into the field. For three months he sent his reports back to the *Times*, stories that countered the prevailing narrative of Indians as savage and bloodthirsty. Lummis revealed, "So long as Arizona whites were not being killed by Apaches, the Indians were good business, especially when they were on the warpath, because then Federal funds flowed into the territory to support the many soldiers necessary to subdue even small bands of Apaches."[6] The *Times* gave readers images entirely different from most newspaper coverage at the time, both of the Apache people and an Anglo man's perception. "If Providence had particularly laid itself out to back up, by sample, what I have said about Arizona economizers of truth and the way Apache war news has been propagated," Lummis wrote regarding the attempts to recapture Geronimo, "it couldn't have done much better than in some of the developments of the last few days."[7]

The railroads opened Arizona Territory to increased settlement and brought it more attention in the last decade of the nineteenth century, and the territorial government produced more publications promoting the place, such as John A. Black's *Arizona: The Land of Sunshine and Silver, Health and Prosperity* (1890). The territorial commissioner of immigration at the time of this 127-page book's publication in 1890, Black assured readers that Arizona was no longer a wild, lawless place, but instead had become the perfect place to settle. "The rustlers and highwaymen were brought to justice," he wrote, "the Apache was placed on reservations . . . the mountains, rich in precious ores, made to re-echo the sound of the miner's pick and the stamp mill. By aid of irrigation the sage brush plains were turned into waving fields of grain and orchards of golden fruit, until today no section of the Union offers better inducements to the laborer, the farmer, the orchardist, the capitalist, and the invalid than Arizona."[8]

As the territory's representative, Black discussed schools, providing evidence of the importance of education to the territorial leaders, stating, "All children between six and eighteen without respect to color or race, are entitled to an admission into the schools and an education. . . .

Teachers are liberally paid with the intent that the best possible talent shall be secured and that the Arizona public schools shall rank with the highest."[9] Access to water was vital in Arizona Territory, and Black addressed land and water laws and reclamation. "Persons making desert land entries must acquire a clear right to the use of sufficient water to irrigate the whole of the land," he explained. "The whole tract, and each legal subdivision, must actually be irrigated. The object of this law is to redeem the unproductive lands, and make them highly productive by artificial irrigation."[10] Black articulated the common viewpoint at the time that land was useless without water, thus the need for irrigation to make land useful, profitable.

William E. Smythe promoted settlement and reclamation in his book *The Conquest of Arid America*, published first in 1899 and reprinted in 1905, declaring that irrigation would turn the barren, unproductive Western desert into fertile green fields. While not specifically an Arizona promotional tract, Smythe's book encouraged the large reclamation and irrigation projects that would eventually water the state. In 1899 he wrote, "The capital city of Phoenix—risen from the ashes of a forgotten people—is the pulsating heart of the new life of Arizona. . . . Phoenix is distinctly modern, and almost wholly the offspring of irrigation."[11] The Anglo farmers of the Salt River Valley took up Smythe's call. They had already repurposed several of the ancient Hohokam canals for their own irrigation systems. Aided by the Reclamation Act of 1902—the federal government's commitment to finance water projects (chiefly dams) through loans that would be repaid by the farmers who used the water produced by the dams' irrigation projects, and eventually by the power generated by the dams—in 1903 the Salt River Water Users' Association was formed to manage the development and construction of Theodore Roosevelt Dam on the Salt River. The dam was one of the first five large-scale irrigation projects across the West authorized under the reclamation act and was completed in 1911, a year before statehood.[12]

While much was made in the decades before statehood of Arizona's mining, farming, and ranching opportunities and successes in newspaper reports and booster tracts, its citizens also embarked on a program of institution building. Normal schools (schools to train teachers) began in Tempe and Flagstaff, and the university was established in Tucson.[13] Recognizing the importance of the historical record, the territorial legislature established the Arizona Historical Society and provided for an official historian in 1864, a year after the territory was established. Twenty years later people who feared that their stories of the trials they endured while overcoming the wilderness would be lost to time organized the Arizona Pioneers Historical Society.[14]

The territory at the time of statehood was also becoming a place of scientific and cultural significance. Casa Grande Ruins was designated a federal archaeological reservation in 1878 by President Benjamin Harrison, providing for the protection and preservation of this fragile site. Six other national monuments were designated by presidential authority, including Montezuma Castle (for ethnological significance), Tumacacori (for historical significance), and Petrified Forest and Grand Canyon (for scientific significance).[15] In 1894 Percival Lowell established his observatory on a hill at the edge of Flagstaff, and in 1899 C. Hart Merriam studied the San Francisco Peaks region of the Colorado Plateau, developing his "life zones" concept.[16]

Herbert Howe Bancroft's widely read *West American History (1902),* published ten years before Arizona became a state, discussed many aspects of Arizona Territory's development. The lack of progress decreed by the *Washington Post* in 1878 had been remediated. A civil society, as westward-looking Anglos defined it, had been planted along with farms and extractive industries. In 1902 Bancroft could remark on the territory's "healthful climate, fertile soil, and mineral wealth" and state that Arizona and New Mexico "are fortunate in their mid-continental position, which has given them railroad communication with the east and west and south. . . . The danger of serious Indian troubles is believed to be past."[17] Arizona Territory was, according to the historian, well positioned to become the nation's next state.

CHAPTER 1

Defining a New State, 1912

ON FEBRUARY 14, 1912, after waiting fifty years, Arizona Territory became the State of Arizona. Its citizens had spent those years advocating for their region, describing its virtues and potential in written narratives, often countering visitors' and nonresidents' narratives that expressed views of the limitations of the place. Both boosters and critics described the characteristics of the landscape and its people as they perceived them, engaging in the work of defining Arizona in words. The written narratives about and coming from Arizona at the time of statehood portrayed an Anglo perspective, written from Anglo experiences, and created an image of the place for Anglo consumption, for English speakers and readers.

At the time of statehood, Arizona was remote and in some ways inhospitable, a space to travel through, not a destination. The population of Arizona in 1910 was just over two hundred thousand.[1] Until railroads were built through the territory, it was accessible only by horse and wagon and on foot. The railroads opened the territory to the nation by making travel easier, and Arizona towns along the rail lines began advertising their districts as destinations rather than simply as stops along the way to somewhere else. The railroads participated in regional boosterism as well, advertising Arizona to travelers in the eastern United States and in Europe. The Southern Pacific Railroad magazine *Abroad*, for example, intended for a European tourist audience, devoted its March 1912 issue to the new state. "Phoenix is cosmopolitan, representatives of every state in the union being here," the guide declared. "We venture to say that the charm of the desert, the sense of freedom out-of-doors, the large spaces, and the beauty of the environing mountains will steadily bring to this entire center men of culture and of original ideas."[2] The descriptions employed here to describe Arizona became familiar phrases in a variety of publications about the place.

Arizona at the time of statehood boasted few roads, and the roads it had were local, surfaced with dirt and gravel, and connected mines, ranches, and small communities with larger towns. Funding for roads was limited. The federal government restricted borrowing by territorial governments, therefore most of Arizona's roads prestatehood were financed and built by the counties. In 1909 the territorial legislature established a two-road highway system. The east-to-west road began in Duncan near the border with New Mexico Territory; it traversed the mining country of the southeast, passed through Clifton, Safford, and Globe on the way to the Roosevelt dam site and the future Roosevelt Lake, then on to Mesa, Tempe, and Phoenix, ending the long trip across the southwestern desert in Yuma. The north-south route began in Flagstaff, ran through Prescott, turned southeast to Phoenix and Tucson, and culminated at Douglas on the Mexican border. None of the roads were paved.[3]

On the eve of statehood, then, the Arizona that most nonresidents knew was one created in words and pictures; and in 1912, before color photography was widely used, written narratives would have reached the largest audience. Residents of the territory wrote about the place in stories, poems, and newspaper articles. Newspapers outside Arizona covered the state with a much different perspective, those reporters writing with an outsider's view. Writers of fiction created an Arizona in their stories that became a familiar Wild West place. Indian people became part of the written narrative landscape of Arizona just as farmers, the desert, and Grand Canyon did. At the time of statehood, however, Native Americans did not have the same access to place-defining and creating words, to the language (English) or the means (publication) that these non-Indian poets, novelists, and newspaper editors possessed. The barriers of language and access, and a bias against oral narratives, meant that the literary Arizona written for the majority of Americans in 1912 was an Anglo Arizona, a place viewed through the eyes of white, English-speaking writers and readers.

As settlers worked to manage the unique yet challenging landscapes, to gain physical control, writers endeavored to define them, to impose an intellectual control, to gain an understanding of the place. In defining Arizona's landscapes, writers employed phrases that became familiar and almost sacrosanct over time. Words described the dichotomy of the state's miraculous growth—an instant civilization juxtaposed against rock-exposed natural features dating from the dawn of time, temporal extremes that continued to define the state for over a century—and of the natural landscape extremes characterized as lush forests and desert wasteland. Natural landscapes cannot be confined within political boundaries, and as writers sought to define Arizona's physical borders, the space that it would encompass within the nation, they found that canyons and deserts overlapped these invisible lines. Descriptions of Arizona's people were as recognizable (and stereotypical) as those defining most western dwellers at the time: the independent pioneer, the rugged cowboy, the motivated businessman, and the subdued yet mysterious Indian. All of these words defined Arizona, characterized it, and gave it meaning.

Sharlot Hall, *Cactus and Pine*

As citizens of Arizona grappled with the process of defining the new state, Sharlot Hall had been defining the place in verse for decades. In 1882, as a twelve-year-old child, she traveled on horseback with her parents from Kansas to northern Arizona, where they built a ranch near Prescott. Hall witnessed the growth and development of the territory and its people. She knew ranchers and merchants, schoolteachers and families, who had emigrated to the place years before the Halls arrived, and she recognized the importance of the pioneer stories, histories that connected the settlers to their place but also defined the place for the rest of the country.

Hall's first published work was an Arizona story; a Hopi creation story, it appeared in a children's magazine in 1891.[4] She wrote essays, poems, and historical sketches and published in venues as varied as the journal *Archaeology*, the magazine *Land of Sunshine*, and Arizona's newspapers. Hall's poetry portrayed the natural landscape of her homeland, and her essays described the history of its people and emphasized their strength and fortitude. In the first decade of the twentieth century Hall put her writing skills to work as associate editor of Charles Lummis's *Out West* magazine and used her familiarity with and knowledge of early Arizona pioneers to begin collecting their oral histories. In 1909 Hall was appointed to the newly created Office of Territorial Historian by Governor Richard Sloan and became the first Arizona woman to hold public office, a position she held until 1912. In addition to oral histories, she collected documents, books, and other written records of Arizona history, creating an accessible past and providing stories defining the place by its own people.

Initially Hall defined the West and its people for readers of *Out West* magazine. Originally published by Lummis in Los Angeles as *Land of Sunshine*, the magazine's name was changed in 1902 to *Out West*, and Lummis commissioned Hall to write a poem to appear on the first page of the first issue. The poem was typical of the verses she would write about Arizona, with larger-than-life landscapes populated by hardier-than-average people. Titled "Out West" to introduce the new magazine, the poem described the landscape as a cliché of extremes, just as Hall's verses would come to define Arizona. She wrote, "The silence of utmost desert, and canyons rifted and riven / And the music of wide-flung forests where strong winds shout to heaven." Hall described the residents of the West as a different breed of fellows (in this poem the place is female, the settlers are male), sturdier because of their western pilgrimage. "And she cried to the Old World cities that drowse by the Eastern main: / 'Send me your weary, house-worn broods, and I'll send you Men again!'"[5] Hall would soon describe Arizonans in similar fashion, in verse and in the essays published in *Out West*.

Hall defined Arizona in the first round of its statehood fight in 1906, when Congress determined that the territories of Arizona and New Mexico should be admitted to the union as one state. Arizonans had waited over four decades to become a state. Designated as part of New Mexico Territory in 1848, Arizona was given its own boundaries and name in 1863. The enabling legislation of 1906 once again joined the two southwestern territories, this time as one state, but the citizens of Arizona would have none of it. Capturing that indignation, Hall wrote, "No beggar she in the mighty hall where bay-crowned suitors wait; / No empty-handed pleader for the right of a free-born state."[6] These words form the opening lines of her poem "Arizona," a tract printed on broadsides and placed on every congressman's desk, words that were read into the congressional record from the floor in both houses of Congress and published in Arizona's newspapers, *Out West* magazine, and newspapers around the country.

In words mirroring her "Out West" poem, Hall defined Arizona for the citizens of Arizona, the U.S. Congress, and the nation. "The men who from trackless forests and prairies lone and far / Hewed out the land where ye sit at ease and grudge us our fair-won star," she wrote, leaving out the Native Americans who had inhabited the place for centuries and instead creating an Arizona that did not exist until Anglo explorers and settlers arrived. Hall defined the territory's natural landscape in words evoking the description of the West in "Out West" and proudly proclaimed Arizona's untamed land and people. She compared what some began calling "The Baby State" to the complacency of older states, writing, "The song of the deed in the doing; of work still hot from the hand; / Of the yoke of man laid friendly-wise on the neck of a tameless land."[7] Her words captured the strength, independence, and determination of the people and characterized the place they had forged into a home. Arizona's citizens believed they deserved statehood, on their own, unattached to and unencumbered by another territory's people with whom they may have shared a past but would not share a future.

"Arizona" appeared again in 1911, as Arizonans took up a second fight for statehood, in Hall's collection of poetry *Cactus and Pine: Songs of the Southwest.* The publication of Hall's poems, most of them about or set in Arizona, in one volume that was nationally distributed, defined Arizona for readers who may not have read her magazine articles. Edwin Markham, poet and editor of the *New York American* morning edition's Book Land, described Hall's poetry as "full of the feel of the Far West, its dare and its dream, its color and its glamor, its vastness, and its valor." He encouraged his readers to buy the volume, declaring, "Everyone will note the fervor of her spirit and the freshness of her attack."[8] The first edition sold out quickly; "None could be had a year later," according to Hall in the introduction to the second edition.[9]

Along with the essays about Arizona published in *Out West* magazine, the poems in *Cactus and Pine* defined Arizona with the authority of one who had advocated for the place for a decade and provided a tool for English-speaking and reading Arizonans to define themselves. The themes of Arizona's dualities are present in Hall's writing, showing the extremes of the temporal (oldest natural landscape and newest settlements) and natural landscapes (forest and desert) and juxtaposing the Old West with the modern. Readers of Hall's articles and poetry would be unaware of Arizona's large Native American population. Indian people are nearly nonexistent in Hall's narratives, mentioned only as a hindrance to settlement. Her Arizona, the one she writes into being, is distinctly Anglo. Instead, Hall readily employs booster language in the articles, using words and tone rooted in the existing literature about the territory.[10]

As Arizonans engaged in their first battle for statehood in 1906, *Out West* magazine devoted nearly an entire issue to Hall's article about the place. The sixty-four-page article reinforced the theme of the stoic, independent, hardworking settler introduced in Hall's poems. "But if [Arizona's] isolation, her transportation difficulties, and her years of strenuous Indian warfare have been to some extent obstacles in the path of Arizona's advancement," Hall declared, "she has been more than repaid by the character they have bred in her people. They have given her a race of 'stayers'; the congenital 'quitters' came and saw and went on in search of easier lands."[11] Hall ignored the contemporary presence of Native Americans, instead placing them in the past, as obstacles to "Arizona's [read Anglo Arizona's] advancement."

Much of the article is of the boosting type, and large sections are devoted to the wonders of Arizona's agriculture, ranching, forestry, and mining. Hall introduced her readers to Arizona's forests and boasted about the territory's farming potential, stating it had "the largest and most valuable forest in the United States—possibly the largest unbroken forest area in the world, covering ten thousand square miles. . . . Nearly one half of the land in Arizona is capable of cultivation, and with water would be immensely productive."[12] As with William Smythe a decade before, for Hall and the readers she was addressing, the promise of Arizona's natural landscapes lay in the usefulness of their resources: wide plains for farming and ranching, mineral-filled mountains for mining, thousands of miles of forest for harvesting. The idea that Arizona's natural landscapes should be left wild, that value existed in undeveloped land, would not be advanced for several decades.

However, even as she wrote about the natural resources available for extraction and harvesting, Hall recognized the beauty inherent in the places she described. Arizona has often been represented as both harsh desert and lush forest in literature, underscoring the dichotomy of extremes, stark and verdant, and the contradictory descriptions of the natural world both as inspirational and as raw material for industry. While much of Hall's writing depicts the possibilities for development, she also describes the beauty of Arizona's natural landscapes.

Of the desert, defining the part of Arizona that most readers would recognize, Hall described the location of Phoenix as being "where the mountains run / Naked and scarred and seamed up to the face of the sun; / His place—reaches of wind-blown sand, brown and barren and old."[13] But she also wrote about the place in words that might have surprised her readers, describing spring in the desert in both essay and verse. In an article for *Out West,* Hall described the scene when the season of rain arrives, writing, "If it is rain in any quantity, the very drops seem to turn into green leaves as they fall; and, almost before the shower is done, a faint, gauzy film of green, like a scarf blown from the hands of Spring, lies on the canyon slopes and along the wide, low sand-washes."[14] While this image does not conjure desert landscapes, Hall made sure the reader was still firmly fixed in the idea of the desert as she added the ever-present cacti to the picture. She described budding and blooming saguaro flowers and the outwardly dead ocotillos suddenly covered with leaves and sprouting flames of orange flowers at the ends of their long branches. "Whole mountainsides are yellow at once with the deep, rich, velvet-textured prickly pear," Hall explained, and she declared, "No other desert growth is more impressive than a great yucca in full bloom," with its "white cluster of waxen bells" on flagpole-like stems.[15]

Hall's poetry also described spring in the desert, creating a life-filled place in what was often portrayed as a lifeless, life-taking landscape. "Every shrub distills vague sweetness; every poorest leaf be gathered / Some rare breath to tell its gladness in a fitter way than speech," she wrote. "Here the silken cactus blossoms flaunt their rose and gold and crimson, / And the proud zahuaro [*sic*] lifts its pearl-carved crown from careless reach."[16] In both the article and the poem Hall described the texture of cactus flowers—rich, velvet, and silk—and calls to the reader's mind the iconic image of the saguaro cactus that symbolizes the desert.

Hall also captured the opposite extreme of Arizona's natural landscapes, the dense forest primeval, in essay and verse. "It will come as no light surprise to many that probably the largest unbroken forest in the United States lies within the land that has been called 'the last stronghold of the desert,'" Hall declared. The forest of yellow pine is "flung like a kingly mantle across the rugged [illegible] mesas of the Mogollon Plateau in Northern Arizona."[17] In 1906 she used the vast forest to argue for statehood, illustrating the natural resources the territory could add to the union of states. Her essay explained the logging process in detail, from the surveying to the cutting of the trees and loading of the logs, and described life in the lumber camps and the output of the mills, all in an unemotional, almost journalistic, manner, quite different from the flourishes she employs in her poem about the Mogollon forests. That poem begins, "In the forests on the mountains sing the pines a wondrous measure, / As the wind, the master-player sways their branches to and fro: / Varied music, full of power; full of passion, joy and sorrow," and it carries the reader along: "And above this earth-born music rings a highbar tone incessant." The song in the forest builds, "Calling: Upward! Upward! Upward! Rise and follow where I go!" until it comes to an end: "Wild with all the pain of living, glad with all life's harmony."[18] Hall's poems and articles reveal tension in her understanding of Arizona and land use; some views could coexist—the extremes of deserts and forests, for instance—but others, such as forests as places for contemplation and as humanity's raw material for development, were incompatible.

Water, or lack of it, was another defining theme as the territory looked to statehood, and it would remain an issue throughout the state's history. "The Trail of Death," a dramatic poem that the *New York Evening Post* called "the most vivid and terrible picture of the desert ever put into verse" when it was published in *Land of Sunshine* in February 1901, was reprinted in *Cactus and Pine*. It describes a stunning and wild Arizona desert. The poem begins, "We rode from daybreak; white and hot / The sun beat like a hammer stroke / On molten iron; the blistered dust / Rose up in clouds to sear and choke." Inspired by the stories of suffering and death on southern New Mexico's Jornada del Muerto, Hall's poem uses harsh words to supplement readers' perceptions of Arizona's deserts and creates a place worthy of the name Death Trail.[19] One hundred years later another story about another trail of death in an expanse of desert, the Devil's Highway in southern Arizona, would be written, this one about Mexican immigrants walking north with hopes of better lives and perishing for lack of water (see the epilogue).

Hall often looked forward, using her poetry and articles to project the coming greatness of Arizona. A history of Prescott published in the first issue of the newly renamed *Out West* magazine looked to the future, envisioning a modern Arizona while also harkening back to the Old West. "There is perhaps no other country quite like this," Hall wrote of northern Arizona, "where the old strong soul of the West, in which manhood was more than dollars, touches hands so amiably with the bustling commercialism of the new. It is a land that inspires to big things—big ventures, big hopes; a land which in its wild beauty so possess the hearts of its dwellers that there is a local proverb that a man who leaves it is never happy till he returns."[20]

Hall's Arizona, a forward-looking place ready for statehood, met resistance in the Arizona of writers who in 1912 looked to the past, back to what Arizona had been. Martha Summerhayes's *Vanished Arizona*, published in a second edition in 1911, described an Arizona of intractable wilderness, few people, and Indian wars. The wife of an army officer assigned to the territory, Summerhayes spent most of her early married years in remote territorial military outposts. The first image of Arizona Summerhayes created with her words was set in the summer of 1874 and was one of dreadful heat, as she and her husband's company traveled by steamboat up the Colorado River: "From [Ehrenberg] on, up the river we passed through great canyons and the scenery was grand enough; but one cannot enjoy scenery with the mercury ranging from 107 to 122 in the shade. The grandeur was quite lost upon us all, and we were suffocated by the scorching heat radiating from those massive walls of rocks between which we puffed and clattered along." By fall she had softened toward the place and expected her readers would as well. She described the views of Tonto Basin from the Mogollon Rim, writing, "The scenery was wild and grand; in fact beyond all that I had ever dreamed of; more than that, it seemed so untrod, so fresh, somehow."[21] Despite the hardships of frontier life, she regretted its passing and created the wild Arizona of the past that many readers in 1911 identified as Arizona still.

Similarly, in a poem published two years after Arizona became a state, cowboy poet and Crazy Horse biographer E. A. Brininstool pleaded, "Take me back to Arizona as it was in the early days."[22] His poem recalled and described an Arizona past, much like Summerhayes's vanished Arizona, Brininstool's early days being Arizona's prestatehood days. He declared, "Let me see the city marshal make a gun-play in the street, / And a victim later buried with his boots upon his feet." This was not the Arizona that Hall depicted, the Arizona deserving of statehood, even though her Arizona, the place she was writing about before statehood, was in the same past that Brininstool longed for. Both Arizonas became the place for readers, a perspective that contributed to one of the temporal clichés that has characterized it for over a century, a place both modern and untamed. "Take me back to Arizona, Arizona rough and wild," the poet sang, "Where the days were dry and dusty and the whisky wasn't mild! / Let me live again those stirring frontier days when all was new, / when the faro banks were frequent but the churches mighty few!"[23] This Arizona was not the place advertised by boosters and editors of newspapers wishing to see the territory grow and develop.

The *Arizona Republican* and the *Coconino Sun*

While Sharlot Hall defined Arizona's natural landscapes and independent-minded citizens in her poetry and essays, many people received information about the place via newspapers. Those published within Arizona described a place of unmatched opportunity, perfect for "homeseekers" (a word that replaced "settlers" in Arizona's booster literature) and businessmen. Articles equally encouraged farmers and grocers to move and implored tourists to add Arizona to their travel itineraries. Whether completely factual, loosely based on truth, or not at all resembling the reality of the place, newspapers' booster words about Arizona formed that place in many readers' minds.

Arizona Republican editor Sims Ely recognized the role newspapers play in creating the places written about in their pages. Newspapers, Ely wrote, "have a large part in the making of history in a new land. Without the aid and encouragement of the press, a large proportion of the successful enterprises for the development of Arizona's resources would have failed of fruition."[24] The land was not really new, and Native Americans and Hispanics had inhabited it for centuries. But the history that Ely intended to make for the "new" land would be defined by Anglo-Americans. Ely declared that the policy of his newspaper was to "[stand] up for Arizona and for Arizona's people, and [make] known to the world the wonderful resources and attractions of this wonderful land."[25] Newspapers described the prosperity already evident while at the same time extolling the possibilities for further exploitation.

The *Arizona Republican* and the *Coconino Sun* employed these boosters' tones when writing about Arizona generally and in describing their own regions. Flagstaff's *Coconino Sun* was the newspaper of record in northern Arizona; published in Phoenix, the *Arizona Republican* was the largest newspaper, in terms of circulation, at the time of statehood.[26] The editors and reporters focused on economic and tourist opportunities and on a concern about the new state's borders. The words reflected what the writers perceived as Arizona, what they hoped their readers would believe was Arizona, and what they intended Arizona to become in the future. The Arizona defined by its newspapers was a place where anyone would want to live, should live, and could make a living within.

In 1910, while Arizona's citizens waited for the U.S. Congress to pass an enabling act providing a path to statehood, the state of Utah was petitioning Congress to redraw its southern border to include the northern Arizona region known as the Arizona Strip. Proposing an amendment to the Arizona statehood bill being debated at the time, Utah's delegation believed that culturally the people residing on the land north of Grand Canyon and south of their border belonged to Utah, most of them being Mormon settlers, and argued that those residents were isolated from Arizona proper by the canyon's chasm, the lack of a bridge to cross it, and the long travel distance necessary to get around it.

The amendment failed and Arizona's newspapers took up the cause of defining the Strip as part of the new state, not on behalf of the people residing there but because of the area's economic value for tourism to Grand Canyon's north rim. As Arizonans voted for delegates to write their constitution, the *Coconino Sun* wrote of this northernmost region, calling on leaders to make sure it remained securely part of Arizona (even as the writer called it the Utah Strip). "One of the greatest assets of the coming state of Arizona is that world scenic wonder, the Grand Canyon of Arizona," the reporter wrote, reminding readers of Grand Canyon's economic potential. "Its value is not only the great amount of advertising of this territory which is done by the writings and talk of the thousands of visitors to it from all parts of the world." The *Sun* assured its readers that "Arizona owns both sides of this world-wonder and it is her finest possession, for with each succeeding year, as tourists advertise the great gorge the number of visitors will increase."[27] Just as Sharlot Hall represented Arizona's forests as both a place of beauty and a product to be harvested, this reporter described Grand Canyon as scenic wonder and economic asset.

As the war of words over the words of the Arizona constitution continued in 1911, Sharlot Hall, in her official capacity as territorial historian, joined the push to define the Arizona Strip as part of the eventual state of Arizona, and she made a nine-week journey to the region to survey its potential. For Hall the importance of the Strip lay not only in its proximity to Grand Canyon but also in the value of its natural resources. She found a country "abounding in a wealth of timber, and of agricultural and mineral resources," with "sublime scenery" and "an ideal climate." The *Arizona Republican* reported that the data Hall collected "ought to be convincing to the people and to the legislature against any proposal to cede that country to Utah."[28]

As the territorial historian and newspaper reporters sought to define the Arizona Strip and Grand Canyon as part of Arizona proper, newspapers also described the canyon's severe landscapes as unpopulated, even though its canyons and south rim had been the Havasupai peoples' home for a thousand years.[29] A northern Arizona reporter wrote the Colorado River's Cataract Canyon (also known as Havasu Canyon) into being for Anglo readers but only included the Havasupais at the end of the article as a curiosity, not as individuals or a community with their own stories to tell. The writer described the "little arroyo" as an uncommon place: "For ten miles down this rocky gorge [Lee's Canyon] into a great red sandstone gap the tourist travels until he arrives at a point where the Lee empties into Cataract Canyon." The journey becomes less a tourist's trek and more an adventurer's toil as the writer describes the place: "The sun's rays beat relentlessly down upon the sandy footing below, the cruel heat radiates from the walls on the sides and everybody perspires freely." As the destination is reached, the article concludes, "at night the frogs bark hoarsely and loud, few stars shine above, and now and then the sound of laughter betrays the whereabouts of the few Indians who inhabit the land of their ancestors . . . the land of the Supais. The trip is one never to be forgotten and one well worth while, though some hardships must be experienced in getting to this branch house of hades."[30] The appeal, it seems, would be to adventure-seeking tourists looking for a place of exciting exploration and beauty. That this canyon was the traditional home of the Havasupai people and had been set aside as reservation land goes unmentioned, as do any of their own stories.

In anticipation of Arizona achieving statehood and with the intent of drawing the attention of an audience the editors hoped would settle, develop and finance, and tour the new state, the *Arizona Republican* devoted an entire edition to recommending Arizona, defining it as a modern place where opportunities abounded. The edition portrayed every region and county, many of the towns, and most of the tourist sites. This edition is *Arizona Highways*–like in its scope, two decades before that magazine existed.

Articles about Arizona cities included several located in the Salt River Valley. Readers learned that many of the successful citizens came as visitors but became residents because of the climate and economic possibilities. "Some of the most magnificent homes and business blocks of the city are owned by men who came here as chance visitors, in many instances as reluctant visitors," the paper stated.[31] In a long article extolling the agricultural possibilities in the valley, potential farmers were told, "Glendale soil is ninety feet deep, and you can't find a pebble in it as big as a marble. . . . Also it is, without a doubt, unsurpassed in [illegible] plant food by any soil in the world."[32] Readers were led to believe that hands to till the soil were the only thing standing between a sterile and a fertile Salt River Valley. The reality was that the river valleys had been farmed for centuries, first by the Hohokam farmers, whose canals laid out across the valleys were evidence of their agricultural acumen, and then by the Akimel O'odham people, who were still cultivating along the rivers even as Anglo farmers diverted the water and growing Anglo settlements dug wells and depleted the aquifers.

Mesa made its contribution to the *Republican*'s boosting edition, appealing to tourists and homeseekers to make Mesa their headquarters because it was the nearest community to the great Roosevelt Dam—a sight, and site, to see—which provided "the best and the most economical water right in the country."[33] Unlike the Arizona depicted in other narratives as a harsh desert or Wild West, the Arizona these writers described offered water and soil for the Anglo settler and wonderful attractions for the tourist; it was a place where people came to visit and stayed to live. As in Sharlot Hall's works, though, Native Americans were invisible in these articles, their existence unmentioned, their stories unwritten.

Tucson was also represented in this state-boosting edition: "The 'ancient and honorable pueblo'—teems with adventure and romance. Prehistoric ruins and many landmarks of the old Spanish and Mexican civilizations add color to the picture the imagination paints of Tucson's early history. The reminiscent pioneer can weave many a tale of the early days more thrilling because truer than even the remarkable fiction of the modern magazine writer on present day Arizona life." Reporter H. V. Failor evoked the Arizona of Summerhayes and Brininstool as a place in history, describing gunplay, bad men, cacti, and rattlesnakes.

He created Tucson as a place of ancient beauty—presenting the ruins of old Fort Lowell and San Xavier Mission as examples—and of natural beauty, citing Sabino Canyon and "pine crowned mountains."[34] Native Americans were again unmentioned, but their stories were as important to the fort and mission as Anglo stories, since the existence of both Fort Lowell and San Xavier Mission was due to Spanish and American campaigns to subjugate and control the Tohono O'odham people. All of these newspaper articles constructed an Anglo Arizona for Anglo readers with their words.

The *Coconino Sun* ran its own version of regional boosterism in a front-page article four months after Arizona became a state. The introduction enthused over Flagstaff's location and attractions: "Flagstaff is located in such a manner that all our surroundings speak in the most enchanting and impressive manner of the creator's desire for beauty in all its variation." Describing all of the wonders northern Arizona had to offer tourists, the article continued, "As a summer resort we are ahead of any other section." Potential visitors learned about Grand Canyon; Walnut Canyon cliff dwellings and Montezuma Castle and Well; Oak Creek Canyon; Sunset Mountain; the Painted Desert, Lava Beds, and Cinder Beds; and "thousands of attractions" east of Flagstaff on the Navajo reservation. Much of the space in the newspaper was devoted to describing the aesthetics of the region, "beautiful bodies of mountain water" and a "fisherman's paradise," for example, tourist destinations situated in a natural wonderland. But in a section titled "Undeveloped Resources," including reservoirs and "good auto high lines," the boosters hoped to attract the would-be investors among the article's readers and once again revealed tension between the ideas of natural landscapes as scenery and as economic assets.[35]

Not only did the editors of Arizona's newspapers attempt to define the territory within their pages, they also provided space in their pages for Arizona citizens to make the effort as well. C. E. Stastny, a former Iowa resident now of Phoenix (one of those visitors to the Salt River Valley the *Republican* described who decided to stay), wrote a letter to his old hometown newspaper, the *Cedar Rapids Daily Republican*. The letter found its way back to his new hometown paper, the *Arizona Republican*, and thus was printed in both papers. Stastny described his new home in Arizona for Iowans, extolling its wonders. "I do not remember of ever having found such a combination of climate and soil as I have found in this valley, and nothing has ever before impressed me as much as the future of this valley," Stastny wrote. He appealed to the farmer and to the investor as he detailed how the land in the Salt River Valley could be used. He included cattle ranching, dairy farming, and other varieties of animal husbandry ("the raising of ostriches, hog farming, sheep raising, both for mutton and wool, horse and mule raising"); the cultivation of grain and other produce ("alfalfa raising for hay and seed, and in the raising of wheat, barley, oats, millet, corn, kaffir corn, sugar beets, sorghum, sugar cane, cotton, potatoes"); and fruit farming ("the raising of grapes for both wines and the making of raisins . . . lemons, oranges, tangerines, grapefruit, dates, almonds, olives, peaches, pears, apricots, plums, figs, prunes, apples, and quinces").[36] In that extensive but simple list, Stastny and the newspaper's editors hoped readers would find enough possibilities to employ as many farmers, and the workers in the agricultural industry who supported them, as would want to immigrate to Arizona.

Stastny's letter presented the Arizona that boosters promoted. Columns in the *Arizona Republican* revealed frustration at the absence of knowledge about the state outside of its borders. Arizona residents traveling outside the state discovered what they considered misperceptions of Arizona based on a lack of information or misinformation. Vacationing in California, Phoenician R. A. Mulford was perturbed to find that people struggled, unnecessarily he believed, in southern California with no idea that life could be better for them in Arizona. He wrote, "California is a disappointment to a great many people. California is a great state for pleasure seekers and capitalists. . . . But some who go there have reached the end of their means and have to stop." But, he stated, "Arizona is not properly advertised. People do not realize how much better conditions are here than in California."[37] Whether these Arizona residents were members of the communities benefitting from Arizona's agriculture, business opportunities, and climate, or whether they agreed with the booster rhetoric (perhaps the boosters' words had created this place for these Arizonans as well as for potential settlers), this was the Arizona that they believed existed, and they actively boosted the place, participating in defining the state with their words.

Often visitors to the state wrote letters to the newspapers to present corrections to the perceptions they held before their visits. These letters provide a picture of the place portrayed by writers who described a different Arizona. In one such letter Charles Moreau Harger, a writer for *Outlook* magazine, explained that the Arizona he had read about, that words had created in the East, differed from the place he discovered when he visited. "To be sure we have been deluged with articles and pictures showing the picturesque," Harger wrote. "The Indians, the cactus, the cowboys and similar features are indelibly impressed on the minds of eastern people as characteristic of the southwest. But when we come here and see the fine buildings, the beautiful homes, the remarkable spirit of enterprise manifest everywhere we get an entirely different view."[38] Often these things of Arizona's past that Harger sets aside are emphasized and reinforced by writers such as Martha Summerhayes, E. A. Brininstool, and Zane Grey.

The Arizonans Harger writes about were also unlike those that some writers encouraged readers to believe populated the state. Harger lauded the settlers of the territory: "I have been surprised to find so many college men . . . men who have come from the best families of the east and who are giving to the southwest the enterprise and education that make the equipment of the eastern college man invaluable to a new country." He concluded by encouraging Arizonans, writing, "It will take time to eradicate from the minds of eastern readers the idea of wildness associated with the territory but it is being accomplished."[39] Ironically, this continued presence of "wildness" is one of the things Arizona would boast of in the 1960s.

Arizona newspapers described and defined Arizonans as businessmen, farmers, and homeseekers. This was how Arizona writers saw themselves and wanted to be perceived by readers outside of the state. Harger was confident that nonresidents would eventually be persuaded. Newspaper publishers and reporters outside of Arizona had their own perceptions of the place.

The *Los Angeles Times* and Writing Arizona from the Outside

Newspapers outside of Arizona played a role in defining it for their readers; the writers' perceptions of Arizona's people and its natural landscapes are revealed in their descriptions. The *Los Angeles Times* reporters described Arizona as a satellite of California, an economic extension of southern California. On promotional trips through Arizona (the Chamber of Commerce Excursion by Train, for example), the *Times* acted as an Arizona advocate and partner in reciprocal tourism. Other national newspapers also wrote about Arizona as a tourist destination, describing the place in words that emphasized its rugged landscapes and Wild West image. These reporters handled words about Arizona's Native Americans in one of two ways. Indian people were either unmentioned (invisible in the narratives), or they were written into the stories as defeated and subdued tribes, as impediments to progress (as the reporters defined it), and as members of ancient civilizations. In none of the articles do Native Americans tell their own stories.

In 1910 the Los Angeles Chamber of Commerce organized a six-day train excursion through Arizona to promote California and gain a better understanding of its neighbor. Affluent Arizonans from the Phoenix and Tucson areas often spent their summers in southern California, on the cool coast and out of the desert heat; the chamber members hoped to encourage more tourism from other areas of Arizona. Via the special train, the chamber members visited Grand Canyon and nearly a dozen Arizona towns, including Phoenix, Tucson, Douglas, and Kingman. Though the purpose of the trip was to promote Los Angeles and southern California, *Los Angeles Times* reporter John S. M'Groarty traveled with the group and documented the trip for the newspaper's readers. His perception of Arizona reveals how nonresidents defined the place; his words also reflect an Anglo perspective that while typical of the time was ahistorical and racist.[40]

M'Groarty's articles characterized Arizona as the marvel of modernization, a civilization grown from the desert wasteland, descriptions that would define it still, fifty years later. His articles also portrayed the Wild

West Arizona, a place just a half step removed from the Apache wars that had been sensationalized in the press a few decades before. Encompassing these themes, one article filed from the excursion described the trip along the Arizona-Mexico border. As the group traveled toward Douglas, the town founded as the smelter site for Bisbee copper mines, "moon and stars alike had faded, but the scroll of the skies was aflame with furnace fires and the never-ending conflagration of the melting pots of the mills. . . . As the gray morning broke across the shadowing buttes we came to Douglas town. . . . It was then that we saw a perfect city upon the desert plain where eight years ago there was no town at all."[41] The furnace fires and melting pots symbolized progress, the city situated on what once had been untrammeled desert represented civilization, labels that Arizona boosters craved and that revealed what both they and the newspaper writer believed were proper uses for the land.

This marvel-of-growth Arizona quickly gave way to a Wild West Indian battleground familiar to readers of fictional Westerns but having no basis in reality. "Under a crescent moon and led by desert stars," M'Groarty wrote, "the train sped into the historic plains, where the white man fought the Apache, gory and red-handed, to the last crimson ditch of death in the immortal conquest of Arizona."[42] M'Groarty's words reflected a prevailing Anglo attitude that identified Apache people as savage but subdued tribes, in narratives that discounted and obscured an entire culture rich in a tradition that granted spiritual power to the mountains of Arizona, New Mexico, and Old Mexico where they had lived before European settlement disrupted their ways of life.

M'Groarty also wrote fiction as history as he described Fort Bowie and reminisced about the "pursuit of old Geronimo into the fastnesses of Mexico, trapping the wily and marvelous Apache at last." He continued, "We passed through starlit vales and the dim mountain passes of the Dragoons and the Chirachuas [*sic*] till the great gash in the mighty hills brought us at last to the stronghold of Cochise, where the last of the fighting Apaches died in his moccasins, with the battle cry of defiance on his lips."[43] Neither the story of Geronimo's capture nor of Cochise's death is correct. Geronimo surrendered and was confined in Florida; Cochise agreed to retire to reservation life in southeastern Arizona and died there of a stomach illness.[44] These fictional war-and-conquest stories characterized Anglo Arizonans' relationship with the Apache tribes at the time of statehood and for years following and contributed to the image of Arizona as a wild western frontier.

In defining Arizona as a marvel of civilization, M'Groarty patronizingly described the Salt River Valley, writing, "There was the land once bare and profitless now fat and verdant. And it made a man's heart glad to look from that once desolate valley and to drink in its clustered groves, its far-flung spaces of growing grain and alfalfa, and its feeding birds."[45] His was the same Arizona that C. E. Stastny described, where orange, plum, and peach orchards, ostrich farms, and profitable land and businesses waited ready for development. Arizona's growth narrative was already well developed at the time of statehood and would continue to influence perceptions of the place and the use of its land and resources for the ensuing hundred years.

Other *Los Angeles Times* reporters wrote specifically about the economic benefits Arizona could contribute to the nation after Congress passed the Enabling Act of 1910, which gave the territory of Arizona a path to statehood. The *Times* explained to its readers that with its "vast mineral resources . . . valley after valley of marvelously fertile lands . . . [and] mountains and mesas in the north which are generally covered with nutritious grasses," the place abounded in natural resources for exploiting. Arizona was described for tourists as having "some of the grandest scenery in the world . . . [and] a climate, which, though hot in the summer, is not very oppressive, while in winter it is usually delightful." And employing another of the common characterizations that defined Arizona, the newspaper described Arizona's natural landscape in temporal terms, emphasizing geologic time in its "many and varied geologic formations; in fact, every period of the world's history since the dawn of life is represented in its geology."[46]

A few months later the *Times* published another article about Arizona, featuring the kind of boosterism and exposure Arizonans could appreciate, that debunked an image of Wild West Arizona in favor of a place where reliable, mature (if inexperienced) citizenry were ready for the responsibilities of statehood. Arizona had addressed its water supply issues, according to E. D. Ewers, and he lauded the results. "Under the Salt River project the irrigated farm of the southwest is believed to have reached its highest stage of development," he wrote. "Fifteen acres is regarded as ample for one family, and with the advantages of Statehood . . . this section looks forward to a large influx of homeseekers." Just as John A. Black had done thirty years earlier, Ewers assured potential relocators that they need not worry about good schools, for "it is claimed [Arizona] will enter the Union with as high-grade common schools as most of the thickly-settled states. . . . Even in the most isolated desert towns one will observe commodious and substantial school buildings."[47] Ewers described a place equal to or better than the established states of the union, a place where farming was easy, water plentiful, and a quality education accessible.

In a description of the Salt River Valley that could have been written by Arizonan C. E. Stastny, the *Times* reporter explained that prosperous (white) farmers grow sugar beets, dates, and oranges. Alfalfa is cut four and five times a year, and a half a million head of sheep are brought to Phoenix each year for shearing and lambing. Readers learned about beekeeping, dairy farming, and horse breeding and were assured that while they might have heard dire descriptions of the harsh heat, it was but a small matter. "Of course, the weather is hot in summer time," Ewers declared. "If it were not, the country would not be nearly so productive. . . . It is a beautiful valley, resplendent under the unhindered sun with green fields and orchards, set in a frame of lovely mountains, red brown, purple, and parti-colored in their coverings."[48] This Arizona, described so often in newspapers' pages, was beautiful in both natural and cultivated ways, already productive and with promise for more.

In an article published a year before Arizona achieved statehood, the *Los Angeles Times* defined an Arizona that was at once prosperous and promising. Within the description of a modern place, Native Americans were left out of that prosperity; this is solely an Anglo Arizona. The full-page article focuses on the Salt River Valley and Phoenix; business and economy are its themes. Repeating the oft-stated image of the fertile valley, the reporter enthusiastically claimed, "None of these garden spots of the Old World are as rich in plant food or as deep or as easily cultivated as the lands of the Salt River Valley."[49] Juxtaposed against a picture of Phoenix as a modern town—"its own water plant, a start made on a $400,000 sewer system, electric lights, gas, two telephone systems, an electric railway system"—the reporter depicts Arizona's Native Americans as indolent. Even though the Akimel O'odham farmers had cultivated the land long before Anglo settlers arrived, the reporter wrote as if the O'odham people had never planted a seed: "The Indians lost their water supply long ago through its being diverted by proud Caucasian farmers farther up the Gila. But the 'gentle savages' can obtain plenty of water by electrical pumping and from shallow wells, and the physical exercise of farming will be of benefit to them."[50] Articles like this reinforced false narratives that absolved Anglo farmers and their settlements of any role in decimating O'odham agriculture. But farming had been the way of life along the Gila River long before the intrusion of white settlers. Because no counternarrative existed at the time, this Anglo version of Arizona was the one written into being in the second decade of the twentieth century.[51]

The *New York Times* and other newspapers not located on Arizona's doorstep defined the territory as a tourist destination, but they described it in words that emphasized its strangeness and wrote about Native Americans using words evoking ancient mystery. These stories often failed to connect the inhabitants of Arizona's ancient structures to the modern tribes whose histories and traditions named them as their ancestors. Casa Grande Ruins was the subject of several articles chronicling the archaeological excavation of the area; the final article in the series explained archaeologist J. W. Fewkes's theories and interpretations of Casa Grande and its surrounds and related "Pima and Papago" creation stories that include the history of the place. "What have hitherto been but oval mounds . . . are being dug away and the houses that exist within them are being brought to life," the reporter wrote. "They are being made to give up the secrets of the people who lived within them and formed a part of a civilization that had fallen into decadence not so many centuries before the Spanish fathers came to this section. They are forming the closest link that moderns have ever found between the present people of the Southwest and those that had earlier left so strong a mark upon the country."[52] Had the archaeologists asked the Akimel and Tohono O'odham people (Pima and Papago in the article), they would have already known of the connections between the "earlier" and the "present" people.

However, the reporter did assert the peoples' direct lineage to the builders of Casa Grande and described a legend told by an Akimel O'odham leader about their ancestors, the canal builders. The story tells of Morning Green, a great medicine man and leader of the people of the Casa Grande area, who "was able, through his herbs, to control the rain and wind and this secret brought great strength to the Casa Grande people in their rivalry with other tribes." Towa, a member of another tribe (which according to the legend occupied what became known as Pueblo Grande in the Salt River Valley), was "a woman of marvelous power, who had control over hard substances, such as stone." Rivalry between the two tribes led to conflicts, but finally peace was made and "the power of Morning Green over the elements and of Towa who controlled hard things, were united, and the great ditches were dug and water made to flow in them, and the people grew in power and the deserts were irrigated and made to blossom as the rose."[53] An Akimel O'odham story told to an Anglo reporter, rewritten for an Anglo audience, and published in a national newspaper defined an ancient Arizona and connected it to a modern tribe.

The *Washington (New Jersey) Star* contributed to defining an ancient Arizona as well, writing the Verde Valley's Montezuma Castle into a place for East Coast readers. Initially this article wrote ancient people into the natural landscape. "Arizona is the greatest museum of natural history in the world, and contains more wonders and freaks of nature than any other similar area in all the universe," stated reporter William E. Curtis. Then he quoted Arizona Antiquarian Society president Dr. Joshua Miller, who corrected that view. "Whatever [the cliff dwellers'] condition or plane in the scale of civilization, they knew how to build a house that would stand," Miller explained. "When we consider that all this timber was cut with stone axes, and, together with the stone and mortar, was hoisted more than fifty feet along a perpendicular cliff wall, we may form some idea of the immense amount of labor required to construct such a building in such an uncanny and inaccessible place."[54] Miller's explanation presented a more sophisticated society than readers were accustomed to learning about. Several decades later, Hopi archaeologists and writers' words connected the ancients to the modern as Hopi stories of the structures as their ancestors' footprints became part of Arizona's written narrative landscape.

Native Americans were also depicted as standing in the way of progress, as Anglo reporters defined it. The power of words to define a place by devaluing some of its people and justifying what happens to them is displayed in a *New York Times* article about the new state. "White men have set their eyes on the riches of the Navajo Indian Reservation," the reporter wrote, "and it may not be long before the proud tribe that has so well preserved its identity will be swallowed by civilization, as other tribes have been." The writer explained that the Navajo reservation contains about 2.3 million acres of land, and the tribe has fewer than two thousand members. Whether or not the statistics were accurate, the words created a northeastern Arizona devoid of all but a few people, individuals who did not need the land and would soon be engulfed by Anglo culture. The writer stated his case, announcing, "This would give 1,200 acres apiece to the members. It is declared that this allotment is unjust, because white citizens could not take up so much public land." The reporter lamented that Anglo men tried to get permission to mine gold and silver on the reservation but were denied. "The Navajos will not let themselves be dispossessed willingly," stated the writer," "but they are averse, however, to progress in any form."[55] The Anglo definition of progress was employed here to designate resource extraction and land development. As historian Patricia Nelson Limerick elucidates, "The argument thus shifted the terms of greed and philanthropy: it was not that white people were greedy and mean-spirited; Indians were the greedy ones, keeping so much land to themselves; and white people were philanthropic and farsighted in wanting to liberate the land for its proper uses."[56] By the time Arizona celebrated its fiftieth anniversary of statehood, the Navajo people were managing their lands' resources—coal and uranium mines and oil fields. But in 1912 no competing written narrative existed, and thus the words of this *New York Times* article defined the Arizona of the Navajo reservation for readers.

When considering Arizona as a tourist destination, one feature nearly always comes to mind—Grand Canyon. In 1912 Arizona was not yet nicknamed the Grand Canyon State; it was never called the Grand Canyon Territory. The canyon was described as isolated and daunting, magnificent and terrifying. A spur line of the Santa Fe Railroad connected the opulent El Tovar Hotel, opened in 1905 on Grand Canyon's south rim, to Williams and the main line. As president, Theodore Roosevelt had called on Arizonans to be guardians of the canyon in 1903, instructing them "in your own interest and in the interest of the country to keep this great wonder of nature as it now is." But the president also stated that Grand Canyon was "one of the great sights" and every American should see it.[57]

Emily Brown Helminger wrote about Grand Canyon in the *Houston Daily Chronicle*: "Imagine a yawning chasm . . . full of sunken mountains, gorges, terraces, domes, obelisks, precipices, cataracts, and cliffs of every hue and color of the rainbow, carved in granite, quartz, sandstone, limestone . . . and you have in part the composition of the Grand Canyon." Why, she wondered, would anyone go to New York City or Europe when "the peaceful quiet of the Grand Canyon of Arizona is within reach?"[58] This was the economic asset the state's newspapers boosted as the reason for the Arizona Strip's value.

Thomas Dowler Murphy's travel book *Three Wonderlands of the American West* explained the canyon's appeal for his readers. He described "a succession of pyramids and palaces of overwhelming immensity and past human imagining in their ever-changing riot of color" that only the "Architect Divine" could have created. "Here the artisans of the ages, fire and wind and flood, have wrought an endless array of gigantic structures which no mortal mind could have conceived," he wrote, and he added that to truly appreciate this wonder, one must view it from the bottom, from the river, as John Wesley Powell had. "For indeed, to appreciate the grandeur and matchless magnitude of these temples and palaces, one must go down among them and look upward to them from the depths," Murphy wrote, "to know the awful majesty and resistless power of that sullen river he must stand on its very bank."[59]

In an article that may be one of the earliest published arguments against development at Grand Canyon, a *Los Angeles Times* reporter argued, on economic and on preservationist grounds, against giving permission for a "trolley railroad" to be built along the canyon rim. Investors would lose their money, the writer contended, because at most only about 2,000 people visited the canyon per month. The reporter figured, "If twice the number were to visit it, an average of 4,000 a month, or 1,000 a week, it would not begin to pay expenses if the fare for riding the road were $2 a trip."[60] Cost was only one reason to deny the project. A greater objection was that "the stupendous proportions of the Grand Canyon constitute the chief features of its grandeur, and wild setting for miles on either side is the proper setting for these scenic wonders. After their stupendous magnificence their appeal to the human eye is on account of the wonderful painting that nature has spread upon the rocks." The writer described a spectacular tapestry of northern Arizona landscape and set it out of reach of many travelers, despite President Roosevelt's call for all Americans to see it, making it all the more desirable a feature and destination. "We would be very sorry to see any permission given," he stated, "to men greedy of gain or foolish in their speculations to change the work of nature in the canyon,"[61] foreshadowing environmentalists' arguments fifty years later.

The Fiction of Zane Grey

Arizona was defined by its residents in poetry, by its local press, and by newspaper reporters outside the state writing for a national audience. Arizona was also defined in fiction written by outsiders who moved to the place and adopted it as their own. Bestselling novelist Zane Grey was one of these writers. He came to Arizona for the first time in 1906 as an adult in his thirties, and he lived and worked intermittently in the place for two decades. He described Arizona's people and landscapes, writing the place into western novels. Arizona in turn created Zane Grey the western novelist, the place providing the raw materials of landscapes and people from which he shaped his stories, and the experiences of his own travels that formed his perspective. Famous for crafting tough western characters and portraying the spirit of the land—making the landscape an essential piece of the stories—Grey defined Arizona, creating a place with unforgiving yet spectacular landscapes and populating it with ruthless and courageous characters. He wrote an Arizona into being that often reinforced readers' ideas of the Wild West.

Grey wrote and published three successful novels during the time of Arizona's statehood quest: 1910's *The Heritage of the Desert*, followed by *Riders of the Purple Sage* (1912) and *Desert Gold* (1913). Grey's first effort at writing an Arizona story recounted the adventures of Charles Jesse "Buffalo" Jones and was written after he had spent time with Jones in northern Arizona. *The Last of the Plainsmen* (1908) was not a bestseller, but it was the beginning of Grey's defining of Arizona's landscape and people, and of Arizona's defining of him. In the prefatory note he wrote, "In the spring of 1907 I was the fortunate companion of the old plainsman on a trip across the desert, and a hunt in that wonderful country of yellow crags, deep canyons, and giant pines. I want to tell about it. I want to show the color and beauty of those painted cliffs and the long, brown-matted bluebell-dotted aisles in the grand forests; I want to give a suggestion of the tang of the dry, cool air; and particularly I want to throw a little light upon the life and nature of that strange character and remarkable man, Buffalo Jones."[62]

Like other writers, and Arizona citizens, Grey sought to understand and define the place physically, within borders, and intellectually, as a cultural place and as a people. The Arizona Strip and northern Arizona served as the setting for several of Zane Grey's novels. His first major success came in 1910 with *The Heritage of the Desert*. One reviewer announced that with this book, Grey "established his right to be classed among the best of those American novelists who have chosen the frontier as their field."[63] The setting was clearly Arizona—the Painted Desert and the Arizona Strip. The same year that Utah was petitioning Congress for Arizona's land north of Grand Canyon and the *Coconino Sun* was emphasizing the place as Arizona, *The Heritage of the Desert* demonstrated the vagueness with which that area was often perceived. Early in the story of Jack Hare, a young easterner rescued by Mormon settlers from certain death in the harsh desert at the hands of cattle rustlers, Grey has Holderness, his cattle rancher-rustler say, "The land is owned by the Government, and though your ranges are across the Arizona line they really figure as Utah land." This combining of Arizona and Utah continues, as Mormon settler August Naab explains to Hare: "'If not overstocked, this range is the best in Utah,' said Naab. 'I say Utah, but it's really Arizona. The Grand Canyon seems to us Mormons to mark the line.'"[64]

In the book's first certain description of Arizona, Naab tells Hare, "That's Coconina there, Fire Mountain in Navajo meaning. It's a plateau low and narrow at this end, but it runs far to the east and rises nine thousand feet. It forms a hundred miles of the north rim of the Grand Canyon. We're across the Arizona line now." Grey continued to describe northern Arizona, relying on his experiences there to categorize the landscape as one both beautiful and challenging, characteristics important to moving his story forward but also characteristics that came to define Arizona for readers who had never been there. The reader becomes Jack Hare, experiencing Arizona the way Grey created it. "He saw a red world," Grey wrote. "His eyes seemed bathed in blood. Red scaly ground, bare of vegetation, sloped down, down, far down to a vast irregular rent in the earth, which zigzagged through the plain beneath. To the right it bent its crooked way under the brow of a black-timbered plateau; to the left it straightened its angles to find a V-shaped vent in the wall, now uplifted to a mountain range. Beyond this earth-riven line lay something vast and illimitable, a far-reaching vision of white wastes, of purple plains, of low mesas lost in the distance. It was the shimmering dust-veiled desert."[65] Descriptions of places both real and imagined create the heritage of Painted Desert for Jack Hare and for the reader.

This became Arizona for readers of Grey's novel, and this landscape defined the people who lived in it. "What then of the men who drifted into the desert and survived?" Hare, and the reader, wonder. "They must necessarily endure the wind and heat, the drouth and famine; they must grow lean and hard, keen-eyed and silent. The weak, the humble, the sacrificing must be winnowed from among them. As each man developed he took on some aspect of the desert."[66] Grey's way with description wrote an Arizona into being. He "paints the surroundings and conditions of this desert life with an attention to detail that makes it all stand out before the reader's eyes exceedingly vivid and convincing," the reviewer declared.[67]

The interchanging and conflating of the regions of northern Arizona and southern Utah continued in one of Grey's best-known works, *Riders of the Purple Sage*. The story of a Mormon ranchwoman beset by Mormon men of authority, familiar characters in Grey's novels, *Riders of the Purple Sage* creates relationships between characters and landscapes in fiction that translate to reality in readers' minds. While the setting is southern Utah—Arizona is never mentioned, Jane Withersteen even telling Lassiter, "I'll never leave Utah"[68]—the novel has come to represent Arizona. The book was immensely successful, became a bestseller, and received favorable reviews. A *New York Times* reviewer wrote, "Grey returns to the scene which he portrayed so powerfully and entertainingly in *The Heritage of the Desert*. The mountains and sage-green plains of *southern Utah* furnish the setting" [emphasis added].[69]

Riders of the Purple Sage may have come to depict Arizona eventually, but in 1912 the novel created Utah. Historian Candace C. Kant sets Surprise Valley—the refuge of Venters and Bess, and eventually of Jane and Lassiter—on the Arizona Strip. Geographer Kevin S. Blake sets the valley in Tsegi Canyon, Arizona.[70] However, nowhere in the 280-page volume is the place Arizona or the Arizona Strip mentioned. The phrase "Utah's southern border" is used twice. That is as close to Arizona as the reader gets. Grey described Surprise Valley, writing, "Before him ascended a gradual swell of smooth stone. It was hard, polished, and full of pockets worn by centuries of eddying rainwater. . . . He had climbed up that wonderful smooth slope, and had almost reached the base of yellow cliff that rose skyward, a huge scarred and cracked bulk." The words describe many places in southern Utah and northern Arizona: Monument Valley, which straddles the state line on the Navajo reservation; Tsegi Canyon, Arizona; and Canyonlands and Arches national monuments in southeastern Utah—all places of "crags and pinnacles, splintered cliffs, and leaning shafts and monuments."[71]

It is an interesting question: When and how did *Riders of the Purple Sage* become an Arizona story? It was a story *written* in Arizona, at

Grey's cabin in the White Mountains; thus the place helped create the story. Perhaps the *Arizona Republican* contributed to the perception of the book being set in Arizona when the first *Riders of the Purple Sage* movie adaptation was released in 1918. Announcing, "Arizona Is the Scene of Zane Grey Film," the columnist wrote, "*Riders of the Purple Sage*, . . . the greatest western story ever written . . . is unquestionably the best western picture ever made."[72] Much of the movie was filmed in the White Mountains and at Grand Canyon. Identifying the book with the state as the movie was released may have created Arizona in the pages of the book. Rather than characterizing and defining Arizona in words in 1912, *Riders of the Purple Sage* may have created Arizona in film in 1918 and the years following. The novel was made into a movie five times, each filmed in Arizona, and has come to be identified with the place even though Arizona is never mentioned in its pages.

While *Riders of the Purple Sage* was wildly successful, it did not create Arizona specifically. *The Heritage of the Desert*, Grey's first successful book, does include Arizona landscapes, real and imagined. Grey's *Desert Gold,* published a year after Arizona achieved statehood and set along the Arizona-Mexico border during the Mexican Revolution, created the southern Arizona borderlands for his readers. Unforgiving desert landscapes once again became synonymous with Arizona in this novel. One of the settings for the story, described first in the prologue, is the desert borderland between Sonora, Mexico, and Arizona. Grey described the Sonoran Desert and the prospectors who traverse it, writing, "It moved Cameron to say that in the years of his wandering he had met no man who could endure equally with him the blasting heat, the blinding dust storms, the wilderness of sand and rock and lava and cactus, the terrible silence and desolation of the desert."[73] A second location, the Belding's ranch at Forlorn River, is set in Arizona: "There's not a spot in southern Arizona that'll compare with this valley for water or grass or wood."[74]

Knowing only the Arizona written in Zane Grey's *The Heritage of the Desert*, *Riders of the Purple Sage*, and *Desert Gold*, a reader's idea of Arizona would be of a wild, uncontrolled landscape full of wild, uncontrolled men. The land is unbearably hot and dry, and it is inhabited by cruel religious fanatics, physically strong and attractive women with little power, crusty old prospectors, and bandits and rustlers. But it is also an oasis of lush vegetation watered by flowing rivers and streams and settled by fortunate, wealthy farmers and ranchers. Two extremes of landscapes, two extremes of people. The uncompromising people and brutal and beautiful landscape with which Grey populated his Arizona defined an Arizona unlike that portrayed by the territory's boosters; Grey's was a Wild West.

Just as Grey wrote an Arizona into being, Arizona made possible the development of Zane Grey the writer. He had already written and published a series of books before setting his stories in Arizona. His Ohio frontier stories, based on family history, did not sell well. "The pubic wanted fresh stories about the trans-Mississippi West," what was considered the real West.[75] Grey's second trip to Arizona, his 1907 expedition with Buffalo Jones to northern Arizona and Grand Canyon, provided a trove of material for his first Arizona-inspired work. Recognizing the value of both the experiences and what he learned from them, Grey gave readers a hint of what would follow in the adventure biography of Jones and in his western novels, writing, "Happily in remembrance a writer can live over his experiences, and see once more the moon-blanched silver mountain peaks against the dark blue sky; hear the lonely sough of the night-wind through the pines; feel the dance of wild expectation in the quivering pulse; the stir, the thrill, the joy of hard action in perilous moments; the mystery of man's yearning for the unattainable."[76] In one sentence Grey revealed how the place influenced, defined, created him as a writer, and at the same time he created and defined Arizona and its people.

Arizona motivated Grey's writing, and from its natural landscapes and the people making a living from them he developed his philosophy that traditional values (hard work, a moral code, and the primacy of a rural society) and the frontier spirit are what made America strong. Grey's heroes and heroines were characterized by stoic individualism, courage, and moral fortitude. These characters came to define the people of the West, including Arizonans, and their characteristics came to define Grey's work. Grey set nearly half of his westerns in Arizona, and half of those that were bestsellers were stories with Arizona as the backdrop.[77] Arizona and southern Utah were the heart of Zane Grey's West, and the material amassed from his experiences in those places and written into descriptive prose and action-romances created the author Zane Grey and the place Arizona.

The Constitution of the State of Arizona

During the same years that Sharlot Hall's collection of poetry depicted in verse Arizona's landscape and people as rugged and matchless, and Zane Grey's novels described an individualistic society in a starkly beautiful land, and newspapers within the territory and outside it boosted and defined the place as both a prosperous wonderland and the Wild West, delegates to the constitutional convention were shaping words to create the State of Arizona in its foundational document. Meanwhile, some of those same newspapers were creating the place as a Progressive haven for socialist laborites as they chronicled the details of the convention for their readers.

Unlike 1906, in 1910 the fight over statehood was not centered on joint statehood with New Mexico but around the words in the document that would create the state of Arizona as a political entity: "Every public officer in the state of Arizona, holding an elective office, either by election or appointment, is subject to recall from such office by the qualified electors of the electoral district from which candidates are elected to such office. Such electoral district may include the whole state."[78] Because these words applied to every elected official, including judges, these words stalled, and nearly squandered, Arizona citizens' statehood bid.

On June 25, 1910, Arizona Territorial Governor Richard Sloan announced the number of and apportionment of constitutional convention delegates; elections for delegates were held in September, and the constitutional convention met in Phoenix over a two-month period that fall. The delegates' insistence on direct democracy provisions in the constitution, and its subsequent three-to-one approval by the territory's voters, created a foundational document and defined a state wherein citizens control governing with the initiative, referendum, and recall.

The State of Arizona also became a place friendly to labor, acquiescing to union leaders' pressure with the words in article 18 and the creation of the elected office of the state mine inspector. Newspaper coverage of the convention and ensuing debate in Congress added layers of defining words, establishing Arizonans as independent and, perhaps, immature, depending on which papers were read.

The constitution is the clearest example of how Arizonans as a society define their state. The constitution says of a people, this is who we are and what we believe is important in creating a government. In 1912 Arizona, authority resided with white men. A 1909 law, passed over the veto of Territorial Governor Joseph Kibbey, prohibited anyone from voting who could not read a section of the U.S. Constitution or write his own name.[79] This law was designed to disenfranchise many Hispanic citizens. Native Americans were prohibited from voting in Arizona at the time of statehood, and women had not yet secured the vote. As a society evolves culturally and politically, state constitutions change. Arizona provided for constitutional change based on popular will as well as legislative agenda; thus the words in the state's constitution reveal a changing definition of place based on a changing political, cultural landscape.

The words in the constitution defined the state in two ways. First, the constitution established Arizona as a remarkably progressive place for the time, a state that would function as a populist direct democracy with recall, initiative, and referendum: "The legislative authority of the State shall be vested in a Legislature, consisting of a Senate and a House of Representatives, but the people reserve the power to propose laws and amendments to the Constitution and to enact or reject such laws and amendments at the polls, independently of the Legislature; and they also reserve, for use at their own option, the power to approve or reject at the polls any Act, or item, section, or part of any Act, of the Legislature."[80] The constitution provided an eight-hour workday and safety and child labor provisions in article 18. Women's suffrage was added in the first election after statehood, eight years before they received that right nationally. The words of the constitution also defined Arizona conceptually, as the idea of a place where citizens were unbeholden to lobbyists, corporations, the federal government, and their own elected officials. Whether or not this was reality, the words of the constitution—with its creation of the Corporation Commission and state mine inspector, its strict control of the banking industry, and the inclusion of direct democracy provisions in spite of the federal government's objections—constructed it that way.

There are other images of Arizona contained in its constitution. The words acquiesce to the Enabling Act of 1910, agreeing in article 10 that public lands given to the new state would be held in trust. Article 20 renounces the state's rights to any federal or tribal lands within its boundaries: "The people inhabiting this state do agree and declare that they forever disclaim right and title to the unappropriated and ungranted public lands laying within the boundaries thereof and to all lands laying within said boundaries owned or held by any Indian or Indian tribe," thus accepting national oversight of those federal public lands.[81] Also important is what the words do not say. Despite the urging of labor union leaders, the delegates refused to include an English literacy requirement. That would occur as a constitutional amendment seventy-five years later (in 1985) and again as the state neared its one-hundredth anniversary.[82]

Constitutional convention delegates met in Phoenix from October 10 to December 10, 1910. Delegates included rancher, former bank president, and Globe's first mayor George W. P. Hunt, the president of the convention, who supported organized labor and women's right to vote. He became the new state's first governor. The vice president of the convention, Morris Goldwater, was also a businessman (the owner of Goldwater's mercantile) and a past mayor of Prescott. George Young, former acting territorial governor, was a mine owner who brought new methods and equipment (including a steam-driven electric power plant and mill) to recover ore from the mines at Goldfield near the Superstition Mountains.[83] Several newspapers condemned the election of these businessmen and other convention attendees as a takeover of the convention by labor unions and Progressives.

Even before the passage of the Enabling Act, the calling of the constitutional convention, or the election of the delegates, the *Los Angeles*

Times stridently cautioned against the influence of labor unions at Arizona's convention. Those unions, the editor wrote, "Propose to make a constitution which shall not stop at guaranteeing laboring people the right to form voluntary organizations as they may see fit. . . . They aim openly at putting into the constitution certain clauses which shall forbid courts of justice . . . to issue injunctions against strikers bent on committing violence." Exercised about this one thing, labor strikes, the *Times* declared, "No State constitution will be acceptable to the Supreme Court of the United States which formally justifies the boycott, picketing, rioting, destruction of property, assault upon persons, and the taking of human life."[84] However, Democratic delegates to the convention had agreed to take up organized labor's causes. The *Times* editor recognized that the decisions belonged to Arizonans, but added, "If being forewarned they fail to be forearmed and permit propaganda to capture the constitutional convention, in one way or another, in fact in every way, it will be so much the worse for Arizona as a Territory or as a State."[85] Fifty years later that newspaper's reporters would be describing Arizona as a place at the opposite end of the political spectrum and Barry Goldwater as the epitome of the conservative state.

But in 1910 the *Los Angels Times* described an immature, unaware Arizona citizenry ready to succumb to the uncontrollable forces of socialism and organized labor. The *New York Times* also sounded the alarm before the convention got underway. The great number of Mexicans and the low rate of English literacy that had been reported about Arizona troubled the editors of this paper. According to the writer, Arizona "will come into the Union with only 200,000 inhabitants, 60 percent of whom are of Mexican blood, and frequently ignorant of the English language. . . . Arizona, it will be seen, is something of a problem at the very outset."[86] Whether true or not, these statistics defined an Arizona with great potential but populated, according to the article, by illiterate Hispanics. This perception provoked similar words, and resulted in English-only legislation, nearly a century later.

National newspapers were not the only publications cautioning Arizona's citizens. The Democrats promoted initiative, referendum, and recall, but according to the *Arizona Republican*, they "centered only on one side of it, the theoretical, in the assumption that all men are perfect and at all times interested in public questions."[87] On the Republican side, the newspaper worried that the professional politicians who lobbied the territorial government for mining companies had sold themselves "like Judas for thirty pieces of silver" and were telling citizens "that the only escape from corporation domination . . . is the surrender of every right the people of this county have." The *Republican* editor viewed the initiative, referendum, and recall provisions as an insult to the intelligence of the taxpayers and "one of the most vicious schemes ever devised."[88] The editor's biggest concern was that Congress or President Taft would not approve a Progressive constitution.

Convention delegates were elected September 12, 1910. In an editorial appearing as the election was being planned, the *Arizona Republican* used dire warnings to alert Arizona's citizenry to the wiles of Washington, D.C. The editor presented his assessment of Arizona and its relationship to Washington as a place under attack by national politicians. "Let there be no mistake about the situation," he wrote. "This 'threat' is an admonition to the people of Arizona to frame a constitution acceptable to the president and the congress, or be prepared to accept the defeat of statehood. . . . If we do want statehood, let us frame a constitution which will meet approval at Washington. If we don't want statehood, if we are determined to frame a freak constitution and, in the words of our friend, the *Arizona Democrat*, are willing that the president and congress shall 'do as they damn please about it,' let us say so."[89] By electing Republicans to the convention, the *Republican* believed, statehood would be assured because that party would not include the direct democracy and labor provisions in the document. But in describing the territory's relationship to the federal government in this way, the newspaper reinforced the us-versus-them mindset that would define the state throughout its history. On the same topic of direct democracy, the *Coconino Sun* portrayed Arizonans as foolish and impatient, animating the debate: "The recall of judges is a mere device intended to meet the demands of those who are too impatient and fickle to submit to any stable government"; the paper called the initiative and referendum provisions "new fangled reforms."[90]

Undeterred by the newspapers' alarmed portrayal of the specter of a radical Arizona if its citizens yielded to the temptation of direct democracy, the convention delegates approved a constitution that was decidedly Progressive. Governor Sloan fought its adoption, fearing, rightly it turned out, that the document would not be approved in Washington.[91] Despite the governor's misgivings, voters accepted the document, changed it under duress after the president's veto, and at the next election reinstated it as initially written.

Congress did approve the Arizona state constitution, including its provisions for labor and with the initiative and referendum provisions intact, but stipulated that judicial recall would be removed. President Taft vetoed the statehood bill on August 15, 1911, stating that the territory must change the document before he would approve it. Congress crafted an amendment to the bill that removed the recall of judges from the language of the constitution. The Nelson Amendment stated, "Article 8 of the said constitution of Arizona, in so far as it relates to the 'recall of public officers,' shall be held and construed not to apply to judicial officers, and that the people of Arizona shall give their assent to such construction of Article 8 of the said constitution."[92] Congress passed the Nelson Amendment on August 21, 1911, and President Taft signed it a day later. Thus Arizona was codified, set down in official language in the state constitution and reinforced in the first election after statehood, when women's suffrage was added and the recall of judicial officers reinstated.

The contentious nature under which the document came to be accepted, the words approved by the state's people and disapproved by the nation's government, signaled the kind of relationship the state would have with the nation's leaders going forward. The words were chosen carefully to leave no doubt where the men (and by implication the state) who framed the document stood on matters of governance. The Arizona and New Mexico enabling acts were designed specifically to guard against a constitution unacceptable to the federal government by requiring the approval of the president as well as Congress.[93] Ultimately Arizonans got the constitution they wanted. The Arizona defined in 1912 was remarkably similar in attitude to Arizona in 2012—independent-minded, stubborn, and defiant of federal jurisdiction—yet markedly different in politics, with its stance on labor unions, women's rights, progressive policies, and English-literacy requirements.

In his first State of the State address to the first meeting of the first state legislature, Gov. George W. P. Hunt presented his idea of Arizona, the place he believed the new state was and could be. In an eighteen-thousand-word message, Hunt described Arizona for listeners and readers, employing not the rhetoric of the recent fight for statehood but rather the clichés that had been and continued to be the defining words of Arizona: "In natural resources and the possession of patent possibilities, Arizona is bounteously blessed. Her acres are broad and fertile, her mountains and streams rich with mineral wealth; her forests are well-nigh virgin; her skies are blue; her climate as of another Italy; her people honest, hardy, self-reliant, brave." Nothing in Hunt's address contradicted the many Arizonas created in words by 1912. The Arizona of the state's constitution and the newspapers' coverage of a state coming into being can be found in his words praising the state's self-reliant people. The Arizona of Sharlot Hall's poetry can be found in Hunt's descriptions of the state's natural landscape. The Arizona of Zane Grey's novels can be found in the governor's portrayal of the citizens as hardy and brave, and the newspapers' booster language can be found as Hunt illustrates Arizona's "bounteous blessings." The governor concluded, "Thus endowed, all things are possible to the forty-eighth state of the union. Whatever of ills there might be—industrial, financial, or social—there is the wherewith to right them. . . . I feel justified on reporting to you that the condition of the state is good."[94] The next twenty-five years would present all of theses challenges—industrial, financial, and social—and would require a broader understanding, a redefining, of the idea of Arizona.

In Summary

Throughout its history, Arizona has often been described and characterized—defined—by outsiders or for the benefit of outsiders. Arizona's narratives in 1912 define the place by the already familiar phrases that describe an independent people and landscapes of extremes—lush forests and stark deserts, modern civilization and Wild West. While its natural landscapes made possible the creation of lyrical poetry and bestselling western novels, the writers of those publications succumbed to and contributed to the characterizations that were already becoming cliché but would continue to define the state in the future. Lacking control of or access to the means of writing in their own words and telling their own stories, Native Americans were written into the stories about the state in stereotypical and racist language. In the future, minority people's access to the publishing apparatus would enable a broader defining of Arizona. The fight over the words in the state's constitution reveals a breach between the state's people and the federal government that would also mark that relationship going forward. As Arizona developed economically and culturally, some of the clichés gave way to a more encompassing perception of the place. However, the old themes remained present and persistent.

OVERLOOK

Booms, Busts, and Borders

WORLD WAR I AND THE GREAT DEPRESSION

"Deputies and Armed Citizens Load 'Reds' onto Cattle Cars," announced the *Los Angeles Times* headline on July 13, 1917. The event occurred in Bisbee, a copper mining town in southeastern Arizona near the Mexican border. Ostensibly "Reds"—reported to be agents of the Industrial Workers of the World—the men loaded onto the boxcars and deported were actually miners striking for a share of the copper companies' increasing profits, the result of high demand due to the ongoing war in Europe. The "deputies" were armed antiunion citizens and businessmen from the towns of Bisbee and Douglas and miners loyal to the mining companies. Deputized by Harry Wheeler, the sheriff of Cochise County, the perpetrators of the deportation donned white armbands to identify themselves and early on the morning of July 12 began rounding up strikers at gunpoint. Newspapers characterized the roundup as warranted, writing of the "strange and foreign" element the reporters believed had infiltrated the mines and using the mining companies' justification of the war effort to rebuff the unions' call for sharing profits with the miners. In the view of mine owners, many citizens, and the newspapers, the strike was unpatriotic and anti-American, and deporting the troublemaking strikers from Arizona was absolutely necessary.[1]

The United States had declared war on Germany three months earlier, and a deportation of seventy-five men from the Jerome, Arizona, copper mines to Kansas occurred on July 10. Rumors abounded that German sympathizers among the striking miners in Bisbee had hidden weapons and explosives throughout the town. Newspaper coverage of the deportation reported that men were stopped on the street and asked about their loyalty to the mines. Actually, many of the men were roused out of bed and hustled out of their homes at gunpoint, in front of their wives and children. Nearly twelve hundred men (not all were miners—some were sympathetic to the strikers' cause and some were bystanders caught in the roundup) were loaded on cattle cars, the floors still inches deep in manure. Two hundred guards manned the train as it traveled east. The deportees were abandoned in the cars in the desert at Hermanas, New Mexico. Rather than denounce the mistreatment of hardworking men, three days later the *Times* declared, "Our soldiers are in France, our engineers in Russia, our sailors in hourly peril stand guard on the North Sea, and hundreds of thousands are training and millions are waiting to go, and fight-win-die. But from Butte to Bisbee, from Seattle to Leadville, that international organization, filled with foreigners, officered by convicts, and attempting vaguely to guise its sabotage behind the specious title of 'Industrial Workers of the World,' is in open warfare against our government."[2]

President Woodrow Wilson appointed a special labor commission to investigate the deportation. The commission determined the deportation was illegal and agreed with Arizona governor Thomas Campbell's assessment: "The constitutional rights of citizens and others have been ignored." According to the commissioners' report, "The function of the local judiciary was usurped by a body, which, to all intents and purposes was a vigilance committee, having no authority whatever in law." However, the commission found no federal law that could be applied to the incident and referred it to the State of Arizona, which took no action.[3]

Copper companies' soaring profits cratered after the war ended. As the nation endured a postwar depression in the early 1920s, Arizona's economy also suffered. Due to a glutted copper market—thousands of tons of copper produced for war use were no longer needed—mines were forced to close. The cotton market also collapsed, affecting hundreds of growers in Arizona who had converted three-quarters of their irrigated land to cotton production. Arizona's lumber industry declined to 25 percent of normal. Drastic budget cuts forced the state highway department to close work camps and put hundreds of men out of work. Labor unions opened soup- and breadlines as the legislature debated what to do with the thousands of unemployed cotton pickers, most of them Mexican citizens brought across the international border in response to growers' pleas for more labor. The state legislature called on the U.S. Immigration Bureau to manage the situation; the bureau in turn declined, stating the growers had demanded the workers and should "do their duty." The Southern Pacific Railroad finally agreed to transport thousands of pickers from Maricopa County back to Mexico.[4]

Arizona's international border proved to be a political, economic, and social challenge for citizens on both sides of the boundary line. In the nineteenth century, as a result of the Treaty of Guadalupe Hidalgo and the Gadsden Purchase, former citizens of Mexico became citizens of the United States. But those political decisions separated people who had once been members of united family groups and communities, placing a political, and eventually physical, barrier to movement across what had once been undivided territory.[5] Arizona's Mexican-born population more than doubled between 1910 and 1920, from 29,987 to 61,580 (Arizona's total population in 1920 was 334,162), as Mexican citizens fled their country during the Mexican Revolution.[6] Prominent businessmen in Arizona's border towns were charged with smuggling arms to Mexican fighters on both sides of the conflict, and the federal government mobilized U.S. troops and the Arizona National Guard to protect the state. Meanwhile, Arizona's mines and cotton farmers employed Mexican laborers and called for more workers as those industries expanded during World War I. After the postwar depression, as the U.S. economy recovered, Arizona cotton growers once again demanded more Mexican workers.[7]

In addition to appealing to the federal government to assist in acquiring Mexican labor, Arizona's agricultural sector played a role in the government's reclamation quest. Wet years in the first decades of the twentieth century and the unpredictable nature of Arizona's rivers—often changing from dry riverbeds to raging floods in a matter of minutes—contributed to citizens' growing sense of need to harness the flow of water for storage and irrigation purposes and flood control. In 1921 Congress gave the state legislatures and governors of seven western states the right to negotiate their use of the Colorado River. Commissioners from Arizona, California, Colorado, Nevada, New Mexico, Utah, and Wyoming met periodically to negotiate an agreement. Approved by commissioners of six of the seven states and by both houses of Congress in 1925 (only Arizona opposed the plan), the Colorado River Compact apportioned the water between the upper-basin states (Colorado, New Mexico, Utah, and Wyoming) and lower-basin states (Arizona, California, and Nevada). As the agreement was being negotiated, the U.S. Reclamation Service announced it would build a high dam on the Colorado River at Black Canyon. In December 1923 Congressman Phillip Swing and Senator Hiram Johnson of California introduced their bill to provide for the construction of Boulder (now Hoover) Dam at the Arizona-Nevada border. As the only river state to oppose the bill, Arizona's congressional delegation worked to block its passage through filibusters and deal making. In 1928 Senator Johnson compromised with Arizona senator Carl Hayden on the amount of water Arizona would receive, paving the way for the passage of the Swing-Johnson Bill in December of that year.[8]

The wet years of the 1920s gave way to the dry years of the 1930s. In 1934 the Arizona Cattle Growers Association informed the federal government that tens of thousands of head of cattle were suffering from lack of feed due to drought. Arizona was declared a drought area, and the government authorized emergency crop loan offices to lend money for ranchers throughout the state to purchase cattle feed. Congressman Edward T. Taylor of Colorado introduced a bill to establish grazing districts, limit the number of livestock permitted in each district, and maintain management of the districts by federal agencies. *Los Angeles Times* readers learned "it is pretty well established that overgrazing has damaged large sections of the free range . . . [and] in some cases destroyed it entirely." However, a subheadline, "Passage Would Bring End of American Frontier," reflected the prevailing attitude, especially in Arizona, that public lands were meant to be utilized to their fullest, which meant unlimited use for grazing by cattle and sheep ranchers.[9]

Anglo ranchers were not the only Arizonans affected by federal land policies, though they did have a hand in writing the legislation.[10] In 1933 the Navajo tribe became the target of a different type of land policy. With no input from Navajo leaders, John Collier, Franklin Roosevelt's commissioner of the Bureau of Indian Affairs (BIA), imposed a top-down program to reduce the tribe's livestock by over a million head of sheep and goats. Concerned about drought and overgrazing on the reservation, Collier was convinced that the lives of the Navajo people were threatened (and feared Boulder Dam would be rendered useless by the soil eroded from the reservation) and was motivated by the new science of soil conservation and the concept of carrying capacity (the number of head of grazing stock a region could sustain). Disastrous and devastating, the livestock reduction program forced the loss of livelihood and cultural cohesion for families and communities across the vast Navajo lands.[11] While the *Washington Post* could report in 1937 that because of the Taylor Grazing Act the cattle industry was "in the best condition, economically, since 1929," it also reported on hearings before the Senate Committee on Indian Affairs regarding BIA policies, including livestock reduction, wherein Navajo tribal members declared that "under [BIA] administration our nation has hit bottom in poverty. . . . They are destroying our nation."[12]

The Great Depression affected how the federal government dealt with environmental concerns and how it interacted with its citizens, especially in the western states. Arizona entered the union perceived as a place of independent, forward-looking citizens. Throughout its first twenty-five years as a state, Arizona's citizens—troubled by uncertainties and fluctuations in the economy and the cyclical nature of the climate, experienced as floods and droughts—increasingly looked toward Washington, D.C., and the federal government for assistance.

CHAPTER 2

Creating Arizona, 1937

ARIZONA'S TWENTY-FIFTH ANNIVERSARY of statehood passed with hardly a mention. Twenty-five years had added a system of roads across the state's vast natural landscape and had more than doubled the state's population, from just over two hundred thousand at the time of statehood to nearly five hundred thousand in the 1930s.[1] The boom years of the 1920s became the bust years of the 1930s. The Great Depression matured the people and changed the land. The place that had been insistent yet independent in its fight for statehood was, in the 1930s, increasingly aided by the federal government in the form of New Deal programs that built and improved the state's infrastructure and described the state in publications to encourage visitors.

Industries that contributed to sustained population and economic growth, particularly copper mining and agriculture, experienced market collapses in the early Depression years. In 1933 Arizona's copper production and sales dropped by 94 percent and employment in the mines fell by 80 percent. Drought coupled with falling cattle prices forced ranchers off the land, and cotton prices fell from eleven to four cents a pound.[2] Migrants traveling from equally devastated regions to the east joined Arizona residents in looking for work.

The state's minority communities bore exceptional hardships as the federal government attempted to manage the effects of the Depression. The Indian New Deal changed federal policy toward Native Americans, including a shift to local rather than boarding schools and the Indian Reorganization Act (1934), which imposed Anglo governing methods on tribal governments. The specter of a southwestern Dust Bowl, and related fears of Navajo people "on the dole" and Lake Mead filled to the brim with Colorado Plateau topsoil, led to the implementation of the devastating sheep reduction plan on the Navajo reservation.[3] Hispanics in central and southern Arizona endured extreme unemployment, in part due to failures in the mining and agricultural industries. As many as eighteen thousand Mexicans may have left Arizona for Mexico between 1929 and 1937 because of unfavorable economic conditions. Many of those people were U.S. citizens.[4]

Federal relief assistance came to the state in the form of employment in the Civilian Conservation Corps (CCC) and programs through the Public Works Administration and the Works Progress Administration (WPA). New Deal assistance changed the natural landscape of the state, raising visitor centers at national parks and monuments, facilitating reforestation and soil erosion control, building dams to control flooding and provide power, and constructing roads across the deserts and through the mountains. Arizona was no longer an isolated, out-of-the-way place. Thanks to federal funds for road improvements, the physical landscape seemed less a wilderness and more accessible. Several towns had airfields. The City of Phoenix purchased Sky Harbor from the Acme Investment Company in 1935. Tucson's Davis-Monthan Airport was the largest municipal airport in the country when it opened in 1927.[5]

New Deal funds also changed Arizona's narrative landscape: directly, as Federal Writers' Project (FWP) writers described and explained the state to encourage tourism; and indirectly, as roads and national park development brought more people including writers to the place, made possible new experiences and perceptions, and added to the layers of words about the state. The FWP work on the Indian reservations added to the narratives about the state, as the lives, landscapes, and stories of the state's native peoples were written into the guides and bulletins. Meanwhile, Native Americans were still excluded as participants in this type of place creation as Anglos continued to control the process as writers, editors, and publishers.

In the 1930s Arizona was represented in images, moving pictures on the big screen. Nearly a dozen Zane Grey novels were adapted into movies during the decade, including *Arizona Raiders* (an adaption of

Riders of the Spanish Peaks) and *Desert Gold* (both in 1936) and *Heritage of the Desert* (twice, in 1932 and 1939). Also in 1939 the iconic John Ford western *Stagecoach*, starring John Wayne and prominently featuring Monument Valley landscapes, was released. The Arizona depicted on-screen was a place of hard landscapes, hard people, and hard lives.

For readers however, whose perceptions of Arizona were shaped by words, the place was more than harsh landscapes and bandits. In 1937 Arizona was a canvas on which a British novelist wrote his vision of America. It was raw material from which writers employed by the federal government could produce a body of literature encouraging visitors to the state. Arizona was not just a place of movie cowboys and Indians but also a land of real Indians negotiating the cultural differences imposed by an encroaching Anglo world and federal powers. American Indians' stories were told through Anglo ethnographers in fiction and autobiography. Arizona's ancient heritage was explored, excavated, re-created, and written up in archaeological reports and popular magazines as Euro-American authors tried to come to terms with a landscape that did not fit within their cultural understanding. The barrier of language and an Anglo bias against oral traditions meant that the Native American histories and connections to these places would not be given credence; these stories too would be appropriated and told by Anglos.

J. B. Priestley and *Midnight on the Desert*

In the winter of 1936, *Harper's Magazine* published an article by British novelist, playwright, essayist, and broadcaster J. B. Priestley. In "Arizona Desert" Priestley explored the location's enchanting environment (masked by the article's plain title), and, inspired by the Arizona desert, he examined America's place in the world. He described the stark beauty of the desert and the bounty of America's natural resources. The presentation was lighthearted, but the undertone was serious. What is this place America? What does it mean and do? What can it accomplish, should it accomplish? These were questions seemingly drawn out by Priestley's time in the Arizona desert.

Priestley employed themes familiar to descriptions of Arizona: the dichotomy of Arizona's age (prehistoric and brand new) and landscapes (verdant and barren), and the wonderland atmosphere of the place. "Everything that happened here [in Arizona] before yesterday is prehistorical," Priestley wrote. "Turn back a page or two, and the Indians are still raiding, the bad men are shooting up the towns, and the traveler whose horse has gone lame is dying of thirst." Men not yet old could remember those times, yet Arizona's children saw dusty dirt tracks paved and towns appear along them. Seen through the eyes of a British visitor, America, and Arizona specifically, was new: "Here along these Western highways, with their fine surfaces, careful grading and banking, elaborate signs, their filling stations, their auto camps, their roadside eating-houses and hotels, their little towns passionately claiming your custom in a startling sudden glare of electric signs, is a brand-new busy world."[6]

Arizona's landscapes were both old and new. On the age of Arizona's natural landscapes, Priestley wrote, "In the north, where you are a mile and a half high, there is the Grand Canyon, which is enough in itself to clear a whole continent from the charge of being dull. But you also have the Painted Deserts and the Petrified Forests. The dinosaurs left their tracks in these parts. When the giant meteor decided to imbed itself in the earth, it chose Arizona, and you may see the crater it made, near Winslow." But Arizona's cultural landscape was new, according to Priestley, and he made no mention of Native Americans, some of whom had inhabited the place for a millennium, or the state's Hispanic population, who had lived there for centuries. "It is all brand-new," he declared. "And most of it, in its pretty frivolity of colored lights and facetious appeals, seems to have no more to do with the savage countryside itself than a jiggling line of chorus girls would have. Yet like America taking its place of leadership in the world, the towns along Arizona's highways were conducting us . . . straight across the waterless wilderness, day and night."[7] Driving along the highways from Los Angeles to Wickenburg, in the vastness of the Arizona desert, Priestley was given to question these things.

The open spaces of desert—connected by paved roads, railroad tracks, and more recently by air travel—caused him to wonder about

America writ large. The youngest state (within what Priestley later readily assigned as the oldest of landscapes) in a relatively young country provoked an ageless question: Is this country and its people up to the task before it? Other nations were following America's lead, Priestley surmised: "America does not know where she is going, but if she walks into some abyss of barbarism, she will not walk alone. This I concluded, was a solemn responsibility." Reflecting on the ingenuity and audacity of constructing miles of highway through the desert, he counseled, "American political and social ideas, though they are changing already, will have to bound forward, to borrow some of the enterprise and courage of the engineers and builders and even of this new wayside population, in order to keep up. In short, you will have to discover where it is you are taking us."[8]

Priestley grieved the unrestrained use, or misuse, of Arizona's resources, writing, "There was a time not very long ago when these ranches in northern Arizona carried feed for vast herds of cattle. But what the cattle left, the sheep that followed almost completely destroyed, pulling up the very roots.... The desert hills have been swept clean of feed for cattle; forests containing easily marketable timber have been massacred without quarter; mines have been worked in what once seemed the cheapest way, but in what since proved to be the most expensive fashion." Yet exclaiming upon the wonder of Boulder Dam, he wrote, "It is worth traveling weeks to see. It is like the beginning of a new world . . . a world of giant machines and titanic communal enterprises."[9] The title of the article, "Arizona Desert," holds the promise and the possibilities of America. Add a little water, build this miracle called Boulder Dam, and watch the desert bear fruit.

Priestley was not immune to the superlatives of boosterism, and he was writing an article about the Arizona desert for a national audience. In describing the Wickenburg area, where he and his family wintered, he could be composing a brochure for the town's chamber of commerce. Wickenburg, he wrote, "has the best winter climate in the state, which means that it has one of the best winter climates in the world." As if he were writing advertising copy, he declared, "The Wickenburg district will become increasingly important, for a winter climate as good as this will prove a better gold-mine than the Old Vulture. . . . There's gold in them thar hills, but the best of it is the January sunshine." He described the air as "enchanting . . . crystal clear . . . [it] gives the Arizona landscape its enduring charm" and depicted the landscape using words like "magically molded" and "unbelievably sumptuous." Just as Sharlot Hall had written about the place twenty-five years earlier, Priestley described Arizona by its extremes: "There are great tracts of virgin forest, as well as hundreds of miles of desert. There are mysterious Indian ruins all over the place. There are strange heights called the Superstition Mountains, where men have gone to look for lost goldmines and have never returned. There is about the whole state a suggestion of the *Arabian Nights*. Its vegetation, with the immense pillars of saguaro cactus dominating everything else, is fantastic. Its rocks hide treasures of gold, opals, and rubies, and are covered with ancient writing."[10] The possibility exists that something inherent in the Arizona landscape caused even a British novelist with a reputation for being caustic in his observations about America and society to wax in exaggerated exposé even while ruminating on American leadership as he drove through the Arizona desert.[11]

The words in "Arizona Desert" became part of Priestley's next book, a combination of travel book, social commentary, and memoir titled *Midnight on the Desert: Being an Excursion into Autobiography during a Winter in America, 1935–36* (1937). In the article and the book, Priestley described the Arizona desert at night: "The nights are even more spacious than the days. No lid of darkness is clapped over you. The spaces are wider than ever, and are lit, night after night, with all the stars of the Northern Hemisphere, as precisely defined as the stars in a planetarium."[12] This description may inform the title of the book; midnight, often symbolizing great darkness in literature, does not symbolize darkness in Arizona. In this book midnight does not describe a time of darkness but a time of looking forward, of looking toward the dawn, and the desert does not depict a hopeless arid wasteland but instead an empty expanse full of possibilities.

As in the *Harper's* article, Arizona was the setting of *Midnight on the Desert*. Priestley expanded on the place, again utilizing time and extremes to emphasize the matchless landscape. He described his middle-of-the-night walk to his writing shack situated at the edge of the ranch thus:

> In the silence, slowly picking my way, I thought about this Arizona country. The New World! It seemed to me the oldest country I had ever seen, the real antique land, first cousin to the moon. Brown, bony, sapless, like an old man's hand. We called it new because it was not thick with history, not a museum and guidebook place. Man had been here such a little time that his arrival had not yet been acknowledged. . . . The early mornings, in winter, are cold, very fresh and pure. Then, under the burning noons, the red cardinals and the bluebirds flash among the cottonwoods, as if nature had turned outrageously symbolic. The afternoons are simply so much sunlight and aromatic air. But at sunset the land throws up pink summits and saw-toothed ridges of amethyst, and there are miracles of fire in the sky. Night uncovers two million more stars than you have ever seen before; and the planets are not points, but globes.[13]

This was the desert and its midnight, thoroughly Arizona to Priestley. With no acknowledgment that people had resided in this place for thousands of years, he creates an Arizona for readers in which the recent American settlers were the first occupants. His descriptions of the natural world paint in prose the increasingly familiar picture of a fantastic landscape. However the book was not all cliché—or completely benign.

From his place of comfort on the desert Priestley made these observations about Arizona: "Thinking, then, of all those Arizona people around me, fast asleep while I smoked and ruminated in my hut, I considered—not too pompously, I hope—the little classless society they had temporarily evolved." According to Priestley, Arizonans had no difference of wealth and still resided in an almost naïve "pioneer" state. "There are few rags, fewer diamonds," he wrote.[14] Priestley may have been observant about Arizona's natural landscape, but he seemed not to have observed Arizonans, seemed unaware of the reservations or the barrios, had not encountered their residents. As he continued his discussion about wealth and privilege, declaring privilege was more insidious than wealth, he wrote an Arizona that exemplified a near-ideal society. Priestley believed, "What is needed is a juster distribution of wealth with as little privilege as possible. Owing to certain local and temporary conditions, a state like Arizona comes nearer to achieving this than the older communities do, with the result that it seems far nearer to our idea of a free and happy democracy."[15] Priestley's unawareness of the state's minorities meant that his representation of Arizona as an ideal was narrow, confined to an Anglo Arizona. Like Sharlot Hall's characterization of Arizona at the time of statehood, Priestley rendered Native Americans and other minority populations invisible in his narrative.

While titled *Midnight on the Desert,* the book was not predominantly about Arizona. Midnight on the desert was the setting, the time and place Priestley chose to get his papers in order. For Priestley the desert brought forth another perspective. It was not only a western novel or a paradise or an adolescent twenty-five-year-old state, though those elements of the place are present in the book, but the arid expanse also enabled a contemplation that is antithetical to the clichés. The idea of rugged western individualism that prevailed in much of the writing about Arizona instead provoked in Priestley a commentary on America's communal aspects. "American economists and politicians and newspaper editors may go on and on shouting about their individualism, but the great unconscious drift of American life," he decided, "was away from it, set towards a very different shore." The opposite, in fact, was the case, he realized. What had made America "so new, formidable, and fascinating" was not its rugged individualism but what could be accomplished by its people collectively. Boulder Dam was the perfect example of this collective effort. "This is a first glimpse of what chemistry and mathematics and engineering and large-scale organization can accomplish when collective planning unites and inspires them," Priestley wrote. "Here is the soul of America under socialism."[16]

"In almost all but his theories," Priestley believed, "the average modern American *is* the collective man. His impulsive advances seem to be always away from that famous individualism. He has no objection to mass movement. Nearly everything he does is being done about the same time by a million others. He likes doing exactly what all the others are doing." This was not a bad thing, according to Priestley. Americans were "a people who, while saluting the old banners of economic individualism, are always busy expressing themselves collectively, and doing it with an ease, force, and natural cohesion." It was this communal mindset that provided work at Grand Canyon for the unemployed through the CCC and built Boulder Dam, and it would lead, Priestley wrote, to "some kind of collectivist state, an ultimate socialism."[17]

Priestley's descriptions of Arizona's natural landscapes bracket the narrative about America. The Arizona desert facilitated his musings about America, and Grand Canyon, Priestley asserted, could facilitate a better America. He began the book with the desert, describing it from his place in Wickenburg, and he ended with descriptions of Grand Canyon. Of his trip to Grand Canyon he wrote, "I have heard rumors of visitors who were disappointed. The same people will be disappointed at the Day of Judgment. In fact, the Grand Canyon is a sort of landscape Day of Judgment." Echoing Thomas Dowler Murphy from a quarter-century earlier ("Here the Architect Divine planned a succession of pyramids and palaces of overwhelming immensity"), Priestley continued, "It is not a show place, a beauty spot, but a revelation. The Colorado River, which is powerful, turbulent, and so thick with silt that it is like a saw, made it with the help of the erosive forces of rain, frost, and wind, and some strange geological accidents; and all these together have been hard at work on it for the last seven or eight million years. . . . It is the world's supreme example of erosion. But this is not what it really is. It is, I repeat, a revelation."[18] Priestley was so moved by Grand Canyon that he declared, "If I were an American, I should make my remembrance of it the final test of men, art, and policies. I should ask myself: Is this good enough to exist in the same country as the Canyon? . . . Every member or officer of the Federal Government ought to remind himself, with triumphant pride, that he is on the staff of the Grand Canyon."[19]

Midnight on the Desert quickly became a bestseller. In a lengthy, two-column review in the *New York Times*, Ralph Thompson called it "a many-faceted and provocative work" and deemed Priestley "an admirable author."[20] What did this book tell the reading public about Arizona? Along with the truths about the landscapes contained within the themes of time and extremes, it also portrayed the falseness of the idea of American individualism. That this reconsideration was generated by a trip to Arizona, a place rooted in the concept, is remarkable. Ostensibly, the book's moment in time is that 1936 night when Priestley organized his papers in Arizona, doing some housekeeping before he traveled back to England. Broadly, the book is about America, its place in the world, its ascending to a position of leadership, and its stereotypical individualism that Priestley believes masks the reality of a communal society.

The Federal Writers' Project: *Arizona Guide* and Bulletins

J. B. Priestley's commentary about the communal nature of American life finds validation in the programs of the New Deal; through opportunities like the FWP, the American people (in the form of their government) took care of each other, making sure even unemployed writers had work. The states and their assets became communal as their landscapes were shared with the nation through the words of the American Guide series. Arizona's people had defied the federal government to get the constitution they wanted just twenty-five years earlier, yet in 1937 the federal government provided a service to the people of the state by publicizing and redefining its resources, residents, and attractions in the *Arizona Guide* and its attendant bulletins, while employing the state's writers.

The bulletins, published by the FWP in conjunction with the Arizona State Teachers College in Flagstaff, reveal that Anglo Arizona and Native American Arizona are not the same place. The bulletins were a deliberate effort by the federal government to represent minority cultures to readers, but the people presented are simply that—presented; they are not active in telling their own stories. The bulletins' forewords took great care to assert the authenticity of the books' contents. "The material was gathered through personal contact on the reservation, verified by documentation, and carefully checked by experts," stated the foreword to *The Apache*.[21] Yet all of the sources cited in all of the bulletins' bibliographies were written by Anglos, predominately by Anglo men. American Indians found themselves amidst an American society addressing the question of assimilation, visible both in the act of writing (Native Americans' stories told by Anglo writers) and in the content of the words: the FWP Indian bulletins, Oliver La Farge's fiction, and the as-told-to autobiographies that became popular in the 1930s. The writers of the WPA, the ethnologists and anthropologists adapting Native American autobiographies, and even La Farge as he incorporated his knowledge of Navajo life into his novels, became interpreters of minority culture. Their versions of the Indian people and reservation life became what the English-reading public in the 1930s knew of the people and their reservations.

The main purpose of the state guides was to describe a place people would want to visit.[22] The *Arizona Guide* repeated the familiar theme of extremes—the temporal (the youngest state with the oldest natural features); the ancient, primitive, and modern cultural landscapes; and the varied, abundant, and stark natural landscape—endemic to descriptions of Arizona: "Arizona is the nation's youngest state, and alive with the spirit of youth. Yet if we count the aeons through which it has been inhabited by man, civilizations that have come and gone, Arizona is an ancient and venerable land."[23] Extreme follows extreme in a passage early in the book describing the contrasts of the natural landscape—"Its mountains tower a mile or more into the air; the rivers have cut miles deep into the multicolored earth. . . . Here are sere deserts and the largest pine forest in the world. Here are fallen forests turned to stone, and forests of trees that have survived the slow change from jungle to desert by turning their leaves to thorns." This is followed by the contrasts of the cultural landscape: "Modern transport planes fly on regular passenger and mail routes, while Hopi grandmothers scatter sacred cornmeal on the newborn infant and pray to the sun for blessings."[24] This was the same Arizona described in 1912, the same place characterized in Hall's *Cactus and Pine* and in newspaper articles. Except for the addition of the airplane, this could have been Zane Grey's Arizona.

These passages reveal how the writers expect readers to view the people of the state. All the descriptions that follow, whether of mining or agriculture or tourism, will be seen through the window that these words frame:

> Arizona has been the home of . . . cliff dwellers who built shelters of stone, learned how to shape clay into pottery, but did not practice even the rudiments of agriculture; of pastoral tribes who built pueblos, planted corn and cotton beside irrigation canals; of fierce raiders who preyed upon their peaceful neighbors; of swashbuckling *conquistadores* and gentle priests who strove to impress the faith and culture of Spain upon the natives they found here; and last of these modern interlopers, the Yankees, who leveled mountains for their copper, laced the face of the land with ribbons of concrete, dammed rivers to make the deserts bloom, and in less than a century worked changes vaster than their predecessors had wrought in thousands of years.[25]

According to the *Guide*'s writers, then, Arizona was the place where primitive cliff dwellers had lived but not farmed, where Native Americans were characterized as agriculturalists and warriors and Hispanics as explorers and priests, and where now resided the Anglo trespassers who had co-opted and admirably used the state's natural resources.[26] This was the Arizona presented to potential visitors and settlers, an Anglo representation with an emphasis on natural resources as economic assets.

A large portion of the *Guide* is dedicated to explaining the state's politics, agriculture, industry, and transportation. Rather than describe using boosterish language and exaggeration, leaving those types of descriptions for the landscapes, the *Guide* writers presented facts about the state in seemingly neutral tones, but in a way that demonstrated its attractiveness. Readers were encouraged to use the *Guide* to plan a trip to and through Arizona, and the writers intended that what they reported, the visitors would actually see. However, the place the *Guide* presented was an Anglo Arizona, the dude ranches and other attractions set up and written down for Anglo consumption as tourists and readers.

The *Guide* emphasized the otherness of Native Americans, revealing that while Anglo Arizonans were mostly indifferent to their state's history, "The 'another-redskin-bit-the-dust' type of reminiscence offers unfailing delight."[27] Was this an exaggeration? Or was it the mindset of writers and readers alike? Probably the latter, considering this viewpoint: "A third of Arizona's inhabitants are Indians and Mexicans, unassimilable into an Anglo-Saxon population, and there are many reasons why the Caucasians have attained only a limited degree of homogeneity."[28] Contrast this with the FWP's *New Mexico Guide*, which, from the first sentence, treats all three groups as part of its cultural tapestry: "New Mexico today represents a blend of three cultures—Indian, Spanish, and American—each of which has had its time upon the stage and dominated the scene. The composite of culture which now, in the union of statehood, presents a harmonious picture upon casual inspection, is deceptive, for the veneer of Americanization in places runs thin indeed." Even with the trend toward "Americanization," rather than characterizing Hispanic and Native American citizens as "unassimilable," the *New Mexico Guide* identified "the interaction of the diverse elements" of a population that was "slowly working towards homogeneity, dominated more and more by the irresistible middle current of Anglo-American civilization and the modern American tempo."[29]

Regarding Hispanics, the *Arizona Guide* stated, "Arizona owes much of its color and individuality to the Mexicans, who largely retain their own culture and customs in an environment constantly growing more alienized. Almost every city and town of any size has its Mexican quarter—squalid, for most of its inhabitants are laborers in the lower wage brackets, but picturesque withal." With this perception as their baseline, *Guide* writers found accomplished, successful Hispanics worthy of mention, yet wrote in a manner emphasizing their strangeness, stating, "History is filled with the names of Mexicans who played a prominent part in the development of the first settlements. Their descendants are respected, prominent, and in some cases well-to-do. In Yuma, Nogales, and Tucson especially, are to be found many families of Spanish extraction enjoying friendly business and social relationships with Anglo-Americans."[30]

However, the writers also stressed what they believed was the more common characterization of the Hispanic character, explaining, "His economic status is such that he has little opportunity to adopt the modes of life followed by the lighter-skinned people who employ him, but it is also true that he has slight inclination to change his ways."[31] The *Guide's* writers relegated Hispanics to second-class citizenship and then placed the blame on them for the writers' having to classify them that way. The stereotypical and racist images in the *Arizona Guide* contributed to an Anglo perception of Hispanic inferiority that increased intolerant rhetoric and culminated in a series of anti-immigrant and English-literacy measures in the 1980s (see chapter 4). Again, the contrast with the *New Mexico Guide* is striking. The *New Mexico Guide* writers recognized that all people within the state's political boundaries became citizens of the United States when their territory became part of the nation. "The people of Spanish descent became United States citizens and were known thereafter as Spanish-speaking Americans to distinguish them from the Indians and the later immigrants from old Mexico," its writers explained. To further clarify cultural differences without subjugating any group, the writers continued, "To distinguish the settlers from other parts of the United States, the prefix 'Anglo' was added. Thus today the residents of the State are spoken of as Spanish-speaking Americans or Spanish Americans, Anglo-Americans, and Indians. It is well to keep these distinctions in mind when thinking of New Mexico."[32]

In describing Native Americans, the *Arizona Guide* stated, "The Indians also afford a bright and novel note for the Arizona scene. . . . More than the Mexicans, the Indians are reluctant to assume the features of American life, although this reluctance is in a measure overcome among Indian children educated in boarding schools maintained by the great white fathers."[33] Indian people may have been novel for new arrivals, but not novel in the sense of new; Native Americans had been in the place longer than any others. The paternalistic belief that the boarding schools were necessary and successful belied the reality of the system's damaging effects.[34]

The FWP writers worked with officials at Arizona State Teachers College to develop some of the material they were collecting about

Native Americans into a useful resource for teachers. This collaboration resulted in several bulletins, each booklet dedicated to the exploration of an Arizona Indian tribe. *The Hopi*, *The Navaho*, *The Apache*, and *The Papago* were published before the *Guide*. In 1937 Native Americans' words were filtered through Anglo lenses or appropriated and re-created by Anglo storytellers. In the 1930s Indian people were still subjects written into Arizona rather than participants writing their own stories about their place.

The introduction to the Hopi booklet served as the introduction to the series of bulletins. It was Eurocentric—more so even than most of the words about Native Americans in the *Guide*. Herein lies the barrier, the boundary that had, at that time, not yet been crossed or even discerned: "The study of any group possessing a written language falls within the scope of history, and such a group thereby becomes a civilized people. The tribes to be discussed are all primitive, in the sense that they do not write their own language. This is the technical distinction between primitive and civilized."[35] In three sentences the FWP writers classified entire cultures as primitive and lacking history—these people had no written language and written language signals civilization; thus the Indian people were not civilized. This conclusion is patently false; written and oral forms of communication are not mutually exclusive, and written narrative does not denote a historical sensibility that oral narrative lacks.[36]

The bulletins, as well as the *Guide*, adopted a tone that made each indigenous culture appear foreign, even as the writers described livelihoods similar to Anglo ways of life. For example, the following description found in *The Hopi* could also be applied to another tribe, to an Anglo western frontier community, or to a neighborhood in a metropolitan area: "A Hopi dance is not only a religious ceremony, but it is a folk art, a holiday, an opportunity for visiting and other social activities, the reward for a tremendous amount of labor on the part of the sponsors, and the focal point upon which all of the other activities converge."[37] Indeed, in a section titled "Mormon Folkways," the *Arizona Guide* describes that community similarly, explaining, "A dance in a Mormon town is usually a community affair. . . . Whatever the occasion, everyone attends, from the oldest to the youngest. The Mormons, unlike some other religious groups, see no harm whatsoever in dancing and lively music."[38] Another example, this a description about Hopi religion from the *Guide,* could be applied to most religions: "Rich in an ancient inheritance of mythology and folklore, the Hopi's religious life resolves itself into an annual cycle of ceremonies that occupy the forefront of their thought and conversation."[39] The *Guide* and bulletin writers contributed to an image of Native Americans as exotic and "other," using words like "ancient" and "mythology" and describing events that occur in most cultures, such as dances, as if they were only practiced by Indian people.

Both the *Guide* and the Navajo bulletin emphasized Indian people's ability to culturally adapt. The bulletin explained that knowledge about Navajo life was disproportionate, that more was known about weaving and mythology than of tribal economics and law.[40] The Apache bulletin was less scholarly or ethnologic than the others and even more patronizing than the Apache section in the *Guide.* The *Guide* stated, "Until they were at last subdued they were the most warlike tribe in the southwest. Their fighting spirit was especially evident in the period 1870–1900, when the encroachments of white settlers roused them to fierce resentment"—at least allowing that the fighting was provoked by white encroachment. But the bulletin drops the hostilities right at the Apaches' feet, blaming a genetic defect: "The Apache is still given to flaring rages of anger and jealousy. In the absence of his ancestral outlet of warfare he occasionally turns on his own tribe, his family, his friends."[41]

The tone of the Papago bulletin was one of admiration. The *Guide* contained only a paragraph about the O'odham people, and combined both Akimel O'odham (Pima) and Tohono O'odham (Papago). The Papago bulletin observed that the Tohono O'odham people had no interest in the politics that affected their region, stating that they "showed no apparent interest in Mexico's revolt against Spain in 1820, the Mexican War, nor the Gadsden Purchase."[42] The main effect of these events on this people was not readily apparent in the 1930s, when free movement across the international border was still possible. The FWP writer acknowledged, with admiration, the difficult lives the O'odham people faced on Arizona's southern desert: "The agriculture plan utilized every drop of the meager water supply and supported hundreds where a smaller number of whites would have starved."[43] This countered assertions made early in the century that the O'odham people "squandered" the land and water (see chapter 1).

The Tohono O'odham people have their own narrative landscape, as do all people, but theirs entered the Anglo written word in the form of the publications of their songs by Ruth Underhill. The bulletin explained the songs, stating, "When Elder Brother founded the Papago tribe he established for all time the custom of meeting every situation in life with a song. The songs are the spontaneous poetic creations of individual singers. Some of them are narrative cycles recounting exploits legendary and personal. Others are lyrical expressions of constant communion with the power of nature. . . . Songs are still being composed and, if they seem especially inspired and gain favor, may be added to the literature of the people."[44] Underhill's translations and explanations of the songs remade them in English for an Anglo audience (see the "as-told-to" section later in this chapter).

The Enemy Gods and the Fiction of Oliver La Farge

One goal of New Deal programs was to help citizens who experienced economic hardships; another was the reform of policies that burdened the poor and minorities. With good intentions, the Indian New Deal attempted to do both of these things. As the consequences of federal policy became clearer, however, supporters of the Indian New Deal began to question some of its results. One of those concerned was Oliver La Farge, often referred to as an "Indian expert" by government officials and citizens alike. La Farge earned bachelor's and master's degrees in anthropology at Harvard and came to know Native Americans through his work as an ethnologist on the Navajo reservation. He was sent by the BIA to the Hopi reservation to assist the tribe in writing their constitution as they strove to comply with the Indian Reorganization Act. A member of the Eastern Association on Indian Affairs, he became its president in 1932. In that role, and as he learned more about the federal government's policies in dealing with what was then known as the "Indian problem," La Farge became aware of the need "for a wedding between ethnology and politics."[45] Ethnological work could inform government policy, La Farge believed. Though his organization worked closely with the BIA, it was La Farge's fiction that illuminated the plight of Native Americans for the public. According to biographer D'Arcy McNickle, "What doubtless was his most significant contribution was that he brought Indians into the consciousness of Americans as something other than casual savages without tradition or style."[46] This contribution, La Farge's narratives about and drawn from Arizona, helped create for readers the Arizona of the Navajo people.

La Farge criticized the results of assimilation policy and wrote his criticism into stories of Navajo people negotiating between two societies: traditional Navajo and reservation culture and the Anglo world imposed on Navajos through boarding-school educations. The Arizona of *The Enemy Gods* (1937), and of La Farge's other works of fiction, was the Navajo reservation—its natural landscape and people—and the Indian boarding schools where the Navajos were forced to send their children. His words revealed a people dealing with destructive and ever-changing government policies. While the stories were sympathetic, even tragic, portrayals, they still were told in Anglo words from an Anglo perspective.

La Farge first experienced the Navajo reservation in 1921 at age nineteen as he participated in an archaeological excavation. His initial impression of northern Arizona was less than complimentary. "The country repelled me," he wrote in his memoir. "Its emptiness, its gaudiness and its sheer size all proclaimed 'not for human consumption.' We were dazed physically by the fierce, color-killing sunlight and emotionally by the mass effect of this sudden presentation." After days of riding through the country and working in it, he had a change of heart. "You could lose yourself in the great spaces of the Navajo country," he wrote. "You could do this literally and die of thirst, or spiritually and forget that the white world existed, like water backed too high against a levee, all around the reservation."[47] La Farge admired the Navajo people, respected their traditions, and embraced the high desert plateau where they lived. His posture was reflected in his writing.

The Enemy Gods tells the story of Myron Begay, a Navajo boy who attends a boarding school and finds that he is happier there than at home on the reservation where his mother's new husband abuses him. He is schooled in Christianity, embraces academics, and refuses to return home during the summers. Myron begins to see his people through the eyes of the Anglo teachers and missionaries, and his goal is to become a leader who can save his people, not from American society but from their backward lives. Myron sets his sights on becoming like Tall Man, a respected member of the tribe whose father was white and whose mother was a member of a powerful clan. As a leader Tall Man could bring to bear both his traditional Navajo heritage and his understanding of white culture and power.[48]

The "Enemy Gods" of La Farge's story are the forces that work to destroy Navajo society in the guise of saving the Navajo people. The Enemy Gods are the U.S. government policies that mandate Indian children must attend boarding schools; the missionaries who lecture about the evils of traditional Native American religions and the risks of backsliding; the teachers and school officials who forbid the speaking of native languages and who teach skills insufficient for life on reservations; and an American society that demands homogeneity and compliance.

La Farge used a conversation between Myron, his school friend Homer Gatewood, and one of Homer's older relatives to illustrate the role education played in Navajo society. Homer does not want to return to school after the summer. Myron wants to be a different kind of Navajo, "civilized," and chooses to stay at school during the summer. Homer's relative is the most conservative traditional Navajo Myron has ever seen. Speaking to Homer, the old man says, "No, my grandson. You want this schooling, even if it is hard. There are many tribes of Long-Haired People, of Earth People, many strong warriors, but this one tribe, the *Bellacana* [white people], conquered them all. Why? Because he knows more, I think. By paper and by wires he talks to his friends in the distance, he leaves his words behind him when he goes away. . . . Therefore we must learn his secrets that we, Navajos, may continue. Long ago we asked for these schools. We want them. It is not pleasant for you, but you need it, I think."[49]

Then he speaks to Myron: "'Now you, grandchild,' he says, 'I think you are making a mistake, too. If you learn all the white man's way and forget the Navajo, if that happens to our young men, then we die, we are destroyed, as surely as if by warfare. The man who will serve his people in the years to come, the man who will strengthen them, is the man who can learn all of the one without losing the other.'" The Navajos intended the schools to teach Anglo ways but not to replace Indian ways. They had asked for the schools. One of the federal government's responsibilities enumerated in the 1868 treaty with the Navajos was to provide a teacher for every thirty students.[50]

Myron and the Navajo people were negotiating between two cultures. La Farge illustrated the Indian people's dilemma as Myron's uncle, Shooting Star, observes, "Did you ever shake water from your hand onto a plate or a board or anything like that? Each drop stands up by itself, with lots of room around it. That's how we were, we and the Mokis [Hopis], the Utes, the Supais, the Apaches, and the rest. The Mexicans, too. They were many, but they were pasturage for us. But you pour a whole barrel of water onto those drops—where are they then? That's what the *Bellacana* is."[51] This seemed to La Farge to be Arizona's cultural landscape in 1937, Anglo culture pouring over and absorbing all of the others. But those minority cultures were not absorbed.

The Enemy Gods was not La Farge's first venture into writing about Navajos. His first novel, *Laughing Boy*, tells the story of the romance, marriage, and tragic end of the relationship between a young Navajo man raised on the reservation and a Navajo girl who has been sent to boarding school and returns to the reservation changed and emotionally distant. *Laughing Boy* won the 1929 Pulitzer Prize for literature; it had its genesis in a short story published in *Dial* magazine in 1927. That story, "North Is Black," also explores the cultural divide between Navajos and Anglos. In this story a Navajo man follows his love, a white woman, to her home in the north, becomes friends with her people, and lives among them for a while. But an absence of cultural understanding, on both the Indian and the Anglo sides, results in a vicious argument, and the man returns to the reservation, alone and bitter.[52]

A prolific writer, La Farge composed stories about the Southwest, the desert, cowboys, and other tribes besides the Navajos. But he was well known for his Navajo stories. Following on *Laughing Boy* and informing the story in *The Enemy Gods,* La Farge published a short story in the *Saturday Evening Post,* again telling the story of the cultural divide existing between on- and off-reservation communities. "Higher Education" is another story with the theme of the effects of boarding-school educations on Navajo children and families. It is told in the first person by an Anglo archaeologist working on the reservation who observes the events but participates in them only peripherally, as an outsider. The story tells of Lucille's homecoming to the reservation from boarding school, her affair with the Anglo proprietor of a nearby trading post, and her subsequent suicide when she cannot find a place in reservation society but has no alternatives.[53] Sardonically naming the story "Higher Education"—many policymakers and missionaries believed that a boarding-school education would elevate the Indian people out of what these Anglos saw as uncivilized reservation life—La Farge demonstrated the complete severance from Navajo society that many boarding-school children experienced and the inability to rejoin that community when they returned to the reservation.

The narrative of Navajo people negotiating between cultures in 1930s Arizona is revealed in nonfiction as well. *Desert Wife* is the autobiography of Hilda Faunce, who with her husband was a trader on the Navajo reservation. Often trading posts were the centers of community on reservations, serving as buyers of arts and crafts, sellers of supplies, and places where news was exchanged from both within and outside of the reservation. The Faunces' trading post was of this type.

Faunce described her first glimpse of Arizona and her thoughts about it from the perspective of a woman who had lived in and was traveling from Oregon: "Each step seemed to carry us farther from every comfort, from the very last trace of civilization. More than once I was panicky. I wondered what Ken could see in country like this. The emptiness, the barrenness, the vastness threatened me. Almost I cried out to him to turn back; I could not face life in a country without one spear of green grass, with nothing but rocks and bare dirt, with never a human being in sight."[54] As with Martha Summerhayes, Oliver La Farge, and others, the Arizona desert grew on Faunce. Like La Farge describing the northeastern Arizona landscape of the Navajo reservation and Priestley describing the sky viewed in central Arizona, Faunce described the landscape during sunset, writing, "Suddenly the sun was gone. The east was a glory unbelievable until one looked at the west. Here was a jumble of blue and purple cloud shadows and scarlet flame high lights with gigantic rays of brilliant yellow shooting high into the heavens. There was color in the desert itself, not in vegetation, but in the very earth and rocks. In the afternoon sun the reds and blacks and blues had seemed unreal enough; but I would never have believed, had I not seen them, what they could be in the light of the sunset."[55]

Faunce also described the people. Occasionally depicting the Anglos who lived and worked at other trading posts and at the edge of the reservation, she mostly wrote about Navajos. Describing an encounter with a Navajo schoolgirl who worked for a missionary family, she wrote, "The schoolgirl sat on the box that held the cooking things and said, laughing a little, 'I may be Navajo, but I can't sit on the ground any more without my feet going to sleep. . . . I am to be here only a few days more. I'm glad; it's too hard to keep my clothes clean and I don't get along very well with "blanket Indians"; I have been away too long.'"[56]

Like the characters in *The Enemy Gods*, the Navajos whom Faunce knew were navigating cultural divides. She described the reaction of parents when the federal Indian agents arrived to take the children to school: "The Indian agent, the highest official on the reservation, wanted one child in each family sent to the government school; but most families hid the children from the authorities."[57] One child sent to the reservation school, John Mitchell, now an adult in Faunce's telling, finds himself in a position similar to Lucille's in La Farge's "Higher Education," having no discernable way to fit in when he returned home. Trained as a mechanic at the boarding school, Mitchell cannot find employment among the white people and has nothing on which to ply his trade on the reservation except the windmills, which many other Navajos can also repair. In *Desert Wife*, John Mitchell was described as a lout of a man. Unable to find his way in either Anglo or Navajo culture, he steals from his people and robs their ancestors' graves. In "Higher Education," unable to bridge cultural divides, Lucille throws herself off a cliff. In *The Enemy Gods* Myron Begay fares little better, committing murder in Flagstaff after betraying his people by telling lies about their ceremonies to a group of missionaries and aid members in an effort to make himself appear more civilized.

The Enemy Gods received favorable reviews in the national media. One reviewer called the book "a powerful and penetrating novel" and remarked on its revelation of the effects of "well-meant attempts to change racial habits, racial beliefs."[58] Another reviewer declared that until "reservation schools or missionary colleges produce" a Navajo scholar with the skills of writing and storytelling, "we shall have, in all probability, no pictures of the Navajo as fine and serious as these Mr. La Farge has given us." This reviewer stated that "in the ordinary way of things," only a Navajo could tell the story of being caught between native and white cultures. That is, if a Navajo who could speak and write English told his story, the rest of the world could finally understand the damage caused by government policies. The reviewer understood the result of policy, that Native Americans had "been so strangely and sometimes so brutally victimized by two conflicting cultural patterns," but she failed to grasp an underlying issue, the destructive policies revealed in the very book under review, as is evident in her belief that only reservation schools and missionary colleges could produce a fine Navajo scholar.[59]

There is a subtle recognition in the words La Farge gave the old man to speak to Myron Begay and Homer Gatewood in *The Enemy Gods*, an understanding of the power of the written word, its supremacy in this case, and the importance of an orally based society to learn to write to gain power. "By paper and by wires he talks to his friends in the distance, he leaves his words behind him when he goes away," the grandfather says.[60] The Navajo people, and all people with an oral tradition but with no written language, have histories, traditions, and stories to share. But the power inherent in the written word—not only to create, but also to control and remain—was recognized, at least by Oliver La Farge, an Anglo author writing stories about American Indians. As Native

Americans learned to read and write English and claimed that power, their own stories became part of Arizona's intellectual landscape and helped to create the place with their words.

As-Told-To Autobiographies

Native Americans' first-person accounts did exist in the 1930s, stories told by Indian people recounting life on Arizona's Indian reservations; these as-told-to autobiographies became popular during the Great Depression.[61] Told by Indian people in their native languages to interpreters, these life stories were translated, transcribed, reviewed, and published by Anglo ethnographers. Wholly unlike the reporting-foreign-peoples style of the FWP bulletins, more detailed and personal than Oliver La Farge's fictional stories of reservation life, and beyond J. B. Priestley and the WPA writers' frames of reference, these autobiographies reveal Native Americans living the way people have always lived. As La Farge wrote, they hoped for "more rain, less sickness (and prayer is effective for both of these), a little more land perhaps, good hunting in the fall, peace within the community, peace all around, not to be pushed around by white people, above all peace and continuity."[62]

Each telling, each book, begins with several paragraphs that describe the process of receiving the story. The ethnologist identified an "informant," usually a person in the community the scientist had a comfortable relationship with and had been working with closely for several years. Rather than ask questions, the ethnologist allowed the story to unfold from the teller's memory in whatever manner he or she recalled. An interpreter translated the story bit by bit, and the English version was written down and clarified. Often the ethnologist structured the story chronologically and removed repetitive details, but otherwise the story remained unchanged, autobiographical rather than biographical.

Anthropologist Walter Dyk spent the early 1930s studying clan and kin relationships on the Navajo reservation. To provide context for the data he was collecting, he began writing the life histories of some of his informants. A "more pedestrian tale was needed," Dyk believed, "some long slow narrative that recalled the ordinary, the petty, the humdrum insignificant affairs as well. . . . I asked one of my informants, an old man, Left Handed by name, to relate what he could remember of his life, insisting that he leave out nothing, no matter how trivial." Left Handed's narrative began in the spring of 1868 with the story of his birth at the time of the Navajo's long journey home after four years at Fort Sumner, New Mexico Territory, and ended with his marriage twenty years later.[63] He was about sixty-six years old when he told his stories, and he provided what Dyk requested: his recollections of daily activities on the reservation. He told of sheep and goat herding, cooking and eating, and playing with other children. The reader learned about reservation social life, dances, visiting relatives, and marriages as Left Handed's Arizona took form. This was Arizona as Navajos knew it.

The importance of sheep to Navajo life and culture is reflected in Left Handed's biography. He told this story from his early childhood: "About this time I began to herd around the hogan in the morning and evening when the sheep came home. But I was so small. I went out with the sheep like a dog. I just walked along with them and stayed right in the middle of the herd. I was afraid to go around them, but while I was in the middle of the sheep I wasn't afraid of anything."[64] This was something new in the body of written narratives at the time, a revelation of the daily life that centered on sheep herding. A reviewer of the book commented on this aspect of the story, noting that the Navajo people's "dependence on these animals and methods of herding and breeding are brought out here."[65]

Ruth Underhill worked as an ethnologist for the BIA on the Tohono O'odham reservation in southern Arizona in the early 1930s. She wrote several books, scholarly and fictional, about the people, called Papagos then. Maria Chona was Underhill's "hostess, guide, and means of introduction to the various villages," as well as an informant. Chona's father had been the governor of a village (long abandoned in 1936) called Mesquite Root.[66] In the book's introduction Underhill explained that Native American storytelling methods differed from Anglo telling styles and "involve a repetition and a dwelling on unimportant details which confuse the White reader." As such, she acknowledged, "It is an Indian story told to satisfy Whites rather than Indians."[67] Underhill revealed a cultural divide that ethnologists believed existed (and perhaps it did) that was created by a lack of Anglo understanding of Native American ways and also by a lack of patience for their narrative style.

Underhill chose Maria Chona for "reasons other than intimacy and opportunity." She explained, "She is not the aberrant type, which so frequently attracts the attention of the White investigator. She accepted her culture completely, and one reason for choosing her was that she had come into contact with so many of its important phases." Underhill was interested in Chona's life because it provided a different perspective from the male informants' lives, though Chona's father was a governor and warrior, and her brother and husbands were shamans and song leaders. However, Chona was not the ideal, or perhaps stereotypical, Papago woman that Underhill identified. As a child she started composing songs. "Making songs is the Papago achievement par excellence, all outward acts being considered merely as a preparation for it," Underhill told the reader. "She had some urge to accomplish, as the men accomplished, and the proper avenue was song making. So Chona made songs and saw visions, and had to have her shaman's crystals cut out by a minor operation" because song making was not a female occupation.[68]

Nevertheless, Chona composed songs as she grew older—simple songs, Underhill explained. Often songs are changed by the composer "only by a word or two," the reader learns, "from songs which had been well known for years. Many Papago compose in this way. . . . None consider it plagiarism, for song making is the spiritual crown conferred on one who has already achieved in the physical world."[69] Studying this aspect of Tohono O'odham culture persuaded Underhill to write *Singing for Power* (1938), a book about the practice of song, which both underlies and girds the Tohono O'odham culture. This book also provided context by citing the origins and purposes of the songs. A song's genesis originates in the power within the song creator. Each song also holds power and confers power.

Sharlot Hall's poetry developed from her life as a pioneer woman in northern Arizona. Tohono O'odham songs arise from lives lived in the southern Arizona deserts. Both are Arizona narratives, in verse. Underhill provided the setting for O'odham songs and created a picture of difficult living in a difficult place, writing in the introduction, "So the Papagos wandered, calm and smiling, back and forth across the waste of brilliant barrenness which Elder Brother, their god, had given them. They shot the ground squirrels and the rats and birds. They picked the caterpillars from the bushes. They shook the seeds from every blade of wild grass. They brushed the spines from cactus stems and roasted them for hours in a pit with a fire over it." The old woman who told this story to Underhill said, "To you Whites, Elder Brother gave wheat and peaches and grapes. To us, he gave the wild seeds and the cactus. Those are the *good* foods."[70]

Tohono O'odham songs are not only methods of self-expression. Underhill's explanation wrote into being a different Arizona: "It was a magic which called upon the powers of Nature and constrained them to man's will. People sang in trouble, in danger, to cure the sick, to confound their enemies, and to make the crops grow. They sang as they fought and as they worked, all together. . . . In such a community, song became not only the practical basis of Papago life, but also the most precious possession of the people. The power of song was an honor to be earned; it could not be assumed lightly at the mere whim of an individual."[71]

The origin of this Tohono O'odham philosophy is found in their creation story. The O'odham live in a land scattered with ancient structures, Underhill explained. She added, "Archaeologists are still hunting for these vanished people, who built the Casa Grande, five stories high. The Papagos know where they went: Iitoi drove them, some to the north and some to the south." The O'odham know what battle was fought at each place, and "they know that the actual conquest came through singing: 'Iitoi had a song for everything.' Though his men did the fighting, Iitoi confirmed their efforts by singing the enemy into blindness and helplessness. So he laid the foundations for the Papago world."[72]

One of the most essential practices for Tohono O'odham life in the desert is the annual ceremony to bring the rains, to "pull down the clouds." The traditional rituals begin in June or July, at the end of the dry season when the saguaro fruit ripens. The fruit is harvested, the pulp mixed with water, and the mixture allowed to ferment for two days. "The making and drinking of cactus liquor is Papago rain magic," Underhill wrote. "It is the duty of every man to drink his fill of this liquor; to drink to a saturation, even as the rain-soaked earth is saturated. In accordance with the rules of Papago magic, which always imitates the desired event, this act will bring the rain to moisten the earth."[73]

Following the ceremony for pulling down the clouds, the season of rain comes and the corn is planted. Underhill described the planting thus: "Night after night, the planter walks around his field 'singing up the corn.' There is a song for corn as high as his knee, for corn waist high, and for corn with the tassel forming":

> The corn comes up;
> It comes up green;
> Here upon our fields
> Green leaves blow in the breeze.
> Blue evening falls,
> Blue evening falls;
> Near by, in every direction,
> It sets the corn tassels trembling.
> The wind smoothes well the ground.
> Yonder the wind runs
> Upon our fields.
> The corn leaves tremble.[74]

This was the place that the Tohono O'odham people knew; their Arizona was collected and translated by the Anglo ethnologist and written for an Anglo readership seeking explanations for a Native American way of life that existed outside of the Euro-American cultural understanding. The Tohono O'odham narratives and songs were co-opted from rather than imparted by the storytellers themselves. The versions Anglos received and consumed were only part of their story, corrupted versions that facilitated a false sense of understanding and contributed to the paternalistic attitudes of American Anglo society.

Similar to Underhill's *Singing for Power,* the book *Truth of a Hopi* (1936) is a collection of Hopi clan stories told by Edmund Nequatewa, a Hopi man from Shongopovi, and edited by Mary-Russell Colton of the Museum of Northern Arizona. However, Nequatewa, who ran away from boarding school as a child but as an adult worked at the museum, wrote his stories in English, providing the translation himself; Colton's role was to clarify, fact-check, and add explanatory footnotes, providing a semblance of Anglo control even as Nequatewa told his own story.[75] Colton explained that the stories "represent the origin, myths, and history of a group of Hopi clans. They carry us from the very beginning of things down to modern times."[76] Countering J. B. Priestley's assertion that all of Arizona's culture was new, the Hopi narratives demonstrated that people had inhabited the place and made lives from it long before the appearance of the paved roads and bright lights that captured Priestley's attention.

Colton explained that Hopi traditions are passed orally from father to son. When boys reach maturity they are initiated into the sacred societies and are taught the stories, traditions, and history of their people. Because of the intrusion of Anglo culture and the imposition of the boarding-school system, Colton wrote, "there has been a consequent breaking down of the ancient customs." Young men were initiated at older ages. Old men complained about the inattention to the traditions and stories. They were "fearful that their history and traditions may fall into confusion and be forever lost to the coming generations."[77] While Colton's explanation for Nequatewa's motivation to set down the stories in writing was his fear of their loss, the publication of *Truth of a Hopi* also provided a Hopi representation of Arizona for readers.

The words in *Truth of a Hopi* represent the Hopi people's understanding of the place, the stories that create their Arizona. The narratives explain how the Hopis came to the mesas, one clan at a time, but one clan lagged behind. "They were traveling away behind," Nequatewa wrote, "and they were rather slow because they would stop to cultivate the land and raise corn to supply them for a few years. They thought that they would build houses and make pottery by which they would mark this land as they went along."[78] The Hopis regard these places where their ancestors paused as the footprints of their people. They call these ancestors *Hisatsinom*; archaeological evidence supports a Hopi connection to sites in northern Arizona.[79] The archaeological study of the ancestral footprints of the Hopis and other ancient peoples provided new narratives in 1937, as archaeologists recorded their findings, and popular print media reproduced the theories and findings for the public.

Archaeological Reports and Popular Works

Archaeological activity increased throughout the Southwest in the 1930s. The public was fascinated with the projects from start to finish. They were interested in the landscape before the excavations commenced, the process of excavating, the reconstructions after the excavations (at that time reconstructing the buildings and villages often was part of the process), the material culture findings, and the archaeologists' theories about the people who had lived in the structures. Native Americans have their own stories about the people who came before them. Some tribes consider them ancestors; the oral traditions of other tribes tell how their own ancestors drove the village builders away. Sometimes the oral traditions and the scientists' theories mirrored one another, sometimes not. This Arizona written into being for the English-reading public complicated the understanding of the place; its cultural landscape was not simply the shiny new cities found in Priestley's descriptions or the abandoned civilizations and simple Indian people described in the *Arizona Guide*. However, archaeologists imagining this ancient Arizona eliminated Native American traditional knowledge and history and dismissed their narratives that claimed the people who built those civilizations as ancestors.

An ancient Arizona was created in layers of written words. In the first decade of the twentieth century, the American reading public became aware of ancient structures in Arizona through the pages of the *New York Times*, in articles that chronicled excavations, explained theories, and connected the ancient to the modern. In the 1930s the archaeologists sent to excavate the sites wrote reports to document laborious and tedious processes and to construct theoretical frameworks. The reports were rewritten for lay readers and published in popular magazines and newspapers, where authors made comparisons between native stories about the ancient peoples and archaeologists' theories. In 1937 the federal government dedicated eight of Arizona's eleven national monuments to preserve ancient structures and impart information about them to the general public, and the public's interest was reflected in high attendance to these sites.[80]

In 1934 excavations began at Snaketown, a site along the Gila River downstream from Sacaton on the Gila River Indian Community, under the direction of Emil Haury. Noted as a "major scientific discovery," the area appeared to be a series of desert mounds whose only inhabitants were the rattlesnake colonies that gave the site its name. However, the archaeologists "uncovered the remains of a sophisticated, prehistoric farming culture that had once spread across the upper Sonoran desert, with influences extending as far north as present-day Flagstaff."[81] The excavations at Snaketown allowed Haury and his colleagues at Gila Pueblo Archaeological Foundation to build on the theory of a new culture—a Hohokam people separate and different from the ancestral Puebloan or Mogollon cultures that had been revealed during an excavation at Roosevelt Lake a few years before.[82]

The Snaketown excavation report was published in 1938. A heavy, thick book, it is full of descriptions and charts, pictures and diagrams, explanations and inquiries on every plot of land explored and piece of material culture excavated during the dig. One of the most interesting finds—something that puzzled the archaeologists, captured public attention, and initiated questions about Anglo understanding of the region—was the discovery of an unusual landscape feature: unnatural depressions in the desert. Large and shaped like oval bowls, these depressions consisted of two parallel earthen banks over sixty yards long, nearly forty yards apart, and almost three yards deep, featuring an open space between the banks and at each end.[83] Similar features had been found in other places in Arizona. Speculation dating to the 1890s labeled them reservoirs or sun temples, corrals or dance arenas.

In 1918 Frank H. Pinkley, the Superintendent of Southwestern Monuments, trenched and excavated several of these depression features near Casa Grande. His report, published in 1935, "showed, beyond doubt, the existence of a floor, of prepared side walls and in the case of the Casa Grande structure, of a stone in the center of the floor under which were bits of shell and turquoise." Pinkley theorized that the structures were areas for ceremonies, games, or festivals. As the excavation of one of the depressions at Snaketown continued and its features were uncovered, the archaeologists began comparing it to the ball courts of Central America. "But to find ball courts 1500 miles from their supposed point of origin," Haury wrote, "was somewhat of a shock and it immediately started questions dealing with origin, relationship, and time implications which [were] impossible to answer."[84]

Considering the possibility that the depression at Snaketown was a ball court similar to those in Central America, archaeologists at other sites began to study their features in this light. John C. McGregor of the Museum of Northern Arizona analyzed two depressions near Flagstaff and found they were comparable to the Snaketown court in many ways.[85] That the inhabitants of this past Arizona could have been culturally connected surprised archaeologists; their theories had not accounted for a communications or trade network that might explain the presence of similar features throughout Arizona.

Arizona Highways documented these finds, making the connection for its readers between the ball courts discovered in northern Arizona during a salvage archaeology excavation for a highway a few miles north of Wupatki National Monument and the courts excavated by Haury at Snaketown in southern Arizona. "Because of the difference in climate and altitude between southern and northern parts of Arizona little thought was given to the possibility of any form of communication between the two areas," Bob Eunson wrote. The excavations "demonstrate some form of communication between the early residents of the south and the prehistoric dwellers of the north."[86]

The *New York Times* also reported on these ball court discoveries in northern and southern Arizona. "Game courts resembling the ball courts of the ancient Mayans were built by the Pueblo III Indians of Northern Arizona 800 years ago," the reporter wrote.[87] The article explained the significance of communication between northern and southern Arizona and between ancient Arizona and Central America using Eunson's *Arizona Highways* article language verbatim. By 1937 it could be shown that the people of ancient Arizona were socially connected to and communicated with communities far to the south. What had seemed prehistoric before the discoveries now appeared somewhat more sophisticated.

Another landscape feature discovered in the Snaketown excavation, an ancient canal system, contributed to the changing representation of Arizona's early indigenous cultures. Until recently the nearby Akimel O'odham people had made use of some of these canals, irrigating hundreds of acres of farmland. Anglos had known of, and used, some of the canals in the Salt River Valley, but the increased archaeological attention to the region added to the number of narratives written about these past farmers in the desert.

The *New York Times* reported on the canal systems of the Salt and Gila River Valleys, informing its readers that there must have been many people living in the communities to have built such an extensive network. Quoting Neill Judd of the Smithsonian Institution, who was preparing an aerial survey of the canals, the *Times* reporter wrote, "These canals are remains of real agricultural communities that existed in these sections of what is now Arizona many centuries ago. . . . It is a true agricultural culture, in which these people used irrigation methods for the growing of their crops." Judd explained, "Many of these waterways would do credit to present-time construction methods. They followed the contour of the land almost perfectly, and often excavations were made through rises in the ground that must have required months or even years to complete."[88]

Of the centuries-old system, Haury wrote, "No single accomplishment of the Hohokam commands as much respect as their canal systems, designed to irrigate otherwise unproductive land. This achievement forms the very foundation of their complex culture and on it all of their accomplishments were more or less directly dependent." The archaeologist estimated the Snaketown canal was over ten miles long and compared it with the Casa Grande canal, which was over sixteen miles in length.[89] The presence of canals added to a growing sense of the sophistication of ancient Arizonans and enhanced the popular perception of the state's indigenous people that had been created in the words of newspaper articles in the 1910s and in the *Arizona Guide* and FWP bulletins.

Another archaeological excavation, Tuzigoot, in central Arizona's Verde Valley, added depth to an understanding of Arizona's cultural landscape, further correcting the idea of the state's "newness." Under the direction of University of Arizona graduate students Louis R. Caywood and Edward H. Spicer, the excavation began in October 1933 with an eight-man crew and was funded by Federal Emergency Relief Administration money. In November the endeavor was reorganized as an Arizona project under the newly established Civil Works Administration. The project, completed in June 1934, undertook the excavation and partial reconstruction of the village, including the preservation of its walls and floors.

The excavation report locates Tuzigoot "on a ridge of horizontal strata of Verde Lake deposits of impure white limestone and reddish sandstone" that rises steeply from the valley floor; it includes the excavation plan, an explanation of the layout of the rooms, and a chronology describing when each room was built.[90] "The first building that took place at the site of Tuzigoot, no doubt, was on the very summit of the ridge," the archaeologists wrote. "The site would not have been selected at all if it had not been planned to take advantage of the most commanding area available, whether for purposes of protection or for sheer beauty of location." The archaeologists estimated that as many as 450 people had lived in the structure at the height of occupation in what had included seventy-seven first-floor rooms and fifteen second-floor rooms.[91]

Gladys Thompson Niehuis's article in *Arizona Highways* about Tuzigoot contains details not found in the excavation report. For instance, it describes jewelry "of rare quality, with its intricate mosaic and its shell work."[92] Another difference, possibly an instance of artistic license, was this description of burials: "Found often under the floors of the rooms [were] remnants of tapestry-like cloth, charred grains, shells from coastal water, pottery from tribes far north or south—all these articles told a story to the skilled scientific minds [of Caywood and Spicer]. To them it was plain that the ancient dwellers of the ruins had been peaceful agriculturists, comparatively unsuperstitious, and skilled at trading with other tribes."[93] However, Caywood and Spicer's report described only one piece of cloth found, although impressions of woven cloth were discovered in the refuse. The conclusions reached in the *Arizona Highways* article may be inferred from the report, but Caywood and Spicer published no outright conclusions like those found in the article. For *Arizona Highways* readers who had not read the archaeologists' report and may not have visited Tuzigoot, the place Niehuis's article created was an ancient Arizona inhabited by wealthy, peaceful farmers.

Niehuis and the archaeologists—and, it can be assumed, the general public as well—wondered what happened to the inhabitants of Tuzigoot. Hopi tradition tells that structures like these across northern Arizona's landscape are their ancestors' stopping places, places where they rested and lived while migrating to the Hopi Mesas. For Hopi people, the structures are not ruins but the footprints of their ancestors. This was not the story the Anglo archaeologists told.[94]

Caywood and Spicer questioned an apparent abandonment of the site at the height of occupation, since it showed no evidence of "decadence . . . no violent and sudden catastrophe in the last quarter of the thirteenth century," although they drew no specific conclusions.[95] Niehuis wondered as well, adding details not found in the excavation report and assigning conclusions to the archaeologists that they had not made. "It must have been something urgent indeed, to have taken them away in the midst of the preparation of a meal, leaving everything, even tables set, in some instances," she wrote. "Scientists have three alternative solutions: invasion and capture by warring tribes, pestilence of a swift and devastating type, or drought that became unbearable."[96] That no set tables or meals in the midst of being prepared can be found in the excavation report leaves one wondering where this information came from. Nonetheless, set tables and interrupted meal preparation became part of Tuzigoot's story because of these words in *Arizona Highways*, and the Native American stories about it remained invisible in the written narrative landscape.

In Summary

At the time of Arizona's twenty-fifth anniversary of statehood in 1937, the state had been created in movies as a Wild West place of tough ranchers, renegade Indians, and rugged landscapes. The Arizona created in words was not that simple, even as clichéd descriptions persisted. The Arizona desert provoked thoughtful reflections on the state's seemingly egalitarian society and on American community and leadership. Many Americans' introduction to Arizona came via the words in the *Arizona Guide* and FWP bulletins. Those bulletins, Oliver La Farge's fiction, and the as-told-to Native American autobiographies revealed an Arizona separate from, but profoundly affected by, the place most Anglo readers knew, yet the stories were still told from an Anglo perspective, were filtered through Anglo words, and retained a measure of Anglo control. Archaeologists' reports and the subsequent rewriting of their theories and conclusions in popular print media created an ancient Arizona.

Future words about Arizona would be influenced by the growing concern over human impact on the natural environment. Words would continue to reflect a booster mentality to increase tourism and investment in the state, as Arizona experienced unprecedented population growth in the years following World War II, but its written intellectual landscape would come to include challenges to the way resources were manipulated and extracted and questions about the influence of the cultural landscape on the natural landscape.

OVERLOOK

Mid-century Growing Pains

WORLD WAR II AND POSTWAR ARIZONA

"Nothing'll stop the Army Air Corps," wrote *Arizona Highways* editor Raymond Carlson in a June 1942 article about the burgeoning flying training schools rising out of the desert around Phoenix. Carlson described the feat of transforming "with a touch of sorcery" raw desert and fertile farmland into a fully functioning military base with headquarters, post exchange, and barracks, its own theater, gas station, chapel, and library, making "every American citizen proud."[1] On July 28, 1941, the Mesa Chamber of Commerce had received a telegram from Senator Carl Hayden announcing the decision by the War Department and Secretary of War Henry L. Stimson to award the contract for the construction of buildings at Mesa Military Airport to Del E. Webb Construction Company, for just over $1.5 million.[2] Twenty-one years later *Time* magazine featured the eponymous founder and owner of the company on its cover, deeming the success of Webb's planned retirement community, Sun City, and its "active retirement Way-of-Life" worthy of national news coverage.[3] In the intervening two decades, Del Webb and his companies had constructed many of the buildings that accommodated the wave of migrating businesses and people that changed the landscape of the West generally, and of Arizona in particular.

When the Japanese bombed Pearl Harbor on December 7, 1941, ushering the United States into another world war, the pace of construction at Arizona's airfields increased. At that time Del Webb Construction crews had completed buildings at Luke Field west of Glendale, Thunderbird Field at Glendale, and Falcon Field at Mesa; by 1943 they would construct 146 buildings at Mesa Military Airport (renamed Williams Field in January 1942).[4] The Army Air Forces fields would be used to train thousands of pilots during the war. Luke Field was the largest flying training school in the country, and Williams Field became the first facility to train jet pilots. The infrastructure and services required to support the increase in military personnel also brought increased growth to those sections of the state's economy.

The service and construction industries' need for workers was compounded by a labor shortage caused by the war. Women entered the workforce in record numbers, recruited for jobs as varied as flying newly constructed training planes to central Arizona airfields and working as graders and checkers in northern Arizona's timber industry.[5] Arizona's farmers feared the labor shortage would jeopardize their harvests, and in 1942, along with growers in other states, they urged the federal government to allow the formal, temporary entrance of Mexican laborers into the United States. The temporary agreement between the U.S. and Mexican governments, known as the Bracero Program, extended over twenty years and allowed millions of Mexican workers to legally enter the United States and work on short-term contracts. According to the agreement, employers were required to provide meals and clean, free housing and insurance; pay the workers the prevailing domestic wage; and provide free transportation back to Mexico at the end of the contract period. However, in practice growers often ignored the rules, which resulted in deplorable living conditions, low wages, and a permanent "temporary" underclass of Mexican workers. Between 1942 and 1964, 4.6 million contracts were signed, making the Bracero Program America's largest contract labor program.[6]

After the war Arizona experienced continued population growth due to returning servicemen and the military's determination for the need of a larger peacetime force. At the end of World War II, the War Department began closing hundreds of bases. In 1945 the government and the armed services planned to disperse their forces and discharge service members. There was no precedent for a large peacetime army. But the reality of the world in 1945 demanded that the United States maintain a strong military presence in Europe to counteract the Soviet threat; strengthen the forces for a prolonged cold war; and, after the Communist invasion of South Korea, commit troops in Southeast Asia.

In addition to hosting the army's flying training schools, Arizona benefited from companies with wartime contracts that relocated to the state. Arizona gained a reputation as a business-friendly place, and following the war more companies relocated to the state. Drawn by the same clear, dry climate that encouraged airfield placement, many aerospace and electronics companies such as Motorola (1948) and General Electric (1957) opened facilities in the Phoenix area. In the decade following the war, Del Webb's construction company was involved in much of the postwar building in the Southwest. It received contracts for the Phoenix Veterans Hospital; air force barracks in Texas, Arizona, and California; casino hotels in Nevada; and an entire town for the Magma Copper Company at San Manuel, Arizona.[7]

Arizona's population more than doubled between 1940 and 1960, from 499,261 to 1,302,161. In 1960 the population of Phoenix nearly matched what the entire state's population had been in 1937. The service and financial industries grew as well, to support the growing civilian population and the high-tech and national defense industries.[8] By the 1950s the desert heat was no longer a hindrance. In 1952 Goettl Air Conditioning developed one of the first affordable residential air-cooling systems; building and manufacturing plants, as well as homes, could be air cooled, making a large part of Arizona livable and workable year round.[9]

In 1946 Arizona became a right-to-work state. Proposition 4, an amendment to the state constitution, was passed by initiative (i.e., placed on the ballot by voters). The measure changed the state's labor-friendly constitution by adding article 25: "No person shall be denied the opportunity to obtain or retain employment because of non-membership in a labor organization."[10] Arizona's veterans led the fight for open (union-free) shops. A welding company owned by decorated veteran Herbert Williams, who employed five other veterans, lost a contract in Phoenix because, the owner believed, his shop was nonunion. Williams and other veterans formed the Phoenix Right to Work Committee, contending that veterans were losing work to union members who had not served in the war, thus making patriotism a key theme of their campaign. The measure passed by ten points, 55 to 45 percent.[11]

The decline of labor's power could be attributed to several factors. The unionized mining industry relinquished its place as Arizona's top income provider to the high-technology industries; the swell of population from the Midwest and South to fill the new jobs brought in people with a more economically conservative outlook; and the presence of large military bases bolstered the economy of many Arizona towns. These trends culminated in a decline of the Democratic Party, which had dominated the state's politics for over fifty years. In 1952 Arizonans voted for a Republican president for the first time and elected conservative Barry Goldwater to the Senate by a narrow margin over the popular Democrat incumbent Ernest McFarland.[12]

While Arizona's population was becoming generally more conservative, the state's minority communities were advocating for equal rights. Native American, African American, and Hispanic Arizonans had fought, and died, for a country where they were rarely treated equally and where their rights had often been denied. The Navajo Code Talkers, for example, a group of men instrumental to the war effort in the Pacific theater, could not vote in Arizona at the time the United States entered the war.[13] Education is often the first civil rights battleground. In 1950 Alianza Hispano-Americana attorneys Gregorio Garcia, Ralph Estrada, and A. L. Wirin filed suit in federal court against the Tolleson School District (in the Phoenix metropolitan area) for discrimination in the segregation of Mexican American students. In *Gonzales v. Sheeley* (1951), Judge David Ling ruled on behalf of the plaintiffs and ordered all schools in the district to end segregation and racial discrimination.[14] In 1952 Hayzel B. Daniels and Herbert B. Finn filed suit in Arizona Superior Court against Phoenix Union High School on behalf of African American students at Carver High School. On February 9, 1953, in *Phillips v. Phoenix Union High School*, Judge Fred C. Struckmeyer Jr. ruled in favor of the plaintiffs (declaring, "a half century of intolerance is enough") over a year before the U.S. Supreme Court decided *Brown v. Board of Education of Topeka* (1954).[15]

As labor and union power in Arizona declined, as minority communities fought for and gained equal rights, and as Arizona's economy and population grew, another demographic came to be identified with the state—retirees. Particularly in the Phoenix area, retirement communities became synonymous with desert living. In January 1961 a special "Sun City supplement" in the *Arizona Republic* declared, "The town that changed a nation's viewpoint on retirement extends its active new

Way-of-Life to thousands more of America's senior citizens." A year earlier, on January 1, 1960, Del Webb Development Company had introduced to the world Sun City, its master-planned retirement community twenty-five miles northwest of Phoenix. A hundred thousand people visited in its first weekend. The Webb team learned from its predecessors, and unlike retirement communities such as Youngtown (launched in 1954), where the residential areas had been constructed first and often the amenities went unbuilt, Webb's developers built the amenities first—a shopping center, swimming pool, community center, and the all-important golf course—and then offered lots for homebuilding. The new opening in 1961, announced in the *Arizona Republic* supplement, doubled the size of the town. "We never sell a home," claimed the Sun City sales staff. The residents of Sun City instead "'bought' the Way-of-Life, the spirit and unprecedented concept that is Sun City. . . . Then they chose a home in which to live while enjoying it all."[16]

By 1962 Arizona was a place where natural resources—uranium, in addition to copper—were extracted in record amounts. It was a place where the population increased dramatically as the new high-tech and electronics industries moved into the state, as former GIs who had received basic and advanced training at the many military bases moved permanently to the state, as retirees relocated to the state's new active adult communities, and as the service industry grew to accommodate new residents and the many visitors drawn by sunny days and outdoor activities. Mid-twentieth-century Arizona also was a place where differing ideas and perceptions of growth and land use would result in conflicts—both in words and actions—between boosters and conservationists.

CHAPTER 3

Becoming Arizona, 1962

ARIZONA MARKED ITS FIFTIETH anniversary of statehood on February 14, 1962. Speaking at the celebration at the state capital in Phoenix, Postmaster General J. Edward Day declared, "We are standing today in the midst of a land once described by Daniel Webster as 'a barren waste of prairie dogs, cactus, and shifting sands, incapable of producing anything, and therefore, not worth retaining.' Look about you at this beautiful, thriving, rapidly expanding city, a fitting symbol of the progress that typifies Arizona today."[1] That barren wasteland comprising the greater Southwest, of which Arizona was just a part, contained abundant quantities of oil and natural gas under its shifting sands and rich deposits of coal within its northeastern mesas. The same sun that warmed the earth for cactus also proved irresistible to tourists and retirees. The juxtaposition of useless wastes and thriving city in Day's words mirrored a national discussion involving questions of land value and use that had real consequences in Arizona.

Day's words, and the publications produced for the fiftieth anniversary, lauded the Arizona of growth and industry. However, narratives written about Arizona in the 1960s reveal a growing concern over environmental questions, a conservation consciousness that addressed land use and doubted the wisdom, even the morality, of resource extraction. These words built on the belief articulated by Wallace Stegner in his 1960 letter to the Outdoor Recreation Resources Review Commission, wherein he advocated for wilderness preservation, an idea of wilderness "for spiritual renewal." "We need wilderness preserved," Stegner wrote, "as much of it as is still left, and as many kinds—because it was the challenge against which our character as a people was formed. The reminder and the reassurance that it is still there is good for our spiritual health even if we never once in ten years set foot in it."[2]

Naturalists and conservationists wrote about an Arizona that had value because of the beauty of its natural landscapes, its isolated spaces, and what these places could do for the soul. Arizona lent itself to examining such questions, and in the examining writers imagined and wrote into being the place they believed Arizona should and could become. Well-known naturalist Joseph Wood Krutch spoke with authority as he wrote about Arizona deserts from the position of a resident, albeit a newly relocated one, not an outsider. Ann Woodin became familiar to readers for her book about Arizona, *Home Is the Desert* (1964). Her descriptions of living in the Sonoran Desert made the place accessible to people unfamiliar with desert life and offered a contrast to other bodies of literature about desert residents such as early pioneers and Native Americans. Woodin's words about living in the desert contrasted with the writing of Helen Sekaquaptewa, a Hopi woman who lived most of her life in Arizona's deserts, and the memoir of David K. Udall, an early Mormon settler whose experiences on the high desert plateau in the 1880s became part of Arizona's narrative landscape in the mid-twentieth century. In a fine example of words creating a place for readers, *The Place No One Knew* (1963), Eliot Porter and David Brower's book about Glen Canyon, created and re-created a place that became the epicenter of the struggle between industry and conservation.

Many of the voices speaking for Arizona—its government (the governor and the Arizona Development Board) and its powerful newspaper publishers and businessmen—wrote as if Arizona had already, finally, arrived and had become what it was meant to be and would continue to be: a growing population center with a multitude of resources to collect and sell. Newspaper reporters within and outside of the state wrote about an Arizona growing miraculously, both in population and in business opportunities. As a southern Californian remembering when his state was the phenomenon, *Los Angeles Times* reporter Gene Sherman wrote jealously about the state. Arizona's fiftieth-anniversary publications reinforced long-standing clichés and continued to emphasize claims of opportunity and already abundant prosperity.

Visual media provided information additional to and in competition with the printed word. Full-color photographs of the state's rugged, rust-red desertscapes and lush green forests appeared regularly in the pages of *Arizona Highways*. Movies such as *3:10 to Yuma* (1957) and *The Greatest Story Ever Told* (1963) brought a version of the Arizona landscape to moviegoers throughout the country. Viewers could tune in weekly to simulacrums of Arizona with television series such as *The Deputy* (1959–61) and *Annie Oakley* (1954–65). These images and stories reflected the ideas of Arizona's past. The Arizona characterized in the printed word revealed a multilayered place. Krutch's publications about the Arizona desert brought a view different than that of developers and boosters, as did Woodin's and Sekaquaptewa's memoirs. Porter and Brower's story of Glen Canyon created in words and pictures a place that would soon no longer exist, and reporter Gene Sherman wrote about the state from an outsider's perspective influenced by his residency in southern California. The theme of extremes, the dichotomy of Arizona's landscapes—stark desert and lush forests, Old West and Modern Miracle—remained present in the words.

Joseph Wood Krutch: *The Desert Year* and Other Desert Writings

Just as time spent in the Arizona desert led to J. B. Priestley's ruminations on American society in 1937, so did the Arizona desert influence Joseph Wood Krutch's ideas of open space and the preservation of natural landscapes. Krutch's observations of and experiences in the Sonoran Desert persuaded him of the value of the natural world beyond that of its material use, an idea that his home in the desert enriched and cultivated.[3] Earlier in his life, Krutch had disliked the desert and used it as "an analogy for despair and alienation."[4] The Sonoran Desert transformed Krutch into a desert lover and an advocate of the natural world, just as he hoped his writings would transform readers' perceptions of deserts and nature. A drama critic for *The Nation*, Krutch began teaching drama at Columbia University in 1937. He became an author of some renown, writing biographies of Samuel Johnson and Henry David Thoreau and exploring issues facing modern humanity. However, it was his desert works for which he became best known.[5]

Krutch's desert home during his sabbatical year from teaching in the early 1950s was in Arizona's Sonoran Desert, about ten miles north of Tucson on Ina Road and only a mile from the Santa Catalina Mountains. He described the mountains as "close to the horizon with stone slopes thinly clad in a dark green which at this distance looks more like moss or lichen than the scattered shrubs which have found there a precarious foothold."[6] The area was sparsely settled, and only a few roofs were visible from his home. Krutch arranged with publisher Bill Sloane to write a book exploring the experiences of a newcomer, believing his "innocence and ignorance might give a special tone to his discovery of the desert and desert life."[7] During that year Krutch and his wife decided to move to Tucson permanently.

Krutch had visited the Arizona desert several times as a "traveler," to use his term. His purpose for living in the desert during that sabbatical year was "to live for fifteen months in a world which will, I hope, lose the charm of the strange only to take on the more powerful charm of the familiar." He hoped "to look at, to listen to, and this time if possible, to be more intimately a part of, something whose meaning I have sensed but not understood."[8] The search for this meaning in the desert, something beyond the material, pervaded Krutch's writing and contributed to his evolving philosophy.

Krutch's descriptions of the Arizona desert reflected the perception of a man whose eyes had seen and whose mind had contemplated landscapes in the eastern section of the United States. Unlike other authors (Oliver La Farge for instance), and despite his earlier dislike, Krutch's response to Arizona's arid landscape was one of affection. "I know that many besides myself have felt its charm," he wrote, "but I know also that not all who visit it do, that there are, indeed, some in whom it inspires at first sight not love but fear, or even hatred. Its appeal is not the appeal of things universally attractive, like smiling fields, bubbling springs, and murmuring brooks." Krutch's list of "universally attractive" sights might be appealing to eastern eyes, but they might not be universally attractive to natives of the Southwest or the desert. "To some it seems merely stricken, and even those of us who love it recognize that its beauty is no easy one," he continued, animating a place that to so many appeared lifeless. He explained, "It suggests patience and struggle and endurance. It is courageous and happy, not easy or luxurious. In the brightest colors of its sandstone canyons, even in the brightest colors of its brief spring flowers, there is something austere."[9]

Krutch recognized that outsiders would view the desert differently than those who were accustomed to it and who understood the reality that belied its lifeless appearance: "Neither the plants nor the animals live under what is, for them, painfully difficult conditions. The vegetation flourishes in its own way. For the desert birds and desert animals this is not an unfavorable environment. . . . Only to those who come from somewhere else is there anything abnormal about the conditions which prevail."[10] Krutch hoped that by living in the desert as opposed to merely visiting, he would no longer see it as an outsider and in that change of perspective gain understanding. In writing about the desert he hoped to facilitate that process of understanding for his readers.

Krutch's time in the desert produced reflections on quality of life and nature's contribution to a better world, beyond any material, extractive uses. Believing desert land could not support masses of people, Krutch argued, "On the one hand, it is a very proper environment for those, including myself, who like it. On the other, it is not crowded either with men or with any other form of life. And for those who dislike crowds of anything, that is a strong point in its favor."[11] While Krutch was wrong in the limits he assigned to what the desert could, or could not, support, at the time he was writing it seemed quite possible that development had reached its limits. Despite what boosters declared, the aridity of the landscape would prevent crowding, Krutch believed, due to the lack of available water.

It is the space, the lack of crowding, to which Krutch attributed to the desert's usefulness on a moral level. He found "this country more than merely aesthetically satisfying. . . . Its spaciousness as well as its austerity are more than merely physically—and nervously—reassuring to those who have found the great centers too crowded and too tense." The problem as Krutch saw it was society's, and individuals', propensity for acquisition. He explored the idea that an abundance of things, jukeboxes and televisions are two examples, results in a lack of abundance, a scarceness, of other things, including natural places and space. "I shall be reminded how whole acres of New York City in which nothing grows have been turned into a desert far more absolute than any I have ever seen in the Southwest," Krutch declared, "and I shall wonder whether man himself can live well in a place where nothing else can live at all."[12] From his location in the desert, Krutch also gained perspective on humanity's place in the natural world, and he developed a philosophy that countered the ascendant theories of science, psychology, and sociology. "No man in the middle of a desert or on top of a mountain ever fell victim to the delusion that he himself was nothing except the product of social forces," Krutch insisted.[13]

In *Voice of the Desert* (1955), Krutch expanded and elaborated on his conservation philosophy and his belief in the value of nature not simply as a material resource but as an intellectual and emotional resource as well. He gave the desert a voice, one he believed had been missing from the national conversation. To draw in people unfamiliar with desert country, Krutch compared the Arizona desert to his former Connecticut home. He was a newcomer to the desert; perhaps he made the comparisons for himself as well. For example: "A really blazing day slows down the restless activity of a community very much as a blizzard does in regions which have them," Krutch explained.[14] "So far as living things go, all this adds up to what even an ecologist may so far forget himself as to call an 'unfavorable environment.' But like all such pronouncements this one doesn't mean much unless we ask 'unfavorable for what and for whom?'"[15] Of course the desert, it could be argued on this basis, is no place for human beings either.

In an article written for the *Saturday Review*, Krutch reached readers who may not have been exposed to his books, thus representing Arizona to a new audience. The article included excerpts from the last chapter of *Voice of the Desert*, and Krutch addressed American society directly on the subject of what makes a natural landscape useful. "To Americans, so often criticized as too practical and too extroverted, [the desert] may still have something to say," he wrote.[16] He emphasized the use of desert spaces as places of retreat, as the desert had provided for him. The thought that nature is for humanity's use only—and whether "use" can be expanded to mean "experiencing" (as a retreat, in Krutch's example)—became a key focus of the conservation movement and Krutch's desert writings.

Krutch argued that a connection needed to be made between the practical consequences of "the reckless laying waste of the earth" and a "large morality," a kindness shown to all living things because they are alive.[17] Articulating Aldo Leopold's land ethic for his own readers, Krutch wrote that the answer, the way to make that connection, is to have love, "some feeling for, as well as some understanding of, the inclusive community of rocks and soils, plants and animals, of which we are a part." Humanity, he believed, must not only live *on* the land but *with* it: "We must be part not only of the human community, but of the whole community."[18] The problem, Krutch believed, is that humanity refuses to admit that it is part of nature. It is the voice of the desert that can enlighten the conversation and enlarge humanity's narrow focus.

But Krutch was susceptible to mishearing the voice of the desert as well. In his book *Grand Canyon*, he described Arizona's northern plateau region through which tourists travel on the way to Grand Canyon. "The road lies straight ahead through that unusually bare desert which is the Navajo Indian reservation," Krutch wrote. Contrary to the perception held by Anglo ranchers and miners at the time of statehood that the Navajo people claimed too much land, Krutch asserted the opposite. Though the reservation encompasses about a fifth of the state's land, "the allotment is not so generous as it sounds. Strange and fascinating as the whole area is to look at, a land less hospitable to a human being who tries to live in it is hard to imagine. Most of the red sandy surface is bare of all vegetation and only dotted here and there by little clumps of straggling vegetation."[19] This description was penned by the man who had written that one should not judge a desert by its seeming lack of vegetation and who had declared that the desert deserves a voice. But he did argue for desert wilderness areas in the book from the perspective of the few who appreciate them.

Krutch's admiration for his adopted environment did not demonstratively hurt the landscape. In a 1962 article he explained, "I was fortunate in that I was a writer who did the desert no harm even when it was the subject of my writing. Physically, I have left it no less beautiful than it was."[20] Yet Krutch's life in the desert presented a dilemma that all modern desert dwellers face. By definition, inhabiting the desert involves harming the landscape. In Krutch's time, as now, sewers and waterlines would have been dug to his house, his household would have used water for many purposes, and the air-conditioning unit would have used electricity; both the water and electricity likely came from some of the sources Krutch wrote about in opposition. But Krutch did voice an argument that would grow among preservationists, one that Edward Abbey championed and articulated succinctly (see chapter 4). As Krutch compared the desert north of Tucson in 1962 to the desert of the 1950s, when he wrote his first Arizona narrative, he noted, "Newcomers are quite right to ask me where are the clean pure air and the sparkling night skies which I described so enthusiastically in my first book about the desert. 'Progress' has taken away from me both my invigorating air and my brilliant stars."[21]

During twelve years of living in the Arizona desert, Krutch's thinking evolved from an ideal—if humans could simply live in such places they would come to appreciate all nature—to the reality that desert landscapes could not sustain even moderately sized populations. His partial solution to the loss of desert space (reflecting his change of heart over the decade, from his opposition in *Desert Year* to simply visiting a place) came to be that rather than occupying the desert, people should, and must, simply visit it. Wilderness should be preserved in parks, monuments, and wilderness areas. "It is far more rewarding to be able to *live* in the desert than merely to visit it," Krutch decided. "But that is at least better than nothing and the recognition of 'wilderness areas' (including desert wildernesses) as having a value for and in themselves is a step forward."[22]

The Memoirs of Ann Woodin, Helen Sekaquaptewa, and David K. Udall

The Arizona desert provided the setting for Krutch's contributions to a growing national environmental consciousness. For Ann Woodin and Helen Sekaquaptewa, the desert was a source of family strength and a learning platform. For David K. Udall and other nineteenth-century Mormon settlers in Arizona, it was a dry, empty space to which they had been called to make flourish. The Sonoran Desert provided the environment within which Woodin taught her sons, away from crowded city streets. The northeastern high desert plateau was the place to which Sekaquaptewa returned after receiving her education in the city. The plateau and mountain region of east-central Arizona became home to a thriving Mormon community led by Udall. The stories of the women's lives, although different, demonstrate life in the Arizona desert. One is the story of a Native American negotiating both tribal upheavals and Anglo prejudice, traveling from desert to city and back again; the other is the account of an Anglo Easterner transplanted from the city to the desert who embraced her new life there. At the time of the state's fiftieth anniversary, the story of a Mormon patriarch—whose sons, grandsons, and great-grandsons became prominent in state and national politics—added the Mormon experience to the body of ever-present Anglo pioneer stories.[23]

The Woodin family's manner of occupying the desert differed from that of Native American desert dwellers such as the Hopi and O'odham people. In 1952 the Woodins arrived in the Sonoran Desert from the University of California at Berkeley (where Bill Woodin had pursued graduate work in herpetology), when Bill took the position of zoologist at the Arizona-Sonora Desert Museum near Tucson in the year that it opened. One of the first of its kind, the museum exhibited living plants and creatures outdoors, providing visitors a chance to experience the Sonoran Desert in a controlled natural environment, unlike the experience Ann Woodin and her four sons would have living in the desert and making it their home.[24]

Home Is the Desert is the story of the family's experiences living in the region north of Tucson, a city that, like many other southwestern cities, had boomed since World War II, growing tenfold, from thirty thousand to three hundred thousand people. Written by a woman who had grown up in New England and attended college in the East, and written perhaps for an audience like her wealthy Eastern family, the book was extremely popular, requiring four reprintings in its first year of publication.[25]

The Woodins embraced desert living. Ann Woodin described the family's wild-animal pets (including bobcats, ravens, scorpions, snakes, and lizards), the stream next to which they lived, and seasonal changes that occur in the desert. The Woodins originated in New England; the book was written from an outsider's perspective and encouraged a new or different perception from those most often held by people unfamiliar with the place or whose only exposure to Arizona occurred through western novels, movies, and television shows. Woodin wrote to rid people of desert stereotypes, as she described her family's habitation of the land. She acknowledged her readers' prejudices, admitting, "An old tradition defines the desert as a wasteland, a place where only scorpions, deadly serpents, and hermits live." She wrote, "A less esoteric attitude toward the desert is embodied by such adjectives as hot, dry, hostile, and lifeless. This is how most people who reside in more benign surroundings think of it, and why they naturally recoil from it. Once this was how I thought of it."[26] Writing for nondesert dwellers, she described the ubiquitous desert symbol, the saguaro, poetically: "Back-lighted by a low-lying sun, their strangeness is accentuated, and I think I will never be able to look at them and feel as if they and I belong to the same world. Whether they are old with many arms, or young with only a first arm beginning to sprout halfway up like a ridiculous bulbous nose, they are equally alien."[27] Of course for people native to the place the saguaro cactus is familiar, not other-worldly at all, and for the Tohono O'odham people its fruit brings the rain.

Once Woodin had her readers' attention and assured them that she is one of them, she was able to draw them into the desert life she and her family experienced. She explained the different ways to see the desert: "through the wondrously revealing eyes of such a naturalist writer as Joseph Wood Krutch, through the startled eyes of the newly arrived Easterner, through the technical eyes of the scientist, through the eyes of small boys." This last perspective, through the eyes of her sons, was how Woodin positioned many of her chapters, revealing, "I am still astonished at the pieces of desert to be found in their rooms and pockets. What a specific, surprising, and varied place their desert is!"[28]

According to Woodin, people unfamiliar with the desert mention the wildlife most often. "Aren't you afraid to *live* out there, with all those things around that sting and bite?" easterners often asked her. To the uninitiated she explained, "The fauna is much more misunderstood than dangerous, and you learn to accept it and live with it much as the city dweller does the car-filled streets." Like Krutch, Woodin compared the desert dwellers' need to spend the summer indoors with the easterners' withdrawal inside in the winter. Like Hilda Faunce and Martha Summerhayes before her, Woodin admitted, "The desert summer does not kindle in my breast the same enthusiasm that it does in the breast of my husband."[29] But she wrote beautifully, lovingly, of the desert landscape when describing the sun's effect: "Most of the day the sun spreads the land with a luminous white wash that diffuses not only color but form and substance. The desert belongs to the sun: it shimmers as the sun shimmers, sears as the sun sears, and it flames red as the flaming sun drops behind the mountains. Nothing is between us and the sun. We are tethered to it."[30]

Woodin employed a form of the comparison of temporal extremes, of old and new landscapes, in describing the southern Arizona desert and its mountains near Tucson and the Colorado Plateau cut through by the Colorado River in northern Arizona. The mountains in the Tucson area "are not the smooth, fleshy mountains of my eastern childhood," Woodin wrote. "They are gaunt and tough, with their ribs showing, and their sinews. It was yesterday that the earth cracked and these pushing shoving mountains were forced up, lifting the dry metamorphosed bottom of the Paleozoic sea high into the air. Slowly over the ages they shook it off their backs, covering their feet with foothills of rubble and filling the valley beyond. Because they are young and because of the lack of continually eroding rainfall, our mountains look new and strong and bony."[31] Describing the Colorado River canyon country from a boat in the middle of the great river, she wrote, "In the 150 miles we had just traveled, over 150 million years had slipped by in the windings of this river. We had brushed our hands over rock that marked the golden age of the amphibians, over rock that marked the dying of the dinosaurs and the materialization of a few mousy little creatures in whose brains flickered unbelievable things to come."[32]

Ann and Bill Woodin took that trip down the Colorado River with specialists in fields such as archaeology, biology, and photography to document southeastern Utah and northeastern Arizona's Glen Canyon before it was flooded by Lake Powell. The Glen Canyon story is a shared story, a shared natural landscape connected by the Colorado River, and therefore a shared intellectual landscape. The dam (completed in 1963) and its hydroelectric power plant (completed in 1966) were built in Arizona, the lake that formed behind it flooded canyons in Arizona and Utah, and the shores of the lake border both states. Woodin described the canyon country, and Glen Canyon specifically, viewed from above as they flew to Hite, Utah, to begin the trip downriver: "Beneath us smoothly slipped an incredibly rough desert of sandstone mesas, upthrust mountains, and deep narrow canyons that wriggled like serpents down to the Colorado. In the middle of this desolation and oblivious to it, the big river had carved itself a long and glorious house called the Glen Canyon."[33]

By the time Woodin was writing *Home Is the Desert*, she noted, "The water is slowly rising in Glen Canyon, submerging the rare and beautiful things we once saw, and the Colorado River, now only a trickle of its former self, flows gently southward." After returning from that river trip Woodin conversed with a newspaperman about the dam and Rainbow Bridge. His response to the river's impoundment mirrored what the proponents of the dam said, and her reaction paralleled responses other opponents had. The newspaperman "waxed enthusiastic at the prospect of this somewhat inaccessible country being, as he called it, 'opened up.' In his opinion it would be just grand to have a paved highway leading to the foot of the Bridge itself so that all one had to do was roll down the automobile window. What cannot be seen by everyone with little or no effort, for him had no value, and a wilderness uncut by roads was therefore a needless waste."[34]

Echoing Krutch, and presaging Edward Abbey and Ann Zwinger, Woodin wrote of the disappearing desert and lamented the destruction of wild places: "In many ways it is an insignificant thing to watch two boys set out on an afternoon's walk through the desert. They will follow a trail they have walked over many times. They will see the same bushes, the same trees, and hear the same birds. Yet this little vignette is increasingly significant as our Arizona desert is covered with houses or turned into irrigated fields."[35]

Helen Sekaquaptewa's words in *Me and Mine* (1969) created a very different Arizona from that described and prescribed by Krutch and Woodin. Born in 1898 at Old Oriabi on the Hopi Mesas in northeastern Arizona, Sekaquaptewa was a child of traditional Hopi parents. Exposed to Anglo culture at boarding school, she embraced Anglo education but was not left destitute by it when she returned to the reservation. Rather, Helen and her husband Emory claimed dual cultural citizenship, taking, according to Helen, the best from both Anglo and Hopi worlds.[36]

Me and Mine had its genesis in conversations Sekaquaptewa and her friend Louise Udall shared as the two traveled once a week from Phoenix to the Maricopa Indian reservation for Latter-day Saints Relief Society meetings. Udall was married to Levi, the son of Mormon settler David K. Udall. Sekaquaptewa told stories about her life, and Udall wrote them down. Unlike the as-told-to autobiographies of the 1930s, *Me and Mine* contains no extensive explanations or stated ethnographic purpose.[37] The title *Me and Mine* indicates that this is not a traditional Hopi story. For example, the title is strikingly different from the Hopi Way, which is a communal way of living. Another indication that the story will be nontraditional is the inclusion in the book's front matter of a Bible passage, beginning, "Who can find a virtuous woman? For her price is far above rubies" (Proverbs 31:10).[38] Sekaquaptewa's narrative is anchored both in her traditional Hopi upbringing and in the Anglo culture she experienced, and as she detailed her life, she described how living in the desert changed over time, from early to mid-twentieth century.

Early chapters of the book described Sekaquaptewa's childhood as a daughter of traditional Hopi parents who did not want her to attend the Anglo day school. "One morning I was 'caught,'" she wrote. "Even then, it was the rule among mothers not to let the child go voluntarily. As the policeman reached to take me by the arm, my mother put her arm around me." Even though Helen liked school, "Tradition required that it appear that I was forced into school."[39] She related the story of the schism in Old Oriabi caused by Anglo influence and education, which pitted traditional tribal members like her parents, who came to be called Hostiles (to U.S. government policies), against the progressive members, called Friendlies. The feud culminated in 1906, when Sekaquaptewa, her family, and other Hopi traditionalists were forced out of Oriabi and many of the men were sent to prison. The traditionalist families moved to Hotevilla, and the children, including Sekaquaptewa, were sent to the boarding school at Keams Canyon. By 1915 she had completed sixth grade at Keams (the highest level attainable there) and asked if she could attend Phoenix Indian School. Her parents would not consent, but Sekaquaptewa was given permission to "go on [her] own responsibility," meaning she could attend school away from the reservation for three years without her parents' consent.

Sekaquaptewa returned home to the reservation in 1918, having been away for thirteen years. "I didn't feel at ease in the home of my parents now," she wrote. Her discomfort, however, did not arise out of a lack of desire for or knowledge of the Hopi way of life. Instead, her refusal to give up the things she had learned at school (reading, for example) in the face of her sister's animosity created discord. After their marriage in late 1918, Helen and Emory moved to Idaho but returned to Hotevilla in May 1920, where their lifestyle combined aspects of both Anglo and Hopi cultures. While they educated their children in the Anglo manner, they worked and kept house in the traditional way, even as other Hopis adopted Anglo lifestyles. "While my neighbors were buying white flour and later bread at the store," Sekaquaptewa said, "I ground the corn for our bread on the stone mata and matake [*sic*]."[40]

Life in the desert for Hopi families at the turn of the twentieth century was much different than the life led by Woodin and her family in the 1950s, and different than modern Hopi families experience. Sekaquaptewa created both the Arizona of the past and of the modern Hopi reservation. Water, and access to it, was vital to the community. When she was a girl, "every spring and fall there was a community cleaning of the well. The sand and weeds that had accumulated within the basin had to be cleaned out and carried away. . . . No one was excused." But by the 1960s, she wrote, "The well has not been used for half a century now. Sand has blown in and piled up on the terraces, and they are grown up with weeds. Some of the retaining walls have collapsed, and some of the sandstone steps are washed away, and the old well is abandoned and forgotten."[41] In addition to water, corn was essential to Hopi survival. "Corn was literally the 'staff of life' in olden days," Sekaquaptewa said. "The Hopis knew how to make their corn grow in the sandy, arid soil. . . . A desperate fear that it might not rain and mature the corn was ever with us."[42]

While portraying life in the desert, in the villages on the Hopi Mesas, and on the family's ranch, and as she described the family's livelihood (cultivating corn and raising cattle and sheep), Sekaquaptewa did not describe the natural landscape in words other than those that related it to the family's living. There are no descriptions of sunsets or mountains or desert vistas. Unlike Woodin, Sekaquaptewa's philosophical musings focused on religion. Her philosophy grew out of both the Hopi and Mormon religions. Sekaquaptewa combined these two views into a dual-religion story.[43]

Sekaquaptewa's philosophy was also formed by and found in education. She quoted her father as she emphasized the importance of the written word. "The white man has kept a written record of the history of the people from the beginning," her father said, "while the Hopis have passed their history from one generation to another by word of mouth. With the telling over the years, some of it has been omitted or misunderstood, and changes have been made. The written record is more accurate and true."[44] Sekaquaptewa's father, once a traditionalist and hostile to Anglo education, now (in the 1960s) agreed with her way of thinking. He advised his grandsons: "You of the younger generation, stand for what is right. Go to school and be diligent, don't play around, but learn the white man's language and his ways so you can come back and help your people and fight the *pahana* in his own way. Who knows? It might be one of you to save our land."[45] Echoes of the Navajo elder in Oliver La Farge's fiction are here demonstrated in reality.

In reviewing *Me and Mine*, Fred Eggan named it as "one answer to how the transition from a society based on kinship loyalties to that of modern America can be made."[46] Eggan made no judgment on whether this was good or bad, but his statement was based on the premise that the transition must happen. He remarked on the book's title, stating, "Hopi children are taught communal virtues. . . . The shift from 'we' and 'ours' is symbolic of the revolution that is required in attitudes before modernization can be effective." The reviewer took it as a given that "modernization" must happen and that modern is "me and mine," not "we and ours."[47]

Louise Udall's father-in-law, David K. Udall, was a leader in the Mormon church communities established along the Little Colorado River in the 1880s. In 1959 his daughter and collaborator Pearl Udall Nelson completed and published her father's memoir. The story of the Mormon colonizing of Arizona in the late nineteenth century became a mid-twentieth-century story, creating the place with the words of this Mormon's experiences.[48]

Words about the Mormon settlement of Arizona had been part of its written intellectual landscape since the late nineteenth century, several decades before statehood. Their stories were extremely important to the Mormon settlers—they kept detailed records and admonished their children to keep journals. But while they wrote prolifically, the words were imparted in letters and journals meant for themselves, family members, and friends and were not often intended for the public. While their narratives created an Arizona for their immediate community, the Arizona that these Mormons experienced was not created for general readers. That place was created by people (often antagonistic toward Mormons) outside the Mormon community, in venues such as newspapers and court documents.[49] As children and grandchildren of the original Mormon settlers began publishing the older generations' journals and memoirs, those narratives became part of the Arizona story writ large.

As a tenet of the Mormon faith, members believe they have been chosen to ready the world for the second coming of Christ. In practice that means taking their unique message to the world, and in the late nineteenth century it meant moving out from their religious and governing center in Salt Lake City, Utah Territory, and colonizing the West. When the calls came from church authorities, members were expected to go, obediently and forthrightly. One of the places church members were called to settle was St. Johns, or San Juan, as it was originally known, in Arizona Territory. San Juan as a town already existed, founded by Mexican laborers and their families who worked for Anglo rancher Sol Barth and his brothers.[50] Less than twenty miles from today's Arizona–New Mexico border, on the Little Colorado River southeast of the Petrified Forest and southwest of Zuni Pueblo, St. Johns became one of several high-plateau Mormon settlements and the place to which David K. Udall and his first wife, Ella (he would eventually have three wives [see chapter 4]), were called in 1880.

Udall's description of Arizona reflects the first views of other writers—Summerhayes, La Farge, Krutch, and Woodin, for example. "We reached St. Johns October 6, 1880," Udall wrote, "having traveled four hundred miles through a wilderness inhabited mostly by jackrabbits, prairie dogs, and roaming Indians. . . . Most of the country through which we passed was desolate beyond description." But he also describes the place as the settlers came to view it later, a place of abundant grasslands and forests but with an unpredictable climate. "As the years passed," Udall wrote, "it proved to be a land of extremes, with alternating periods of drouths and floods, undependable seasons, and devastating spring winds. Washes and gullies grew deeper and deeper from the forces of erosion."[51]

Udall's words about settling and making use of the land created and re-created an Arizona for readers. His descriptions about reservoir building at the turn of the twentieth century can be compared with the discussions about water and dams occurring mid-twentieth century (see the next section, regarding Glen Canyon Dam), words set down at different times but read concurrently in the 1960s. "Reservoirs had to be built to maintain the Mormon people in Arizona and farming was primarily my vocation in life," Udall explained. "In those days in the northern part of the state, with no engineers and in our own way—for we did most of the work by ourselves—we stopped the water from going to the sea,"[52] presumably, he and the other farmers believed, where it would be wasted.

In the 1960s, at a time when women's voices and their stories were becoming part of Arizona's written narrative landscape, Udall's memoir reminded readers that this had not always been the case. In a section titled "Reminiscences of Our First Years in St. Johns," which follows his journal entries for 1882, Udall wrote, "Of course, the sisters did not take part in our priesthood meetings where community problems were considered, but they sustained and encouraged us. . . . I have always felt to say, 'God bless our pioneer sisters.'"[53] The biography of Udall's second wife, Ida Hunt Udall, would tell the women's side of the story more than thirty years after her husband's memoir was published.

The Mormons settled in St. Johns at a time of increasing animosity and prejudice toward them. Just as Sekaquaptewa's childhood experiences of the struggle between traditional ways and federal policies on the Hopi reservation became part of Arizona's written landscape in the mid-twentieth century, so too did the Mormons' experiences of conflict. Udall recounted the Mormon version of events in 1885, explaining that non-Mormons viewed the increasing number of Mormon settlers as a threat to their power. He described the political organization that Mormons termed the "St. Johns Ring" and its efforts to keep Mormons from holding office: "By deceit, fraud, ballot-box stuffing, miscounting of votes, and even by forcibly preventing Mormons from voting, the 'Ring' sought to dominate the affairs of the county. In a few cases where Mormons were unquestionably elected, they were prevented by force and fraud from holding office."[54] Mormons responded by sending representatives to Salt Lake City; the church called one hundred families to mission in St. Johns, and the Mormon settlements continued to grow. Udall's description of the Mormons' political struggles at the turn of the twentieth century contrasted greatly with mid-century readers' reality wherein one of David K. Udall's grandsons (Stewart Udall) served as U.S. secretary of the interior.

Both Woodin and Sekaquaptewa concluded by discussing what they learned through their experiences and what they imparted to their children. Woodin's lesson was a desert philosophy similar to Krutch's. "The desert, in fact the world of nature, because it is wholly impartial, is a teacher from whom children can learn spontaneously, without resentment," she wrote. "I hope the desert has taught our sons that they do not *own* the earth, that it is lent to them for as long as they treat it properly and respect the creatures with whom they share it."[55] Home is the first place of edification and forming; this was what her boys learned at home, in the desert.

Sekaquaptewa's final thoughts also reflected on the lessons she taught her children: "When I think upon my children and the kind of people that they are, a feeling of joy and pride fills my heart, and I say to myself, 'I have had a good life.'"[56] On the dual cultural citizenship she and her husband shared, she wrote, "Most of my chums gave up and went back to their Hopi ways when they returned home from school. They gave in when their parents urged them to forget what they had learned, although they admit that many of the ways of the *pahana* are better. I was stubborn and held on and would not give up. . . . My children would not be what they are, or doing the things they are doing, if I had forsaken the good that I learned at school. We chose the good from both ways of living."[57]

These are opposing lessons: the desert, the natural landscape, and what Woodin believed it taught her boys; and "civilization"—Anglo society, modernism—and what it taught the Sekaquaptewas and their children. Woodin wrote of the desert as the only place to teach and learn values that can sustain the world, and she and her family moved from a crowded Eastern place to "out there" in the desert and lived out those values. Sekaquaptewa's experience was the opposite, and her travels took her from the Hopi Mesas to the "civilized" Keams Canyon boarding school and then to Phoenix Indian School. Experiences like these, she believed, would advance the Indian people. For one woman, the desert, its space and land, would be society's redeemer; for the other, formal education in Anglo schools and the adoption of the Mormon religion redeemed.

Udall, too, believed the Mormon religion redeemed, and he also believed it was the Mormon people who redeemed the land on which they settled. "It must have been the Lord's will for us to go through these experiences in St. Johns," Udall stated. "When I look around me now, July 1930, I ought not to feel sad anymore. I see roads, reservoirs, shade trees, orchards, fields, this big home, and above all the men and women and children this country has produced."[58] Sekaquaptewa's autobiography created in words the Arizona of the Hopi people's experiences, describing both turn-of-the-century reservation life and a life spent navigating Anglo and Hopi cultures simultaneously. In Woodin's work, readers found an Arizona desert of the mid-twentieth century occupied by an Anglo family learning to live within and embrace its characteristics. Woodin's informal prose and outsider-becomes-insider viewpoint created her family's Arizona. Udall's memoirs complicated the Arizona that readers encountered by adding to the 1960s narrative landscape the stories of Mormon colonization along the Little Colorado River. The Mormons' 1880s experiences become part of the state's fiftieth decade.

Glen Canyon: *The Place No One Knew* and Popular Publications

In the winter of 1962 to 1963, a narrow, remote desert canyon in northern Arizona and southern Utah became the location for the filming of *The Greatest Story Ever Told*, the story of the life of Christ, starring Charlton Heston as John the Baptist. Heston described the region as "not just like the Holy Land but more as the Holy Land should be."[59] Within a few months, that canyon—known, but not widely, as a place of quiet beauty carved deep into sand- and limestone by the relentless wearing of the Colorado River—would be inundated by the water backed up behind Glen Canyon Dam and would be eventually filled with silt settling out of Lake Powell. While the lake filled, Glen Canyon became an epicenter in the escalating conflict over land use in America, a battle over whether and how natural landscapes and resources should be utilized: as assets for extractive exploitation or as resources to be experienced.

Just a year after Arizona's fiftieth anniversary, on March 13, 1963, Glen Canyon Dam's diversion tunnels were closed and Lake Powell began to fill. On that same day David Brower, executive director of the Sierra Club, composed the foreword to Eliot Porter's *The Place No One Knew*, a nearly two-hundred-page, full-color, exhibit-format coffee table book dedicated to the canyon that would no longer exist, depicting scenes that could no longer be viewed and documenting places that could no longer be visited. Most of Glen Canyon is in Utah, but its story is a shared one. The canyon is part of a natural landscape divided by a political line drawn on a map, not by any physical barrier on the actual landscape; therefore, its story becomes a narrative landscape shared by both Utah and Arizona.[60]

Construction on Glen Canyon Dam began in 1956, and while the Sierra Club's book may have envisioned the place as unknown, Glen Canyon had been considered as a location for a dam at least since 1924. Every year from 1924 to 1929, Arizona had submitted an application for a Glen Canyon dam site as an alternative to the Boulder Canyon dam. Another proposal was offered in 1947, this one by Los Angeles officials for the purpose of generating power for expanding southern California cities.[61] Conservationists played a role in choosing Glen Canyon, finally, as a dam site. In the early 1950s they successfully argued against a dam inside Dinosaur National Monument and acquiesced to one in Glen Canyon as an alternative. Initially, this seemed to be a fair trade; however, in the summer of 1956 the Sierra Club sponsored a boat trip through Glen Canyon (the same trip Ann and Bill Woodin joined; see the previous section) and the expedition members discovered the rugged and pristine landscape that would be lost. Determined to right that wrong, conservationists enlisted words and images to press their case against construction of the dam at Glen Canyon.

By the time *The Place No One Knew* was published, Glen Canyon was beyond saving. The book used Glen Canyon as a pictorial rosary with which to do penance so as to never commit this particular sin again. The heart of the matter for conservationists, in Porter's words, was that an "invasion is taking place—one that will obliterate all the places that bear the nostalgic names, wipe them out for all foreseeable time. . . . The waters impounded by this plug of artificial stone spread back through Glen Canyon for one hundred eighty-six miles in all, inundating the sparkling river, swallowing its luminous cliffs and tapestried walls, and extinguishing far into the long, dim, distant future everything that gave it life."[62] That the canyon was little known contributed to its demise.

The book was designed to move the reader emotionally through images. Yet pictures could not tell the whole story. Brower and Porter borrowed words from a variety of writers whose original intentions had not been to lament the loss of Glen Canyon. Photographs could not have done the job alone. Brower's words in the foreword, for example, create a Glen Canyon beyond what any image could. "Glen Canyon died in 1963 and I was partly responsible for its needless death," Brower declared. "So were you. Neither you or I, nor anyone else, knew it well enough to insist that at all costs it should endure. When we began to find out it was too late. . . . So a steel gate dropped, choking off the flow in the canyon's carotid artery, and from that moment the canyon's life force ebbed quickly."[63] No picture could evoke the death of a canyon so clearly.

Porter began his career as a biochemist at Harvard. An amateur photographer when his work was shown in a New York gallery in 1938, the success of that exhibit prompted him to pursue photography full time.[64] Porter's first publication for the Sierra Club, *"In Wildness Is the Preservation of the World,"* was an exhibit-format book of New England landscape photographs coupled with Henry David Thoreau's words.[65] Porter took his initial Glen Canyon photographs on a trip through the canyon in 1960, before the lake began to fill. He came back to the canyon several times in the 1960s, twice accompanied by Georgia O'Keeffe.[66] The very marked differences between the landscapes of New England and Glen Canyon stimulated Porter's creativity, and he produced stark and vivid images of a place that would soon cease to be. The resulting collaboration between Porter and Brower demonstrates the emotional appeal of entwining words and images to create a place.

Reflecting an opinion also held by Krutch (that nature, not progress, will advance humankind), Brower stated, "The natural Colorado—what is left of it—is a miracle, not a menace. The menace is more likely the notion that growth and progress are the same, and that the gross national product is the measure of the good life."[67] Porter's words evoked images that even his photographs could not depict. This description can be found in both "The Living Canyon" essay and in text paired with a picture of Hidden Passage.

> It is reflection that imparts magic to the waters of the Glen Canyon and its tributaries. Every pool and rill, every sheet of flowing water, every wet rock and seep—these mirror with enameled luster the world about. In narrow chasms streams of melted gems flow over purple sand past banks of verdant willow. Small puddles, like shining eyes, fuse the colors of pink rocks and cerulean sky, and wet ripples of mud may do the same thing. In the changing light nothing remains the same from year to year or hour to hour. Flood and drought, heat and cold, life and death alter the finer details incessantly, but they leave unchanged the grand plan and the enchanting quality of the Colorado's masterwork.[68]

The book's sponsors hoped that after reading descriptions such as these, no one could think damming such a place was a good idea.

Porter's final essay, "The Geology of Glen Canyon," is an evocative, *longue durée* telling of the canyon's story. "At the beginning of the great upwarping the seas drained away and in their place a meandering river carried the waters of the plain into the western ocean," Porter wrote. "Its dark mahogany waters must have supported an abundance of life which in turn supplied the food needs of many of the riparian birds and animals of the Eocene. But as the continent continued to rise, the character of the river changed. Tributaries, loaded with debris, flowing down the western slopes of the newly born Rocky Mountains, gave it the tools needed to cut its way downward as fast as the land itself was rising." The river cut its way through the layers of time, until "today still, it is cutting into these rocks, which can be seen exposed on the somber walls of Granite Gorge at the bottom of the Grand Canyon."[69]

Many of the quotes paired with Porter's images were words written for other purposes but appropriated to create a place, Glen Canyon, that was no longer the place in Porter's photographs. Several describe Grand Canyon, such as this quote excerpted from Clarence Dutton's *Tertiary History of the Grand Canyon* (1882): "The lover of nature, whose perceptions have been trained [elsewhere], would enter this strange region with a shock, and dwell there for a time with a sense of oppression, and perhaps with horror." Henry David Thoreau's much-quoted passage from *A Week on the Concord and Merrimac Rivers* (1895) was also adopted as a description of the forming of Glen Canyon: "The finest workers in stone are not copper or steel tools, but the gentle touches of air and water working at their leisure with a liberal allowance of time."[70]

Other passages do describe Glen Canyon, including Wallace Stegner's words from *Beyond the Hundredth Meridian* (1954), anchored in the very stone they describe: "Its walls are the monolithic Navajo sandstone, sometimes smooth and vertical, rounding off to domes at the rims, sometimes undercut by great arched caves, sometimes fantastically eroded by slit side canyons, alcoves, grottos green with redbud and maiden-hair and with springs of sweet water."[71] The reviews of the book also tapped emotion and created the place for people who would never see Glen Canyon as *The Place No One Knew* portrayed it. "There is an apprehensive—perhaps a mournful—note in much of literature of nature today," stated the *New York Times* book reviewer. "A book of magnificent outdoor pictures becomes an elegy on a Colorado River canyon that is in the process of being obliterated."[72]

Not content to let conservationists have the only word, Floyd Dominy, commissioner of the Bureau of Reclamation, published an *Arizona Highways*–style book about Glen Canyon, focusing on the lake that the dam created. Describing the Colorado River Storage Project, the dam, the lake, and the future, Dominy made his case for reclamation and created a very different place for readers, declaring, "Man has flung down a giant barrier directly in the path of the turbulent Colorado in Arizona. It has tamed the wild river—made it a servant to man's will. . . . Built of rock and cement and sweat and skill, Glen Canyon Dam stands as a monument to the talent of its builders. . . . The manmade rock of the dam has become one with the living rock of the canyon. It will endure as long as time endures."[73]

Dominy not only described Lake Powell in tones similar to those used by the conservationists describing Glen Canyon, he also described the same features: "Over eons of time, wind and rain have carved the sandstone into shape to please ten thousand eyes. The graceful, the dramatic, the grand, the fantastic." Secretary of the Interior Stewart Udall described the lake in a similar manner, stating in the foreword, "Once in a blue moon we come upon almost unbelievable beauty. Such was my reaction at my first sight of Lake Powell and its setting of incomparable grandeur." But Udall and Dominy's landscape is viewed from the shores of the lake that has drowned the canyon. From that position, Dominy wrote, "You have a front-row seat in an amphitheater of infinity."[74]

Though the most adversarial, the Sierra Club's and the Bureau of Reclamation's narratives were not the only words writing the place into being. And as the Colorado River was dammed and as Glen Canyon filled, descriptions of Lake Powell began to compete for place-creating attention. *Arizona Highways* dedicated an entire issue in 1958 to the Colorado River, including stories that encompassed it from its headwaters in the Colorado Rockies to its delta in Mexico. Raymond Carlson editorialized, "The Colorado can be a torpid, muddy laggard dozing in the sun, or an angry monster roaring with thunderous fury, chewing away millions of tons of the good earth as it lunges recklessly down, down toward the impatient sea." Taking the side of reclamation, he concluded, "A lot of millions of dollars and a lot of time have been spent on gentle Old Red. Every cent and every minute spent in the process has been worth it." A year later, in describing the growing dam, Carlson wrote, "The dam will be another shackle to control the mighty Colorado and will be another triumph of reclamation in the West."[75]

In 1964 a full issue of *Arizona Highways* was dedicated to "Lake Powell, America's Newest Playground." In the article from which the issue's title was drawn, and which is illustrated with her husband Joseph Muench's vivid color photographs, Joyce Rockwood Muench described the new lake. The couple was prepared to dislike Lake Powell, having known and loved Glen Canyon, but they were surprised at the beauty that still encompassed the landscape. The words and pictures in the article, an account of their seven-day boat trip on the lake, dispute the notion that the dam should not have been built. After spending the week experiencing this new landscape, Joyce Muench became a booster of the newly made place, creating it for the magazine's readers and declaring, "Having revisited Glen Canyon and been completely conquered by the wonders of Lake Powell so that my enthusiasm, tinged with amazement overflows to anyone who cares to listen, I rather want to stand on some high point and using my biggest voice proclaim: 'Hear Ye! Hear Ye! Lake Powell is open. Come and see for yourself the world's most dramatic lake. There will never be anything like it anywhere else. Come play in the sunshine of America's finest and newest water playground. Lake Powell!'"[76]

Thelma Hall Towle wrote about Glen Canyon and Lake Powell from a local perspective. She knew Glen Canyon before the dam, lived in Winslow for twenty years, and visited Rainbow Bridge six times in those years. She refused to embrace the new lake with enthusiasm, although she also acknowledged its benefits, both scenic and utilitarian. "Red cliffs and deep blue buttes are more bewildering than in the old days when the river was deep within the sheerly secluded walls, the river shallow, and shadowed, and the rich and secret feeling of intimacy with the brooding walls is gone," she wrote. "Perhaps one of the saddest aspects of the change is not being able to identify exactly where some of the treasured landmarks now lay drowned—to be so unsure of your location in your own bailiwick." But she ends convinced, in part, because of a trip to Rainbow Bridge, this time via the lake that made it more accessible. Of the eleven on the trip, only Towle and her husband had previously been to the Bridge. One woman had longed to see it for years, but before the dam was built she had been physically unable to make the trip from the river to the arch. The shorter hike, now reduced to a mile and a half, allowed the woman to attain her dream. Echoing the words of Ann Woodin's newspaperman, Towle decided, "If nine people who would not have seen Rainbow Bridge under the old circumstances can now see it, and if one out of those nine is as elated as she, then I and others who so deeply regret the changes can certainly feel the sacrifice of primitiveness has been in a good cause."[77]

The *New York Times* outlined the conservationists' dilemma early in the fight for Glen Canyon, before *The Place No One Knew* was published. The legislation authorizing the dam prohibited any water from inundating Rainbow Bridge National Monument; conservationists expected the ban could keep the diversion tunnel from being closed, at least until Rainbow Bridge was made safe from rising lake water. In 1961 a group of engineers, conservationists, and congressmen led by Secretary of the Interior Udall made the trip by helicopter to the Bridge.

According to the *New York Times* reporter who accompanied the group, "To prevent the waters of the Colorado River impounded at Glen Canyon from backing up to the foot of Rainbow Bridge, engineers now estimate that they will have to build a series of small dams and tunnels" at the cost of fifteen million dollars. A dam would be built in Bridge Canyon downstream from Rainbow Bridge to prevent lake water from reaching the arch. Another dam and a diversion tunnel would be built above the Bridge to prevent Bridge Canyon water from backing up behind the downstream dam and flooding the area below the span. The project would be costly and would detrimentally affect the surrounding landscape, adding roads, gravel pits, and more dams.[78] The sides had switched. The engineers used the conservationists' own arguments against them, and the conservationists found themselves arguing for activities that they had condemned developers for doing in any other instance. In the end, Rainbow Bridge remained unprotected and the water rose to within a mile and a half of the span.[79]

Both the *Washington Post* and the *Los Angeles Times* published articles praising the dam and the lake. Merlo J. Pusey's article in the *Post* argued that this human-made lake was as beautiful as anything nature had created; it had improved the desert desolation it covered, Pusey believed, and he taunted conservationists for that reason. "Can man ever add anything to nature? Most conservationists reply with an emphatic 'no.' Even the rank and file of outdoorsmen doubtless agree in principle. . . . But in the minds of increasing thousands, Lake Powell is posing a formidable challenge to that sweeping generalization," Pusey wrote. "It has created a new aquatic paradise in one of the most arid parts of the country." Pusey made sure readers understood the remarkableness of this achievement, writing to induce emotions opposite those cultivated by Porter's book: "People not familiar with the Four Corners region . . . can have little concept of its desolation. Bare clay hills and parched prairies extend for hundreds of miles." How, he implied, could anyone not approve of flooding such a place? "For centuries [this country] has repelled human invasion. But water in some measure subdued it, turning scorching and impassable canyons into cool coves where a person may fish or swim or sit and drink in the beauty around him."[80] According to Pusey, this was the triumph of Lake Powell. But his version left out the original inhabitants of the Four Corners region. These indigenous people, and Native Americans' traditional knowledge about them, go unmentioned, invisible in Pusey's narrative.

The *Los Angeles Times'* message also was aimed at conservationists. Lake Powell, the article began, "is a wonder in spite of itself." The author added, "If Lake Powell had sprung up full-blown from nature, like Grand Canyon or Tahoe, it would be viewed by Man the Discoverer as an unqualified blessing. But man did not discover Lake Powell. He created it, and its beauty is thus tainted in the eyes of some." Taking direct aim at readers who would be swayed by the Sierra Club book, the reporter wrote, "Because the purists remember the loveliness that existed there before, Lake Powell is suspect as a substitute blessing, a counterfeit."[81] Both places existed: the Glen Canyon no one knew, gone but still present in stories, and Lake Powell, now known, loved, and hated, standing as a testament to what was important to both sides in the conflict over natural resources.

Gene Sherman and Arizona's Fiftieth-Anniversary Series in the *Los Angeles Times*

In February 1962 Pulitzer Prize–winning reporter Gene Sherman, on hiatus from reporting crime and politics, wrote a series of articles for the *Los Angeles Times* about Arizona at fifty. A well-known war correspondent in the Pacific theater during World War II and an eyewitness chronicler of the atomic bomb tests in the early 1950s, Sherman won the 1960 Pulitzer Prize for Public Service in Journalism for his reporting on the narcotics traffic between Mexico and the United States. His coverage led to negotiations to halt the flow of illegal drugs between the two countries.[82] Yet he was a nearly lifelong resident of southern California and had been a *Los Angeles Times* reporter for his entire career; thus he represented Arizona from that perspective. In his mid-forties at the time of Arizona's fiftieth year of statehood, Sherman gave the impression of a much older man longing for California's youth. In both tone and substance the articles in the series are superficial, revealing as much about southern California and what one reporter believed about his state as they do about Arizona.

The series' uncredited introductory article sets the stage, giving California a starring role in Arizona's development, much as the *Los Angeles Times* did in the 1930s. "A new chapter in the growth and development of the West is being written by our neighbor, the state of Arizona," the writer declared. Arizona's "story of expansion, gaining substance in the shadow of California's great growth" included factors such as climate, location, the development of water resources, and the advent of air conditioning.[83] The *Times* reporting expanded on the idea of Arizona's newness, naming it the "Miracle of Arizona's Growth." In part, according to the newspaper, this growth miracle was due to an expanding light industry, a post–World War II boom led by AiResearch and Motorola and bolstered by the subsequent arrival of General Electric, Sperry, and Canon Electric. This Arizona was rarely portrayed in popular media in the 1960s, writers rather focusing on the tourist and Old West storylines. These themes are also present in Sherman's reporting; fifteen million tourists visited the state in 1961, "lured by winter sunshine, old western history, and magnificent scenery."[84]

The first article in the series, published three days before the official Statehood Day, reflects these common perspectives of what Arizona had become, but it casts the state as a kid brother in California's story rather than the star of its own. "One is struck hard by its similarity to California of two generations ago, particularly Southern California," Sherman wrote. "TWA and American Airlines yearly swoop eastern travel writers out of the blizzards and deposit them gently but firmly in the Valley of the Sun with the enthusiastic co-operation of the chi-chi hotels, restaurants and dude—oops!—guest ranches. When the junkets are dampened by rain, there is anguished teeth-gnashing, good-natured shoulder shrugging and joshing all around. . . . How nostalgic for an old Californian!"[85] Despite his words, Sherman's tone was less sentimental than scornful, disclosing perhaps a southern Californian's bias against a state that had become increasingly successful in competing for visitors and investors. The population of Los Angeles in 1960 was five times that of Phoenix and had grown by a respectable 25 percent in the preceding decade; however, the population of Phoenix had increased 300 percent during that time.[86]

Sherman labeled Arizona "yeasty." Did he mean restless, energetic, frivolous? Arizona described as each of these terms can be found in Sherman's articles. A new characterization of Arizona also emerges—the newcomer theme, which implies that everyone who lives in the state is from somewhere else. Even as he told about native sons such as Barry Goldwater and artist Ted de Grazia, he remarked, "Almost everyone seems to be from elsewhere" and added that half of the population "are newcomers within the last decade."[87] Sherman did not consider the Native American population of Arizona in this or any of the other articles in the series.

Sherman attributed the astronomical growth, in part, to the air-conditioning unit. "When the West was won, Arizona got tossed half-heartedly into the kitty," he scoffed. Sounding like Daniel Webster describing the Southwest in 1850, Sherman stated, "It was tucked out of sight and mostly out of mind, a barren patch of wasteland populated mostly by Indians and cows, tolerable in the winter but unbearable in the summer." Arizona would have remained underpopulated without the invention. "Air-conditioning is to Arizona what the iron horse was to California," Sherman declared, "the key that unlocked the frontier. Without it, the murderous summer temperatures would shrivel the ambition of those who spur the State to maverick prominence."[88] California's distance from the rest of the nation kept it isolated until the railroads provided the means to cross the western expanse. Heat kept the Arizona desert less attractive until air conditioning provided a more habitable environment.

In the series' second article, Sherman paused his mocking tone and with seriousness took up the Miracle of Arizona's Growth story—echoing *Arizona Republican* articles published at the time of statehood—telling of people who came to Arizona to visit and became residents. Sherman gives as an example Motorola executive Don Noble, who became one of those visitors-turned-residents and pressed his company to open a plant near Phoenix. Arizona is a right-to-work state, Governor Paul J. Fannin explained: "Wages are ten to twenty-five percent lower here than in larger industrial areas while per man production is ten to twenty-five percent higher." Sherman also interviewed Phil Theiss, regional director of the AFL-CIO Central Labor Council of Arizona, who stated, "This is a good place to live if you have money, or are making money, but it's a hell of a place to live if you're making fifty or sixty cents an hour. Then all you get is sunshine."[89] These words, quoted in an article published in a nationally read newspaper, described two Arizonas, one for businesspeople and one for the people who work for them. An investor or entrepreneur contemplating starting or growing a business would consider Arizona, based on these words. Laborers and wage earners considering a move would not.

Sherman once again framed Arizona from a southern Californian's viewpoint in an extra article on day two of the series. This was Sherman's fairytale of Arizona: "There is an air of ascendancy in Arizona, California's gawky neighbor. . . . She's getting into the act on the electronics circuit and shaking the sand out of her slipper in the fond hope of becoming the Cinderella of the Union by the end of the century." The picture drawn here in words is of a grubby hearth servant with visions of grandeur. What role does California play in this fairytale? Sherman's tone implied an evil stepmother or mean stepsister. Instead, Sherman cast California as fairy godmother, writing, "With California her godmother, she hopes to see her cactus turn into the golden coach of industry which can ride to meet the Prince of Prosperity."[90] Like the *Los Angeles Times* reporters of the 1930s, Sherman's Arizona was dependent on California, a satellite of the older state.

The third article in the series reveals an Arizona that had moved away from its progressive roots, ideologically becoming the place it would be at its one-hundredth anniversary. For example, state leaders' words of explanation regarding the rejection of federal aid—"we'll do it ourselves"—would be reflected in newspapers fifty years later. Unlike 2012, in 1962 conservatives embraced the philosophy but rejected the label. "We elect the man, not the party," Sherman frequently heard. "This attitude stems from the lingering frontier personality of the state that not so many years ago counted more cattle than people," he wrote. However, his tone is less glib and sarcastic in this article. He explored the idea that "Deep South thinking shades its politics" and quoted politicians admitting, "Arizona has a 'slight heritage of state's rights.'"[91] A look back at the statehood fight confirms this statement, but that conflict was embedded in progressive ideals. By 1962 Arizona had become a conservative state. At least that was the perception, and proving that perception can create identity, Sherman noted, "If Arizona were not in fact a conservative state, it would now be conservative by association" because of Barry Goldwater.

Goldwater's was not the only conservative voice in the state. "True, the state turned down urban renewal," said Valley National Bank's Walter R. Bimson. "We don't want federal aid. And the same applies to federal aid to education. We'll do it ourselves. . . . I'd say the state is independent rather than conservative." The results of this "independent" thinking, according to Sherman, could be seen just down the road from the state capitol building: "Nowhere is the expression 'the other side of the tracks' more apropos than in Arizona's capital. The demarcation between north and south Phoenix is stark, a miserable commentary on lack of urban renewal." Sherman wrote of an Arizona seldom described: "Pavement virtually ends at the tracks and south of them lies a large Mexican and Negro community of depressing squalor, muddy with the rains and dust-ridden with the sun." A clergyman whose church was located in south Phoenix said, "They refuse federal aid and say they'd rather do it on their own. But they never do."[92] This is an Arizona much different from the place readers would discover in the state's booster literature.

Sherman became the California partisan again in the fourth article. Published on Statehood Day, this article about water development reflects the view of a person whose home state and Arizona had always been at odds over water. Sherman did not mention the Colorado River Storage Project, Hoover Dam, or the new Glen Canyon Dam. Arizona "hasn't acted like a state withering from lack of water, although of course the plea is that water is the key to the future," he wrote. "Like all desert states, Arizona depends on water for progress—and in Arizona, progress is its most important concern,"[93] this from a longtime California resident whose state also proclaimed the necessity of progress, pleaded the need for more water, and participated fully in water politics.

Sherman's final article in the series begins with the state motto, "God enriches." He followed with the statistics: the growth of bank deposits (more than doubled from 1950 to 1960), industrial employees (again, more than twice as many), and industrial payroll (three times as much) in the last ten years. "God enriched Arizona with breathtaking scenery, an octave of climate, an abundance of natural resources, and one of the world's wonders in the Grand Canyon," Sherman declared. Despite his reporting in the "Far Right Label" article (and overlooking God's command to take care of the least), Sherman concluded that God "also helps those who help themselves, and a purposeful bunch of natives and perspicacious outlanders has benefited by the bargain. In the last decade they have done God's work well in Arizona."[94]

Of this assignment, to write about Arizona at fifty, Sherman said, "It's an extremely interesting assignment, digging a little under the façade of a state designed for tourist consumption. Not that that's bad, but it's often too superficial and self-serving to give any indication of what makes the state tick."[95] However, Sherman did not dig under the surface, did not apply the skills of investigative reporting that led to a Pulitzer Prize, and seems not to have traveled beyond Arizona's capital city. He did not explore the burgeoning environmental conservation movement or the relationships of Native Americans with industry or state leaders. He did not interview people such as Joseph Wood Krutch or Helen Sekaquaptewa to get diverse perspectives, deeper perceptions about Arizona, the place it had been and what it was becoming. Instead, with an eye to his own state of residency, he employed the time-tested truisms of climate, scenery, and tourism and added the expression of the Miracle of Arizona's Growth and the newcomer cliché.

Other newspapers published articles about Arizona on the eve of its fiftieth year. Despite Sherman's posture on frontier versus modern Arizona, the Old West was still profitable for tourism. Thomas E. Lesure of the *New York Times* described where visitors could find this Arizona, even as he referenced the Miracle of Arizona's Growth. Lesure wrote, "The magic word in Arizona is 'growth'—amazing, colossal, stupendous, as Hollywood writers say. All that people seem to talk about is how fast the state is expanding." But, he assured readers, the Wild West Arizona, "this land of cowboys and Indians," remained beyond the metropolitan areas.[96] Where were these wild, remote places where Old West Arizona could be found? One region, according to Lesure, lay in northeastern Arizona on the Navajo reservation, where development due to oil and uranium discoveries saw roads being graded and highways paved. Another remote area could be found in Palm Canyon in the Kofa Mountains north of Yuma: "More than all else, the gorge, where the trail follows a well-worn mountain sheep path, practically duplicates locales that gold-seeking prospectors stumbled over in search of El Dorados. And it is just as harsh and lonely."[97] Lesure assured the seekers of the Old West among his readers that they need not fear.

Joe Alex Morris chronicled his automobile tour around Arizona for the *Saturday Evening Post*, discovering the place for himself and creating it in words for national distribution. Morris reinforced the prevailing views of Arizona and offered a more thorough (yet still Anglo) perspective in writing about Native American Arizona. Arizona's dualities, its extremes of natural and cultural landscapes, are reflected in Morris's descriptions. "Arizona is a big state full of contradictions," he wrote. "It has splendiferous scenery, including the Grand Canyon, the Painted Desert, the Petrified Forest and miles of gigantic saguaro and organ-pipe cactus. But you can also drive for hours through the most desolate terrain this side of the Sahara, and hunters still regularly and perilously get lost for days in the treeless, rocky back country." But Phoenix was the epitome of Arizona's progress and modernity. "Modern plumbing and manmade lakes have brought phenomenal growth to this hot, colorful land," Morris wrote. "Millionaires now infest the hills where fierce Apaches once held sway."[98]

However Phoenix, "with its 459,000 people and 8,000 private swimming pools," was not the only Arizona.[99] Morris took the reader to the Navajo reservation, describing it in more detail than Lesure did, writing, "The most forbidding and, in some ways, the most exciting area I visited is the northeastern quarter of Arizona, a land of high barren mesas that is dry and hot in summer and bone-chilling when swept by winter winds." Visiting the Apache reservations, Morris granted the same progress there that had occurred in other areas of the state, remarking on the tribal cooperatives, recreation areas, and fine herds of cattle. Even with the state's miraculous growth and progress, Morris assured readers (just as other reporters had), the Old Arizona still existed: "All of this might seem to suggest that Arizona has shed its frontier ways, become sedate and mature and lost the spicy, rambunctious flavor of the Old West. Any such assumption would be reckless, indeed."[100]

Arizona's Fiftieth-Anniversary Publications

Advertising and place promotion often occur simultaneously. At Arizona's fiftieth anniversary, the partnership between boosterism and advertising produced several noteworthy publications. Created for consumption by readers beyond Arizona's borders, the anniversary publications reveal Arizonans' views of themselves and their state. The clichés of extremes are present in Arizonans' own words. "Arizonans have been men and women of rugged adventurous spirit, befitting their 'frontier spirit.' . . . Writers of national reputation refer to 'the miracle of the Southwest' as they report on our progress," Governor Paul Fannin proclaimed. "This half a century built a bridge from buckboards to jet engines, from mud huts in the mesquite to the gleaming towers in the sky," declared Arizona newspaper publisher Eugene C. Pulliam.[101]

The reality was that frontier life in Arizona had not been uniformly romantic, not all stories about its colorful past were true, and not all participants in the exploration and settling of Arizona were victors, as the state's large Native American population could attest. These stories remained untold in the semicentennial literature (this unfortunate term is found throughout the fiftieth-anniversary literature). Similarly, the

Miracle of Arizona's Growth was not experienced by all of the state's residents, nor were all of the effects of growth positive. As Gene Sherman's reporting demonstrated, Arizona's increasing prosperity did not reach many groups, such as Hispanics, African Americans, and Native Americans.

The most substantial anniversary publication was not an official state publication. The magazine-sized, 560-page, three-pound special edition of the *Arizona Republic*'s Sunday magazine *Arizona Days and Ways* included histories of the state and its branches of government and laws; histories of the state universities and utility companies; detailed stories about dozens of the state's businesses coupled with their advertising copy; columns and letters by prominent state and federal officials and well-known Arizonans; and reports covering every facet of life in Arizona—cattle and mining industries, housing and retirement, government and education, the medical field, and religious institutions, just to name a few. Subtitled *This Is Arizona: Fiftieth Anniversary*, the book is a demonstration of what a group of people—the *Arizona Days and Ways* editorial board and those whom they chose to write for the issue—perceived as Arizona, and it marked their endeavor to create and promote a place in which people would visit, invest, and relocate.

In the preface to the publication, the Arizona Development Board, whose self-stated purpose was "to tell folks everywhere how wonderful Arizona is," described the fifty-year-old state as a place of endless opportunity for all and evoked the post–World War II standard description of the Arizona Miracle: "We're salesmen for a product that sells itself. . . . This dynamic economy of ours requires a continuing influx of new talents, new tourist money, new retirement residents, new investment capital."[102] The book contains no articles by naturalists or coverage of the developing conservation movement; this publication is strictly devoted to growth.

Built from a rough but wondrous landscape, Arizona was now the land of opportunity, according to the publisher of the *Arizona Republic*, Eugene C. Pulliam. He employed the temporal cliché of oldest landscape in the youngest state: "The land that is Arizona, youngest of the states but two, was already old with fossils when the Rockies and Sierras thrust their backbones above an ancient sea. In no other place in America have so many tireless centuries of wind, sun, flood, and irresistible time itself etched great pinnacles against the sky, gouged out vast canyons in the earth, painted the sands a thousand hues, raised up the great mesas, and laid out the vast valleys." But the Arizona of 1962 was thoroughly modern, Pulliam assured readers, and people need not fear a missed opportunity. "Here are the people with the indomitable courage," he wrote. "Here are the great forests and the cool high country, the rolling plains of the southern grasslands, the warm living deserts, the placid inland lakes. Here, in short, is opportunity untouched that dwarfs even opportunity realized."[103]

Governor Paul Fannin described how Arizona's rough land fostered a frontier spirit that still permeated the place. "Today, we are a highly developed modern state, with towns and cities which are booming," Fannin wrote. "Yet, Arizona has never lost that territorial spirit of expectancy, the belief that greater things are yet to come, a spirit which has always been the hallmark of the American frontier." Fannin too evoked the Arizona Miracle, writing, "Time and again the spotlight is thrown on 'amazing Arizona.'"[104] Even the president of the United States contributed to the story of Arizona's frontier-to-modern growth with a letter to the people of Arizona, declaring that the Arizona Miracle resulted from the land and the pioneer spirit that built a marvelous, forward-looking place and people. John F. Kennedy wrote, "Arizona has reached a rich maturity after a phenomenal growth in population, industry, and scenic recreation. . . . The pioneer vigor and breadth of vision which built Arizona are essential well springs of strength for the nation and the continued development of a free and forward looking society in the decades ahead."[105]

Native son Stewart Udall also ascribed Arizona's independence to its rugged land and determined people. "Most of us from Arizona," wrote Udall, "believe we have developed a character all our own, based on the values of imagination, daring, and independence which carved Arizona from the desert land." Reflecting on his position as secretary of the interior, Udall described how the people had changed the land: "From Arizona's once-arid acres, we have wrought an agricultural economy which supplies the tables of housewives everywhere. We have developed a minerals industry which is essential to our nation's prosperity and defense. With nature's bounty, we have created a mecca for vacationing America." In discussing Arizona's challenges, Udall presented ideas that would become part of his 1963 book, *The Quiet Crisis*. "To achieve the material things of an urbanized and industrial society, we have at times ignored, denied, and exploited our Arizona landscape and the resources which it holds," Udall lamented. But Arizonans could change their course and "determine what kind of an environment we will leave to our children's children. Given this opportunity, we must act quickly to preserve and protect our natural resources—our mountains, forests, deserts, and places of history."[106] Rivers and canyons are not on the list, even as the diversion gates at Glen Canyon Dam were being readied to close.

On Bud Kelland's first sight of the Arizona desert (in the late 1930s, when he arrived with his son), he liked it immediately and decided to stay, becoming another visitor-turned-resident. "Before us spread to infinity the sun-drenched desert of Arizona," Kelland described, "incredibly rich in color, embellished by such flora as we never before had beheld. It was Wonderland." A once-well-known fiction writer and longtime Arizona resident (*Days and Ways* calls him "America's Best-Known Fiction Writer"), Kelland attributed the state's conservatism to its landscape. He stated, "One cannot live in close touch with our beautiful deserts and our stern, majestic mountains without breathing in an air of honesty and solidity and reverence which they inspire." This may sound like a call to conservation rather than conservatism, but he continued, "Our environment, our historical background, the character and integrity of those pioneers who wrested this state from the wilderness and set its fertility to produce riches, will never permit it to go blundering off in pursuit of the heathen idols of radicalism or socialism or other isms that threaten our most precious possession—human liberty." This certainly was not the Arizona that inspired J. B. Priestley's ruminations on communal America twenty-five years earlier. In case the reader still was unsure of Kelland's—and, by inference, Arizona's—politics, he wrote, "The conservatism of the United

States centers in Arizona under the splendid leadership of Senator Goldwater."[107]

Women contributed six articles in this 560-page book, writing about retirement living; food; the arts; horses, rodeos, and dude ranches; women's bowling leagues; and Arizona's clothing styles. While women reporters received a small amount of space in the book, minority authors received none. However, they were written about. In an article titled "Arizona's Earlier Residents," a piece actually about the state's contemporary Native Americans, reporter Ralph Mahoney described the dynamics of Arizona's Indian tribes. His eight-page article discussed each of Arizona's fourteen Indian tribes (without quoting any tribal members) and described their languages, religions, agricultural and farming methods, arts, and reservation lands from the perspective of an Anglo reporter who was certain all of these cultural identifiers will eventually fade away: "They are part of a society that is ready to engulf them before they are able to adjust to its demands."[108] Mahoney also wrote of the people who built Arizona—Chinese, Japanese, Italians, Hispanics, and African Americans among them. "None could have envisaged the wealth in people that followed the path across the continent to hack towns and cities out of an arid desert and a virgin forest," Mahoney wrote.[109] Though they dug pits for the mines, cut trees for the timber companies, and built houses in the growing suburbs, none of these groups were found in the anniversary edition articles about these industries. Unmentioned are the contributions of minority workers in turning the frontier into this modern state.

The only piece contributed by an ethnic minority in this huge book is a letter to the people of Arizona from the Chinese Chamber of Commerce. The Phoenix Chinese Chamber of Commerce was incorporated in 1939, at a time when discrimination against Chinese was customary and widespread. By 1962 Chinese Americans had achieved significant prosperity in Phoenix.[110] Perhaps from this position of quiet prosperity they felt secure to comment. The chamber employed a nonthreatening tone, yet still asserted their role in Arizona's development, "We, both the American-born and those of us from the old country of China, are proud of whatever influence—quiet, reserved, more felt than seen—that we might have had in fostering the cultural, financial, and civic growth of our beloved State of Arizona."[111]

To mark the beginning of the semicentennial year, the *Arizona Republic* produced an anniversary supplement to be distributed with regional newspapers in January and February, inserted within the regular newspaper editions. Titled *Arizona's Golden Era: Arizona's Fiftieth*, the twenty-four-page, four-color supplement focused on images of Arizona's progress. Each newspaper printed its name and the issue date in the space provided on page one. One article retraced Arizona's history and explored the relationships between Anglo-Americans and Indians. The authors allowed for the provoking of the Apaches by Anglos: "Antique newspapers and traditional western writers cast all cowboys and miners as strong silent saints, all Indians as red demons. History, on the other hand, casts reds and whites alike as human beings."[112] The supplement included articles on Arizona's growth, which listed all of the requisite numbers in population (a 959 percent gain from 1900 to 1960), tourists (which accounted for $290 million of the state's 1960 income), bank deposits (375 percent of the 1950 total), and income from manufacturing (an increase of $300 million from 1956 to 1960), numerically demonstrating the Miracle of Arizona's Growth.[113]

Arizona Highways, the state publication with a national audience, combined its February and March issues into one large anniversary publication. Echoing the prose of Sharlot Hall (and mirroring her practice of classifying the state as feminine), Edward H. Peplow, the writer who coauthored the newspaper supplements, wrote of the epic Arizona chapter in the equally epic American story. "Nothing about Arizona has been small," Peplow claimed. Her story could be found in "the turbulence of her geologic history and the treasures laid down then in her rugged vastness; the unsung accomplishments of her prehistoric inhabitants which parallel those of early Egyptians; the ironies of her first explorations by white men; the treacheries, struggles, tragedies and heroisms which marked her Americanization; the vision and work which have guided her from a position as baby sister among states to that of most dynamic in a dynamic nation."[114]

The vice president of Valley National Bank, Herbert A. Leggett, took up the booster language to encourage visitors and investors. Employing the temporal cliché writ large, Leggett wrote, "As one gazes into the colorful depths of Arizona's Grand Canyon, it begins to dawn on the viewer that fifty years is but a fleeting instant in the eternity of Time. Here is a creation that took not centuries, not millenniums of time, but millions upon millions of these units men call 'years.' To us mortals there are normally allotted but three score and ten of these units, i.e., less than a century but more than enough to encompass the period of Arizona's statehood." His concluding statement shouts from the page in all uppercase letters: "ARIZONA MAY NOT BE PERFECT ITSELF—BUT IT DOES SPOIL YOU FOR LIVING ANY PLACE ELSE."[115]

In another collaboration between boosters and advertisers, *Pictorial America* published an Arizona fiftieth-anniversary edition, celebrating the state in a 175-page, magazine-sized book with color photographs interspersed with advertising and information about towns and state history. Part 1 includes full-page, full-color photographs of Arizona scenery placed between chapters of Arizona history; prominently displayed advertisements for Arizona's businesses accompany each picture. The second half of the book is given to discussions of Arizona cities, listed alphabetically from Ajo to Yuma. On the first page the author asked, "What is Arizona?" He then lists, in paragraph form, dozens of things that Arizona is, separating the items with ellipses. Arizona is "land of towering peaks and outstretched deserts . . . last frontier of the Great West." Further on, Arizona is "where music is the clicking of Mexican castanets . . . the weird chant of the melancholy Indian peoples . . . and the pounding of hoofs on the range." And still further on, it is "a land whose vast panorama of color . . . beauty . . . and romance . . . no one book can completely portray. This is Arizona."[116]

In Summary

At the time of its fiftieth anniversary, stories about Arizona were still dominated by white men writing about the state's progress and possibilities, themes that had created and defined it for half a century and longer. In 1962, however, new voices were being heard, new words being written, and an Arizona very different from the dualities of ancient-modern, desert wasteland–verdant promised land was emerging. Joseph Wood Krutch's desert works helped make Arizona's natural landscapes part of the national debate on land use while simultaneously making words about that debate part of Arizona's narrative landscape. Eliot Porter and David Brower's *The Place No One Knew* set Glen Canyon as an example of what would be lost if the conservationists' words went unheeded. That book, and other publications about Glen Canyon that followed, created a place being made and unmade—the lake becoming as the canyon disappeared, as Lake Powell displaced Glen Canyon. This Arizona story continues to be written.

Ann Woodin's *Home Is the Desert* was a modern contribution to a long line of historical works about life in the desert. Juxtaposed with Helen Sekaquaptewa's *Me and Mine* and David K. Udall's *Arizona Pioneer Mormon*, the three serve as examples of the multilayered and entwined aspects of natural, cultural, and intellectual landscapes. Sekaquaptewa's words at first may appear to be another in a series of Native American as-told-to autobiographies, but hers displayed a different perspective. Her words did not demonstrate an opposition to Anglo culture but an embracing of it. Concurrently, there was little conflict within the author over Hopi culture; it was equally embraced. Instead, *Me and Mine* depicts a woman and a family who claim dual cultural citizenship. Yet the book was still edited by an Anglo and filtered through the Anglo publishing apparatus. Two decades later, Native Americans would control their own Arizona stories and the means to publish them. The publication of Udall's memoir demonstrated that the Anglo male pioneer perspective still played a role in creating the place in words and added the Mormon settlement experience to the narrative landscape.

Reporter Gene Sherman's *Los Angeles Times* articles provided an outsider's perspective, an almost adversarial view, written for non-Arizonans. While the perception in these pieces displayed one man's and one newspaper's viewpoint, the articles may have represented the idea of Arizona for many people and contributed to many others' perception of the state. That Sherman failed to dig deeply or broadly created a shallow, narrow perspective of the place. Arizona's own fiftieth-anniversary publications presented the historic voice of Arizona—Anglo men—writing Arizona for the nation. Themes that had been dominant in Arizona's narratives up to 1962 still found voice, still prevailed in these publications, but other voices were beginning to be heard. These new voices, new words, and new stories threatened this dominant storyline and instilled a fear that found purchase in the 1980s in an effort to make English words the only official voice of Arizona.

OVERLOOK

Water Rights, Civil Rights, and State's Rights

THE 1970S AND 1980S

In 1961 Avon Books published a slim paperback pocketbook titled *Barry Goldwater—The Biography of a Conservative*. Written by two journalists from Arizona who had reported on the state's politics for years, the book was published just a year after Goldwater had stepped aside for Vice President Richard Nixon at the Republican National Convention in Chicago after giving an inspirational "we are all Republicans" speech that solidified his place as a conservative Republican Party leader. Goldwater "is against an all-powerful federal government and for individualism," the authors declared. "He is for a militarily powerful America and against any attempt to pacify, or do business with, the Soviet Union. He is for strict interpretation of the Constitution. He wants a tight hand on the purse strings of government and an end to federal aid programs at home or abroad."[1]

At the same time, though, Goldwater and Carl Hayden (who had served Arizona in Congress since 1912, spending fifteen years in the House of Representatives and over forty years in the Senate), worked on the state's behalf for passage of the Central Arizona Project (CAP), the plan that would bring Colorado River water across the desert to Phoenix and Tucson. Yet Goldwater voted against the Civil Rights Act of 1964, believing it was unconstitutional and amounted to federal overreach into the rights of business owners. This vote earned the derision of Dr. Martin Luther King Jr. as Goldwater ran for president that year and was soundly defeated. King penned a piece in the *New York Amsterdam News* calling Goldwater's nomination by the Republican Party "unfortunate and disastrous," and he told the *New York Times* if Goldwater was elected president it would be "'a dark night of social disruption' in the United States."[2] However, in the late 1980s and early 1990s, Goldwater supported the paid federal holiday honoring King and backed Arizona's attempts to declare the holiday in his state.[3]

Barry Goldwater became synonymous with Arizona in the 1960s

as the state transitioned from solidly Democratic, with progressive politics and a vocal and powerful union presence, to reliably Republican. Both Goldwater (on the federal level) and state government maintained a philosophy of individualism that contrasted with requests for federal spending on massive water and power projects. While the state became more conservative politically, more federal dollars were spent on the dams, canals, power plants, and pumping stations of the CAP. What began as an irrigation project to bring water to Arizona's agricultural land became a vital source of municipal water for the state's growing cities.

The CAP was part of an immense, intricate plan, the Colorado River Basin Project, a forged compromise that brought upper- and lower-basin states together through deals that gave each state a share of an ever-decreasing supply of Colorado River water. The deals' drafters used an average annual flow amount based on numbers calculated for the Colorado River Compact, which had measured the average flow between 1899 and 1920, some of the wettest years on record.[4] Each expansive deal based on the questionable river flow—giving participant states projects, and rights, that the actual water amounts would not sustain—was necessary for the whole deal to be approved.[5]

Initially introduced in 1947 by Carl Hayden and Ernest McFarland, the CAP legislation was backed by and reintroduced by Arizona's congressional delegation over the next twenty years. Congress finally authorized CAP in 1968, five years after the Supreme Court had ruled in Arizona's favor in *Arizona v. California*. The ruling adjudicated the rights to Colorado River use between the two states, supported Arizona's claim to the 2.8 million acre-feet allocated in the Colorado River Compact, and agreed that the Gila River watershed would not be included in the total. Eventually, an immense aqueduct would carry the water from the impounded river at Lake Havasu 336 miles across the desert to central and southeastern Arizona. The water would be lifted two thousand feet in elevation from the river to Tucson via power produced by a coal-fired power plant at Page.

One of the necessary components of state and federal water and power policy was the mining of coal for power plants, among them the

Navajo Generating Station that would make pumping CAP water possible. Black Mesa, a coal-rich plateau encompassed by the Navajo and Hopi reservations, was key to this plan. Both tribal councils signed leases with Peabody Coal Company allowing the strip-mining of twenty-five thousand acres of Black Mesa.[6] The environmental effects of the massive amount of groundwater needed for the strip-mining, and of the strip mines themselves, proved detrimental to the Navajo and Hopi peoples' health, as did the smoke pollution emitting from the power plants' stacks. Astronauts orbiting the earth reported that "they could view but one man-made creation: the particulate matter spewing forth from Four Corners."[7] Thanks in part to the Navajo Generating Station, twenty years after CAP was authorized Colorado River water began reaching its engineered destinations—Phoenix in 1985 and Tucson in 1989.

In 1977 a group of business and government leaders formed Arizona Tomorrow Inc. to orient and move the state toward the future. The group contracted with the Hudson Institute, an entity that at the time specialized in futurist projects, which issued a report in May 1979. Proving that perception does create place, the study's authors declared, "Arizona has become largely responsible for redefining the very term 'desert.' Before 1950, a desert was widely perceived as a harsh, forbidding wilderness area incapable of supporting any considerable population. Today, a desert has become an appealing landscape, an attractive place to live, and a new kind of adult playground."[8]

Three years later journalist and columnist Peter Wiley perceived a very different Arizona and desert. In *Empires in the Sun* (1982), he wrote of Phoenix, "It is a potent vision, the empire on the desert. A strong sense of violation permeates the urban landscape. The city looks something like a war zone. Unfinished roads pass through agricultural fields or barren land and then run adjacent to half completed new subdivisions. . . . A civilization, they say, is in its formative stage as America moves west, and its newest power center emerges, superimposed on the desert terrain."[9] As has been the case throughout Arizona's history, undocumented workers from Mexico performed much of the labor on the construction of that civilization. In 1986 Immigration and Naturalization Service commissioner Alan Nelson declared, “We are seeing the greatest surge of people in history across our southern border,” and the *New York Times* reported apprehensions (of workers crossing the border without documentation) were up nearly 40 percent from the previous year.[10] Congress responded with the Immigration Reform and Control Act of 1986. Intended to address all of the issues, the legislation sanctioned employers for hiring undocumented workers, increased the number of Border Patrol personnel on the southern border, and gave permanent resident status (amnesty) to undocumented people who could prove they had been in the United States since January 1, 1982.[11] Barry Goldwater was one of eleven Republican senators to vote against the bill.

Goldwater retired from the Senate in 1986. Though he epitomized the term “conservative,” in the two decades following his run for president, the state and national Republican Party had moved further right of Mr. Conservative, and he found himself disagreeing with his party, especially on social issues.[12] Goldwater had voted against the Civil Rights Act in 1964 on constitutional grounds. In October 1987 he called for the resignation of Evan Mecham, Arizona’s Republican governor who had been in office for only ten months, in part because of Mecham’s rescinding of Arizona’s Martin Luther King Jr. holiday on constitutional grounds.[13]

A paid federal holiday created by Congress in 1983 and first observed in 1986, Martin Luther King Jr. Day became a political football in Arizona, a contest between its opponents (independent-minded states’ rights advocates) and its proponents (who believed the civil rights leader deserved the recognition) that ultimately cost the state a real football game, Super Bowl XXVII. Between 1984 and 1986 Arizona’s state legislators attempted to create the state’s version of the holiday, to no avail. Governor Bruce Babbitt, a Democrat, designated the holiday by executive order in 1986.

In one of his first acts in office, Mecham (who replaced Babbitt) rescinded the holiday, declaring the former governor had no constitutional authority to proclaim it. In 1990 Arizona voters had the chance to decide the issue, and confusion reigned when two different versions of the holiday were placed on the ballot. The voters rejected both and the NFL promptly pulled the Super Bowl, scheduled to be played in Tempe's Sun Devil Stadium in 1993. Voters finally passed Proposition 300 in 1992, creating the state's version of MLK Day, and received Super Bowl XXX in 1996 as reward.[14] Goldwater's evolution from Civil Rights Act opponent to supporter of the Martin Luther King Jr. holiday, and his opposition to any form of immigration reform, illustrated the tension that increasingly became apparent in Arizona's cultural and intellectual landscapes as minority voices were included in the narratives.

CHAPTER 4

Realizing Arizona, 1987

IN 1962, AT ITS FIFTIETH YEAR, Arizona's population stood at 1.3 million. Twenty-five years later the population had nearly tripled, to over 3.5 million.[1] By 1987 the phrase "Arizona Miracle" was no longer in vogue, but the conditions that gave rise to the moniker still prevailed. Arizona led the nation in creating new jobs and businesses and in stimulating the growth of new companies. According to business analysts interviewed for *Inc.* magazine's annual economic report, Arizona "benefits from lower wages, warm climate and the surge in defense-related industries under the Reagan Administration." The survey, reported in the *Los Angeles Times*, reflected each state's economic successes (or failures) over a four-year period; Arizona's job growth from 1984 to 1988 was over 23 percent, and it led the nation with the addition of nearly eighteen hundred new businesses with at least ten employees. The high-tech industries accounted for 48 percent of Arizona's jobs.[2]

However, Arizona as the land of prosperity and opportunity was not the only narrative available to readers in 1987. Other narratives about Arizona revealed a diverse cultural landscape. The seventy-fifth anniversary went nearly uncelebrated. *Arizona Highways* included the traditional statehood stories in its February issue, as did the state's newspapers on Statehood Day; the event earned no mention in the national press. The history department at Arizona State University sponsored an anniversary conference, providing a forum for scholars to look back on and explore the state's previous seventy-five years, but also to look forward at what the next twenty-five might bring. The conference resulted in a publication, *Arizona at Seventy-Five: The Next Twenty-Five*

Years, perhaps the only book marking the date. Unlike the fiftieth- and one-hundredth anniversary publications, which were supported by advertising and contained articles lauding the state's extractive industries and encouraging tourism and new business ventures, the publishing of *Arizona at Seventy-Five* relied on grants and donations, and the essays examined "the gap between image and reality," the real place inhabited by real people rather than the image of the place portrayed in popular culture. It illuminated an Arizona that readers of novels and newspapers rarely encountered.[3]

At the time of its seventy-fifth anniversary, Arizona was a place beginning to be realized, to be known and understood more broadly. No longer the distant, isolated frontier or the young state miraculously growing, concepts that had defined and created it in words since statehood, in 1987 Arizona's diverse cultural and natural landscapes were reflected in its written landscape; the multifaceted and multivocal place Arizona had always been was now revealed for readers.

In the 1980s Native American authors and poets wrote their own stories and published their own poetry and songs reflecting Native American perspectives. No longer were their words subjected to Anglo control and refracted through Anglo perceptions. Arizona publishers specializing in Native American works facilitated an understanding of the state that had been missing. The Navajo Community College Press and the University of Arizona's Sun Tracks series provided an outlet for American Indian authors and their stories that had been unavailable twenty years earlier, and each publisher released several volumes at the time of the state's seventy-fifth anniversary. However, with the books it chose to publish, the Navajo Community College Press obscured any lines between Anglo and Native American control, demonstrating the complexity of Arizona's written landscape. Native American author N. Scott Momaday's memoir *The Names* (1976) was reprinted in 1987, and poet Wendy Rose published several collections of her work during the decade. Both wrote about a connection to land and place that described their lives and experiences.

At the time of the state's fiftieth anniversary, the memoir of Mormon settler David K. Udall created in words the experience of early Mormon missionaries from the male perspective. Shortly after the state marked its seventy-fifth anniversary, Udall's granddaughter published the biography of her grandmother, Ida Hunt Udall, Udall's second (plural) wife, and the Mormon mission experience from the women's perspective was created. Maria S. Ellsworth's biography illustrates the changing nature of Arizona narratives over time. Appearing decades after her grandfather's memoir was published, the book shifts focus from stories dominated by Anglo men to an increasing inclusion of stories by and about women and minority groups. Reflecting a growing number of works by women authors, Barbara Kingsolver's novel *The Bean Trees*, a book about a group of Tucson women affecting change in their community, was published in 1988 and was decreed Arizona's most famous book by *Business Insider* editors.[4] Her nonfiction work *Holding the Line*, which tells the story of the 1983 Phelps Dodge copper mines strike, followed a year later. Both Kingsolver books present an Arizona inhabited by strong women advocating for powerless people who lived in the shadows.

While state leaders continued to promote progress in the form of more growth and development, in both actions and words naturalists and environmentalists targeted that unrestrained growth and humanity's careless, often willful, destruction of the natural landscape and resources. The process of recharacterizing Arizona as a place mindful of environmental change and humanity's impact on the natural world accelerated in the 1980s, as new voices added to those of the 1960s and the Sierra Club's *The Place No One Knew* and the desert writings of Joseph Wood Krutch and Ann Woodin. In 1987 *Arizona Highways* included articles addressing environmental concerns, in addition to its standard tourist fare. Naturalist Ann Zwinger wrote *The Mysterious Desert Lands* (1989), an informational book laced with moving descriptions of the land and the natural life within it. Edward Abbey's *One Life at a Time, Please* (1989) was published at the end of the decade; this collection of essays reinforced his critical, action-driven environmentalism but also presented some surprises as he detailed his stance on immigration.

Arizona was no longer simply the place described by boosters and advertisers in their written words. It had never been solely that place.

The diversity reflected in the words written in the 1980s finally fully revealed the multicultural place the state had always been. Yet this diversity discomfited many Anglos.[5] In that decade, as the state's (and the nation's) cultural landscapes became more diverse and polarized, groups worked toward moderating or silencing the many voices being heard and the stories being told. English-only language measures were introduced to amend the federal constitution and many state constitutions, including Arizona's. In addition to the words of minority groups, the words imbedded in the discussions about language and the state's Official English law presented a contentious, conflicted Arizona and became part of an understanding of the state.

Navajo Community College Press Books and Sun Tracks Publications

Controlling access to narratives—controlling the publishing process—is as important as controlling the words themselves. Native Americans' words and stories were not fully represented in Arizona's written intellectual landscape until the 1970s. Before 1960 Anglo authors, editors, and publishers monopolized the publishing of Native American stories. Beginning in the 1960s, and accelerating in the '70s and '80s, Native Americans gained access to non-Indian editors and presses to publish their own stories in their own words. By 1987 the Navajo Community College Press at Tsaile, Arizona, was publishing original and reprint publications about Navajo people and other tribes. Sun Tracks, which began as a literary magazine published out of the University of Arizona's American Indian Studies Program, became, in partnership with the University of Arizona Press, a publisher of book-length Native American titles.

The Native American publishing industry originated with various tribes and tribal members' need for information. Vine Deloria Jr. explained, "During the sixties and early seventies whenever Indians would gather together at conferences, the discussion would inevitably turn to the question of gaining access to information concerning programs, funding, and eligibility requirements." At the same time, federal program managers sought ways to get information to the people whom they served. Out of this dual need rose an informal network of tribal newspapers and newsletters.[6] As with non-Indian publishers, Native American presses developed an array of publications to meet a variety of needs. They employed different genres (tribal newspapers, community newsletters, literary magazines) that were sponsored by tribes, schools, and advocacy groups and that provided news, education, and employment information.

In Arizona two venues were established to publish manuscripts for and by Native Americans. Soon after its founding in 1968 as the first tribally controlled community college in the United States, the Navajo Community College (NCC, now Diné College) developed a press at its Tsaile, Arizona, campus. In 1971 a group of students at the University of Arizona in Tucson published the first edition of *Sun Tracks: An American Literary Quarterly*, a magazine dedicated to Native American creative endeavors.[7]

Shortly after its move from the Many Farms Bureau of Indian Affairs high school to Tsaile in 1973, NCC established a press, initially with the purpose of creating publications by Navajo people, for Navajo people. The books published by the press in the 1970s exemplified this mission. Ruth Roessel, a Navajo tribal member born in 1934 on the reservation at Round Rock, was educated in BIA boarding schools and graduated with bachelor's and master's degrees in education from Arizona State University. She was deeply involved in the founding of Rough Rock Demonstration School (the first community school in the country controlled by Native Americans) and the establishment of NCC. Her husband, Robert, became the first president of the college. The author of five books, several published by NCC Press in the 1970s, Roessel wrote about Navajo history, culture, and education, and she edited collections of oral history. Works such as *Navajo Stories of the Long Walk* (1973) and *Navajo Livestock Reduction* (1974) finally added Navajo experiences to the narrative landscape of these events.[8]

In the 1980s, however, as Arizona turned seventy-five, the books published by NCC Press presented a confusing landscape of narratives—stories both by and about Native Americans—and revealed that the process of constructing the place that Native Americans knew as Arizona was still subject to Anglo influence. Three books demonstrate the continuum along which that influence could be found. *Southern Athapaskan Migration, A.D. 200–1750* (1987) was a classic monograph about early indigenous people by an Anglo scientist. *The Myth and Prayers of the Great Star Chant* (1987), similar to Edmund Nequatewa's *Truth of a Hopi* and Helen Sekaquaptewa's *Me and Mine,* was a Native American story with an Anglo editor; a white ethnographer collected the chants and stories, which were originally published by a museum specializing in Navajo ceremonial art. The editors of the book collaborated with Navajo medicine men, who were given credit throughout its pages. Martha Blue's *The Witch Purge of 1878* (1988) entwined Navajo oral history with Anglo documentary evidence to present a more complete picture of the witch-purge events. The representations of Navajo Arizona found in these three works still reflected various degrees of Anglo control of the storytelling and place-making processes.

Anthropologist and archaeologist J. Loring Haskell's *Southern Athapaskan Migration* addressed the lack of synthesis he saw in the scholarly literature about the migration of indigenous people into the Southwest. The book was entirely anthropological and contained no references to Navajo or Apache origin narratives or traditional knowledge. Considering some of the science in the book—its reliance on "reexamining the osteological remains in light of current archaeological knowledge," for instance—it was remarkable that a Native American press published it. In addition to comparing skeletal remains, the author used North American language patterns to plot the Athapaskan migration, but the dense scientific language makes it nearly impenetrable for the lay reader.[9] *Southern Athapaskan Migration* created a Native American Arizona similar to the ancient Arizona described by archaeologists of the 1930s in their reports and echoed by the popular news stories drawn from them.

Though published by the Navajo Community College Press, the songs and chants in *The Myth and Prayers of the Great Star Chant* were collected and edited by Anglos. David P. McAllester treated his subject, the oral histories of these chants, with respect and deference, explaining the backgrounds of the medicine men who performed the ceremonies and including plates of the sand paintings that were an integral part of the ceremonies described. "For the Navajo, the interrelationships of stories, chants, and ritual express ideas that are experienced," Rain Parrish, curator at the Wheelwright Museum, explained. Harmony and beauty are essential, vital, as is the "deep kinship we have with the earth," and all are exemplified in song.[10] Like the Tohono O'odham songs in Ruth Underhill's *Singing for Power*, the words of the songs belong to Native Americans but are presented by an Anglo editor.

Martha Blue's short (thirty-five pages, including references) history of the Navajo reservation's 1878 witch purge is less pedantic than *Southern Athapaskan Migration* and is not as explicative as the Great Star Chant book; rather, it is almost an outline. Blue collated oral histories collected from Ganado-area Navajos with nineteenth-century Indian Service and military records; in addition, she utilized Indian agent John E. Pyle's diary and correspondence between traders Charles Hubbell at Ganado and William Leonard at Fort Defiance. "An ethnohistorical analysis" of the witch purge, an incident in which Navajos killed other tribal members suspected of witchcraft, the book "chips [at] the historical view that Navajo leaders orchestrated it as part of their political gamesmanship."[11]

Blue compared the documents with the oral histories, quoting Hubbell's letter to Leonard of May 31, 1878: "There is a big row going on here, among the Indians, they just killed one of them and we are in danger of our lives. . . . A big crowd just passed here and are going to fix themselves to go on a fight at Canon De Chelle [*sic*]." In 1970 Amos Johnson, a grandson of one of the participants, described the event this way in an oral history interview: "They led him around there [Ganado Lake] for awhile and finally killed him by hitting him with an object." Johnson explained the curse that Haloishjohn spoke before he was killed: "Hastiin Biwosi is our leader and we have buried some of your belongings, we have talked you into the ground, and now you will all die."[12]

Blue's use of Navajo oral history provided depth to the shallow representations of the Navajo people found in the FWP bulletins and the *Arizona Guide* of the 1930s; she exposed the Navajo stories in

Arizona's narrative landscape, where they had previously been invisible and unheard. *The Witch Purge* entwined Anglo documents (letters and diary) with Navajo oral history to expand the story of the purge and provide a deeper understanding than the version that relies on the Anglo documents alone. Blue compared the conclusions of the Anglo version and those resulting from the inclusion of Navajo oral history to a type of flower that blooms in bright sunlight: "The witch purge in the Anglo-American reports is like datura at night—small and shriveled. The Navajo accounts flesh out, like sun-opened datura, these dramatic incidents with a detailed chronology from a cultural perspective."[13]

The University of Arizona, through the Sun Tracks series, began publishing original works by Native American authors as well as offering reprint editions by native writers. When its first issue was published in August 1971, Sun Tracks became "one of the first publishing programs to focus exclusively on the creative works of Native Americans."[14] Students in the university's American Indian Studies Program developed the literary quarterly, which would present their own contributions as well as work from well-known authors and artists. They chose the name of their journal from a poem by Atoni (Choctaw), which contained the line "the Track of the Sun across the Sky leaves its shining."[15]

When the series evolved to include book-length projects in 1980, editor Larry Evers sought the assistance of the University of Arizona Press. Initially the press was a reluctant partner, declining to collaborate with the explanation that it did not publish literature. However, its editors decided, "because the subject matter has to do with Indians, and anthropology is a strength of our list," they could partner with Sun Tracks. Just as stories of the Native American past were once found in natural history museums (as anthropology, not history), the press categorized Native American literature as anthropology. Evers explained that this mindset was typical among university presses and many other publishers at that time.[16] In 1987 Sun Tracks published three volumes: one a book about Yaqui deer songs, another a collection of interviews of Native American poets conducted by Joseph Bruchac, and the third a reprint of N. Scott Momaday's memoir *The Names* (see the next section in this chapter).

In the 1930s Anglo ethnologists had collected and published Native American songs (such as Ruth Underhill's book of Tohono O'odham songs, *Singing for Power*) and had edited Native American traditional stories (such as Mary-Russell Colton's work with Edmund Nequatewa on *Truth of a Hopi*). In the 1980s collaborations between American Indians and non-Indians resulted in a more encompassing understanding of Native American ceremonies and songs, and the Native American voice stood preeminent. *Yaqui Deer Songs* (1987) is an authentic rendering of Native American oral tradition into the written word. The songs are presented in Yaqui and in English translation and include historical context—the reason for or the event at which each song is sung.

The Yaqui tribe "are the most widely dispersed native people of North America," according to Claudia Sadowski-Smith. They inhabit an area from southern Mexico to southern California, including their federally recognized land near Nogales and south of Tucson.[17] Yaqui deer songs belong to Arizona's narrative landscape in their oral form. *Yaqui Deer Songs* the book is a Native American contribution to the written narrative landscape of Arizona; even as the authors recognized and emphasized the importance of oral tradition, the songs and explanations create for readers the Yaquis' experience of Arizona and their representation of the place. Yaqui deer songs are both traditional and contemporary, Larry Evers and Felipe Molina explained. The songs "continue to be sung in Yaqui communities in both Sonora and Arizona. These are translations from a living tradition which stretches back past the time the Spanish slave trader Diego de Guzman first encountered Yaquis in 1533 into time immemorial."[18]

Evers and Molina began the project in 1979. Molina was a native Yaqui speaker and a deer singer who lived in Yoem Pueblo, a Yaqui community between Picacho Peak and Marana, Arizona, who met Evers while studying at the University of Arizona. Evers was a native speaker of English who studied the Yaqui language with Molina but did not speak it. In discussing their collaboration, they explained, "The historically exploitative aspects of the relationship between Euroamericans and Native Americans, teachers and students, investigators and informants, employers and employees, all cast long shadows around our effort to make this a fully collaborative project. It would be arrogant for us to suggest that we have avoided them completely. . . . We want to remind you that we have tried."[19] The authors did not want their collaboration to be confused with the earlier Anglo-Indian relationships found in older ethnologic works.

Unlike *Singing for Power* and *Myth and Prayers of the Great Star Chant* (which use only English), the songs in *Yaqui Deer Songs* are presented in both Yaqui and English; the Native American–language version is as important as the English-language version. The songs bring forth the Yaquis' place, stories and songs emanating from their experiences. For example, "Flower-Covered Fawn" is the first song of the *phako,* the ceremonial occasion. In an accompanying essay, Molina explained that the Yaqui people consider flowers "to be sacred and beautiful"; the deer live in the flower world. In his commentary for the book, Molina wrote, "In this song we talk about [the fawn] coming out to walk around and to play in an enchanted opening in the flower world. When I sing, my mind is always in the flower world. That is where I think the songs take place."

> Over there, in the flower-covered
> enchanted opening,
> as he is walking,
> he went out.
> Flower-covered fawn went out,
> enchanted, from each enchanted flower
> wilderness world,
> he went out.[20]

As each song is set down, in Yaqui and in English, the flower world of the Yaqui singers is created for people who would not otherwise have known it.

The Navajo Community College Press released books that complicated an understanding of Arizona by adding Native American stories while reinforcing a measure of Anglo control over those stories, and the Sun Tracks series expanded the available literature by Native American authors and poets. However, these narratives were but a small part of the available body of literature about Arizona and may not have reached a wide audience. Other Native American authors and poets writing about Arizona, and their words drawn from its landscapes, were better known and their works were consumed by a wide readership.

The Nonfiction of N. Scott Momaday and the Poetry of Wendy Rose

During the 1980s N. Scott Momaday and Wendy Rose were part of a growing contingent of Native American authors whose works became well known and widely read. Joseph Bruchac, a Native American poet and publisher, interviewed Momaday and Rose, among others, for *Survival This Way* (1987), volume 15 of the Sun Tracks series. Both Momaday and Rose contributed Arizona stories; each came to the place in a different way. Momaday spent much of his youth on the Navajo reservation and knew that part of Arizona intimately. He paved the way for other Native American writers with his Pulitzer Prize–winning novel *House Made of Dawn* (1969).[21] His novels, memoirs, and essays weave place, whether Jemez Pueblo in New Mexico or communities on the Navajo reservation, into the fabric of living. His memoir, *The Names*, first published in 1976, was reprinted in 1987 in the Sun Tracks series as volume 16.

Rose did not live in Arizona; she visited the state as a child and as a college student. But she imagined Arizona, and the Hopi people from whom she was descended, as if she had lived her whole life there among them. Rose wrote poetry as a Hopi woman unable to officially claim that identity and place because of tribal traditions. Rose's poetry explored that dichotomy, as well as the challenges she encountered as a Native American anthropology student and her anger at the treatment of Indian people by Anglo society.

In the 1930s Indian autobiography had occurred in the as-told-to genre; ethnologists interviewed and collected stories from Native informants, deleted and rearranged the words to appeal to Anglo sensibilities, and published the stories for Anglo audiences. *Survival This*

Way is a thoroughly Native American endeavor. Bruchac conducted the interviews; the Native American poets' words were transcribed as they were spoken, allowing no reordering or omissions to comply with Anglo tastes; and the volume was published in a venue specifically focusing on Native American creative work. The poets' words in *Survival This Way* explained their relationships to the natural and cultural landscapes, adding the Native American dimension to the place and portraying an Arizona unlike the place Zane Grey or J. B. Priestley or even Joseph Wood Krutch described, rewriting the place that had been created in the FWP narratives and early newspaper articles.

Momaday "defined" (Bruchac's word) a Southwest landscape for the readers of his poetry, explaining: "I think it's a much more spiritual landscape than any other that I know personally. And it is beautiful, simply in physical terms. The colors in that landscape are very vivid, as you know, and I've always been greatly moved by the quality of light upon the colored landscape of New Mexico and Arizona."[22] Even as Momaday spoke of writing places into being, referencing "Man Made of Words" (see the prologue to this volume), he recognized the effect the place, its people and landscapes, had on his writing. "I would say that much of my writing has been concerned with the question of man's relationship to the earth, for one thing," Momaday explained. "Another theme that has interested me is man's relationship to himself, to his past, his heritage. When I was growing up on the reservations of the Southwest, I saw people who were deeply involved in the traditional life, in the memories of their blood. They had, as far as I could see, a certain strength and beauty that I find missing in the modern world at large."[23] These were the same people who had been described in older literature as declining and disappearing.

Poet Wendy Rose explored a different type of landscape with Bruchac—cities. On the problems of modern cities represented in her poetry, Rose said (echoing Krutch and Woodin), "I don't think there should ever be more than, at most, a couple of thousand people living in one unit. I think beyond that it is impossible to be governed with any sense of integrity when you don't recognize each other and have no obligation to each other. . . . I become intensely uncomfortable in cities and I see cities destroy people I love." Rose also discussed Native American influences in her work and revealed the difficulty of classifying cultural influences. "I'm being fairly careful not to cite tribe here because I was born and grew up at a distance from my tribe," she said, "so I'm trying to deliberately separate myself from saying Hopi literature or Miwok literature—my community is urban Indian and is *pan* tribal."[24]

Rose's poetry explored this cultural heritage: half Indian and half Anglo, growing up in an urban community far from the reservation. On the topic of her family and identity, she explained, "I was in that situation where the white part of the family had absolutely no use for any other races that came into the family. . . . The Indian half is in a situation where, among the Hopi, the clan and your identity comes through the mother, and without the Hopi mother it doesn't matter if your father was fullblooded or not, you can't be Hopi."[25] Rose's words reveal an intricacy in relationships that had been absent in older, less personal works *about* Native Americans rather than *by* them, complexities in the cultural landscape that had always been present but had remained invisible to those who knew of the place only through stories written by and facilitated by Euro-Americans.

The University of Arizona's reprint of Momaday's memoir *The Names* followed the publication of *Survival This Way*. Much of *The Names* is stream-of-consciousness memory recording, as a child might remember, or as an adult might put into words his childhood memories. Momaday remarked on the power and magic of language and words. "Children trust in language," he wrote. "They are open to the power and the beauty of language, and here they differ from their elders, most of whom have come to imagine that they have found words out, and so much of magic is lost upon them. Creation says to the child: Believe in this tree, for it has a name."[26] The learning of names, of words and language set down in long, unpunctuated paragraphs ("fragmented and confused, images . . . which are mine alone and which are specially vivid to me"), pervades the book.[27]

Just as J. B. Priestley's experiences in Arizona caused him to rethink American individualism, and just as the place drew out of Joseph Wood

Krutch a conservation ethic, so did Momaday's experiences bring forth an idea of how words and place entwine. Bruchac asked Momaday about the magic of words in his interview for *Survival This Way*. "Words are powerful beyond our knowledge," Momaday replied. "They are created in the imagination and given life on the human voice. You know, we used to believe—and I am talking now about all of us, regardless of our ethnic backgrounds—in the magic of words. The Anglo-Saxon who uttered spells over his fields so that the seed would come out of the ground on the sheer strength of his voice, knew a good deal about language, and he believed absolutely in the efficacy of language. That man's faith—and I may say, wisdom—has been lost upon modern man."[28] This, too, was the experience of the Tohono O'odham people and the power of their songs.

Momaday was born in Lawton, Oklahoma, in 1934. His family lived on the Kiowa Indian reservation until he was two, when his parents went to work on the Navajo reservation. In Shiprock, New Mexico (*Naat'aaniineez* in Navajo [Tall Chief]), his father worked as a truck dispatcher with the Office of Indian Services roads department and his mother as a switchboard operator at the Shiprock Agency. Place and language would be entwined for Momaday from the time he was a child. Whether told in Kiowa, Navajo, or English, the stories he heard were attached to the land in those languages. The family lived in Shiprock and in Tuba City and Chinle, Arizona, and lived on the San Carlos Apache Reservation in Arizona during World War II. "But 'home,'" Momaday explained, "was particularly the Navajo country, Diné bikeya. My earliest playmates and schoolmates were Navajo children and the children of the Indian Service employees. Just at the time I was learning to talk, I heard the Navajo language spoken all around me. And just as I was coming alive to the wide world, the vast and beautiful landscape of Diné bikeya *was* my world, all of it that I could perceive."[29]

His description of the desert in winter re-created the experience in words: "Dawn is on the desert for a long time, and the air is clean and cold; it feels like frost, and it draws the skin tight about the hands and face. Look across the dunes wrinkled with light and shadow; the colors, before they deepen, are the colors of shells or of birds' eggs."[30] In his description of Monument Valley, a place that bestrides the Utah-Arizona border and transcends political boundaries, Momaday involved all of the reader's senses:

> Monument Valley: red to blue; great violent shadows, planes and prisms of light. Once, from a window in the wall of a canyon, I saw men on horseback, far below, two of them, moving slowly into gloaming, and they were singing. They were so far away that I could only barely see them, and their small, clear voices lay very lightly and for a long time on the distance between us.
>
> The valley is vast. When you look out over it, it does not occur to you that there is an end to it. You see the monoliths that stand away in space, and you imagine that you have come upon eternity. . . . I believe that only in *diné bizaad*, the Navajo language, which is endless, can this place be described, or even indicated in its true character. Just there is the center of an intricate geology, a whole and unique landscape which includes Utah, Colorado, Arizona, and New Mexico. The most brilliant colors in the earth are there, I believe, and the most beautiful and extraordinary land forms—and surely the coldest, clearest air, which is run through with pure light.[31]

The reader can almost hear the men's far-off song and feel the cold air as well as see the marvelous natural monuments. This was not Zane Grey's hard, bereft landscape. The place Momaday described is life-filled and spirit-sustaining. With these words, this place became part of readers' understanding of Arizona, broadening their perspectives.

Wendy Rose used words in poetry to bring herself into being ("to name," in Momaday's words), to give existence beyond herself to her pain at being rejected by both sides of her family, to voice her sense of belonging to a place and a culture she lived apart from, and to document her anger at what she and other Native Americans, present and past, endured at the hands of Anglo society. As Rose explored these issues in verse, she also created an Arizona in verse.

Rose was born in 1948; her father was Hopi, her mother Anglo-Miwok. Her poetry declared her Hopi ancestry and revealed her sense of abandonment by both the Hopi and Anglo sides of her family. "More than respect," she wrote, "I have needed to be claimed by someone as their own, someone who is wanted."[32] As an adult Rose discovered her Anglo roots, Scots and Irish. "This is not the heritage I would have picked—to be the daughter of the invaders. It is not where my sympathies lie," she confessed. However, she added, "The colonizer and the colonized meet in my blood. It is so much more complex than just white and just Indian."[33] That complexity can be found in her words as she juxtaposes the various facets of her identity to explore the intricacies of Arizona's, and the nation's, cultural landscape, where a Native American woman is "too dark to be Anglo, too white to be Indian."[34] She grew up in an urban Indian community but felt connected to the Hopi Mesas, and she majored in anthropology so that she could write a dissertation about Native American literature. Because Rose's reality was complex, so too was the place she constructed in her poetry.

Rose's discontent, and sense of disconnect, in growing up in an urban Indian community is clear:

> It is I in the cities, in the bars,
> in the dustless reaches of cold eyes
> who vanishes, who leans unbalanced
> into nothing; it is I
> without learning, I without song
> who dies and cries the death-time,
> Who blows from place to place on creosote dust.[35]

She felt cut off from the people she claimed as hers, both physically ("[blown] from place to place") and spiritually ("without learning" and "without song"). However, Rose's words about Hopi land and people demonstrate that even at a distance, this is the place to which she feels connected. Rose's Home-going poems, published in *Lost Copper*, document her 1977 journey from California, where her mother lived, to the Hopi reservation and her father's people:

Thirty years ago
a shred of brown cotton blew
from the cottonwoods
of Hotevilla; the sky lightened
to give it a passing to the west.
I remember: one lone Hopi
made it to the sea. It was 1947
. . . .
California moves my pen
but Hotevilla dashes through my blood
like a great and
crazy dragonfly.[36]

Rose imagined a Builder Kachina (supernatural being), the title of this poem; it is not part of the Hopi tradition. She imagined it "based on the things my father really said to me. . . . I've invented lots of Kachinas. I hope that it's not thought of as too sacrilegious. But I've invented Kachinas that go into outer space. I've invented Kachinas that are in the ocean and a lot have appeared in the visual arts. This particular one appeared in poetry."[37] Like Edmund Nequatewa, Rose depicted religious aspects of her people in her writing, and like Helen Sekaquaptewa, she blended aspects of the traditional with the modern.

Rose also wrote about being a graduate student in anthropology, bringing the unique perspective of an American Indian anthropologist to an Anglo-dominated discipline. While a dissertation involving a "cultural-historical perspective" on published Native American literature should be housed in an English or literature department, Rose explained, in many universities "Native American literature is not part of American literature."[38] Just as the University of Arizona Press agreed to publish the Sun Tracks books by classifying Native American literature as anthropology, Rose discovered that the University of California at Berkeley made the same categorization. During her first years in college in the mid-1960s, her archaeology classes "caused a crisis" of cultural identity: "It seems that I could *feel* the trowels, *feel* my bones smother in paper bags in a lab, *become* extinct in a museum display.

Rather than peering down into the excavated pit, I found I was, instead, staring up at the archaeologist from below."[39] Rose's perspective was entirely opposite those of the archaeologists and popular journalists who were creating an ancient Arizona in their reports and articles. She wrote these experiences into being in verse.

> In this university
> I am a red ghost
> touching handprints
> that gleam, bleached
> . . . .
> There is somewhere
> a woman
> built from earthen blocks
> who is not
> specimen,
> sideshow evidence
> for "affirmative action."[40]

Rose reminds readers that the past inhabitants of Arizona were people, not specimens, and that connections exist between those early residents and Native Americans today.

As a writer of poetry, and as a person who studied literature in academia and wrote about literature in various venues, Rose declared: "My position is that *all* literatures may be viewed ethnographically. All literatures provide information about the culture of both writer and subject. All literatures are potential tools for the anthropologist—but not one literature more so than any other. Native Americans are not 'more ethnic' than Polish-Americans or Anglo-Americans; they simply may be called upon more often and more intensely to deal with their ethnicity."[41] Although the Anglo Arizona created in stories had been the dominant version for over a century, it was no more valid or real or important than the Arizona written about by Native Americans or Hispanics or even by the ethnic Russians who worked the sugar beet farms west of Phoenix.[42] Rose's poetry and essays presented another image of Arizona and added another layer to the state's narrative landscape.

Ann Zwinger and Edward Abbey

Arizona's population grew by nearly 30 percent in the 1980s, and in 1987 the state was in the midst of a population increase second only to Nevada's. The Phoenix and Tucson metropolitan areas absorbed much of that growth; the population of Maricopa County, which includes Phoenix, increased by over 40 percent during the decade.[43] Suburbs fanned out from central Phoenix and replaced cotton fields and citrus groves with single-family homes wedged together sardine-style, sometimes six or seven to an acre. Environmental quality concerns (groundwater depletion through suburban and industrial use and air pollution exacerbated by tens of thousands of daily commuters, for example) that had been the focus of conservationists for several decades became mainstream issues and were reflected in the narratives about the place.

Arizona Highways supplemented its usual tourism and promotional articles with pieces describing the adjustments to these environmental concerns. Dennis B. Ferrell explained how municipalities adapted to groundwater regulations by increasing the use of treated effluent to irrigate parks and golf courses. Jan Barstad described Arizona ranchers embracing goat ranching and holistic resource management to mediate the effects of overgrazing. (Readers learn that goats prefer shrubs to grass and will forage on steep slopes, unlike cattle and sheep.)[44] The appearance of these topics demonstrated the importance of such issues to the magazine's readers. The editors did not take sides in the debates, however; instead, they chose stories illustrating the resourcefulness of Arizona's people and communities while remaining silent on the underlying reasons for the need of innovations. They did not question whether a desert landscape is a suitable environment for millions of people to inhabit.

Naturalist Ann Zwinger and environmental activist Edward Abbey both contended with the issues of conservation, preservation, and environmental degradation, but each brought very different perspectives and tones to their writing. Zwinger facilitated understanding and appreciation with lyrical and informative text supplemented by her own illustrations. Abbey advocated an adversarial stance, pursuing an us-versus-them, by any means necessary activism in strident tones. But both agreed the issues are vital. In Zwinger's words, "I suspect that the fierceness in our point of view may be much the same, we just go about it differently."[45] Zwinger's and Abbey's descriptions of Arizona and their narratives drawn from the state's natural landscapes added to the body of literature about the place and brought a sense of urgency to their representations.

Ann Zwinger did not set out to be a naturalist. An art history major, and a graduate of Wellesley like Ann Woodin, she commenced writing her first book when she was a housewife and the mother of three young girls. That book, *Beyond the Aspen Grove* (1970), and her career as a naturalist began as she made notes and sketches of the flora surrounding Constant Friendship, the family's retreat in the Front Range of the Rocky Mountains near Colorado Springs. Echoing Woodin's *Home Is the Desert,* Zwinger's book described her family inhabiting a wild area, albeit a high-mountain place rather than a desert. Zwinger's method, however, was more analytical and encompassing than Woodin's, incorporating botany and zoology into her narratives.

A writer whose words embraced equally the biology, zoology, and geology of a place, Zwinger explored the natural world in places as varied as mountains above tree line (*Land above the Trees,* with Beatrice E. Willard, 1972) and canyons along river bottoms (*Wind in the Rock,* 1978). The story of her journey down Wyoming and Utah's Green River, *Run, River, Run* (1975), received the 1976 John Burroughs Award. "'Naturalists are generalists,' people who explore broad workings of nature," Zwinger explained.[46] *The Mysterious Desert Lands* (1989), her examination of the four deserts of the American West, was also an exploration of Arizona, the only state that encompasses all four.

Desert is often the predominant image of Arizona, and it is often depicted as a one-dimensional tract of sand. Zwinger's desert book gave depth to that perspective. *The Mysterious Desert Lands* is a natural history of the Chihuahuan, Sonoran, Mojave, and Great Basin Deserts. Like Glen Canyon and the Navajo people's homeland, deserts know no political boundaries; their stories are shared, and their narratives, like their natural landscapes, are of a piece. So, for example, while Zwinger wrote about the Chihuahuan Desert based on an experience in West Texas, her words described the desert of a small corner of southeastern Arizona as well. Zwinger began the story of the four deserts' natural history with the Chihuahuan Desert in Texas and took the reader on a journey northwestward, through the stereotypical Arizona landscape of the Sonoran Desert, to the sliver of the Mojave Desert in the state's northwestern corner, and finally to the sagebrush-covered reaches of the Great Basin Desert on Arizona's northern border.

Zwinger described each desert's geologic and natural history, both lyrically and scientifically explaining sediment and rocks, plants and animals. Words that could have been written in language as dry as the desert being described are instead infused with expression. Describing the ever-present creosote, Zwinger illustrated it in words: "A breeze stirs the branches and the aroma swirls out of every leaf. I inhale that marvelous scent that graces the air, not cloying, not sweet, but resinous and clean. It's what the world ought to smell like when it rains. . . . I pull off one of the round white furry seed clusters and separate the five dark seeds. Although seeds could have reached southern Mexico and dispersed from there, there is also the possibility that they made the leap in one jump."[47] Like Momaday, Zwinger laced her descriptions with words that draw on all of the senses, bringing the Arizona desert to life.

The Sonoran Desert, the ecoregion most associated with Arizona, is the state's predominant desert landscape. Like other authors before her—Sharlot Hall, the FWP writers, and Ann Woodin, for example—Zwinger depicted the Sonoran Desert's unique yet stereotypical flora, writing, "It is the only North American desert with sizable 'subtrees' and treelike cacti, along with numerous deciduous and evergreen shrubs, and a marvelous variety of succulents. This particular assemblage of desert plants has been in place for only about four thousand years. An Egyptian ecologist, seeing the Sonoran Desert for the first time, exclaimed that this was not a desert at all but a veritable flower garden."[48] As did Hall and writers for *Arizona Highways*, Zwinger emphasized the beauty and life inherent in the state's major desert landscape.

In writing about the human-caused changes in the Sonoran Desert, Zwinger employed strong imagery, a creating of Arizona that followed on Woodin and Krutch. Exploring along the San Pedro River east of Tucson, Zwinger rested in a bosque, "grateful to be out of the noonday sun." She wrote, "Black mesquite intertwine like Gothic tracery, the black trunks like ruins of ancient cathedral columns against brilliant emerald grass." The bosques were disappearing, she noted, a result of lower water tables and arroyo cutting that left "graveyards of mesquite along the watercourses." Zwinger portrayed a landscape marred by human use, or misuse: "If not sequestered in a national park or monument, the sparse plant growth of unprotected desert is frequently miserably overgrazed. One March night I camp in southern Arizona. . . . I've thrown down a sleeping bag in some scruffy places in my life, but this cow pie-studded terrain is one of the dreariest. A landscape I know as so satisfyingly beautiful, so in balance, is here so tattered and beleaguered."[49]

Zwinger described the stark difference between grazing and nongrazing areas in a story with an ironic twist. The Cabeza Prieta National Wildlife Refuge, an 860,000-acre tract established in 1939 along the Arizona-Mexico border, is also part of the Barry M. Goldwater Gunnery Range. Grazing is not allowed within the gunnery range boundaries. "The landscape changes markedly the minute we enter the cloistered area," Zwinger explained. "Although unmistakable desert in its openness, stalked with great regiments of saguaro and ocotillo, there are so many more plants, so much more variety in size and shape, such a wealth of colors, compared to the overgrazed area outside the fence."[50] This is the natural desert, protected, as it were, from above (if one ignores the areas where the ordnance lands).

Just a sliver of the Mojave Desert lies in Arizona, a small area at the state's northwestern corner. Zwinger described its creation with words that bring exactly to the mind's eye what occurred: "Originally the Great Basin, Sonoran, and Mojave were a more or less homogeneous stretch of arid land. About two million years ago, the Mojave Desert uplifted as a block, rotated, and became a transitional desert, intermediate in climate and elevation."[51] The region of Arizona encompassed by the Great Basin Desert is also small, a section along the state's north-central and northeastern border. Just as Ann Woodin's perspective of northern

Arizona's landscape broadened as she and her husband flew over it, the nuances of the Great Basin Desert gained depth and became a textured, boundaryless landscape as Zwinger described the view from a plane:

> From twelve thousand feet the Great Basin Desert has a past-finished aspect, as if all that could be done to it has been done, and now it is old and tired and worn-out, grizzled and gutted, faded and weatherbeaten. Sometimes the land has a worn velvet look, tucked with arroyos, pleated with mountains, a landscape seemingly without seasons or eternally half past autumn, a landscape left out to dry, forgotten, tattered with rain, wrinkled with sun, and yet, in a peculiar sense I cannot explain, always vital and never forlorn. Because big sagebrush is the same color winter or summer, the landscape has a changelessness that grants it an aura of stability.[52]

It is this northern Arizona–southern Utah desert, changeless and stable, that drew Edward Abbey, and through his writing people learned that the land's stability has one threat—humans.

Abbey wrote compellingly about natural landscapes, and his words forcefully condemned human actions against nature. He became identified with, and his writings helped create, a militant environmentalism that found an outlet nationally in Earth First! and similar groups. Like Zwinger, Abbey did not intend to be a nature writer. A native of the Appalachian Mountains of Pennsylvania, Abbey first traveled west in 1944 as a seventeen-year-old, hitchhiking across the country before he was drafted into the army. On that trip he saw Grand Canyon, walking the last mile to the Rim because it seemed "disrespectful, even irreverent, even blasphemous to ride to the edge of the Grand Canyon seated on one's backside inside an upholstered, jiggling, clanking, mechanical contraption like the automobile."[53] Abbey attended college at the University of New Mexico in Albuquerque on the GI Bill at a time when the metropolitan areas of the southwest began to see the first waves of postwar growth and as the number of Americans traveling around the nation sightseeing increased. The ceaseless growth labeled "progress" by boosters and leaders became a recurring theme in Abbey's work.

Abbey's two seasons as a ranger at Arches National Monument, in 1956 and 1957, became the raw material for his first national success as a writer, as he turned his journals and experiences into *Desert Solitaire: A Season in the Wilderness* (1968). Set in the canyon country of southeastern Utah, the book offers the ideas and themes that became Abbey's hallmarks. He began *Desert Solitaire* in fine Krutch-like, nature-writer form: "It seems to me that the strangeness and wonder of existence are emphasized here, in the desert, by the comparative sparsity of the flora and fauna: life not crowded upon life as in other places but scattered abroad in spareness and simplicity, with a generous gift of space for each herb and brush and tree, each stem of grass, so that the living organism stands out bold and brave and vivid against the lifeless sand and barren rock."[54] He also expounded on the themes of unrestricted development and "industrial tourism" that are found in many of his later works. His novel *The Monkey Wrench Gang* (first published in 1975 and, like *Desert Solitaire,* reprinted in the 1980s), influenced environmental activists. *The Monkey Wrench Gang* follows a group of anarchists disgusted with industrial development as they act on their beliefs and inflict damage on the timber industry, road and bridge builders, and dam construction on the Colorado Plateau. Abbey continued to build on the themes of economic development and degradation of the natural world, this time in fiction, in a story encompassing much of the Southwest, including Arizona.[55]

All of Abbey's themes and arguments are brought together in a collection of his essays, articles, and speeches, *One Life at a Time, Please* (1988). In the book's essays he criticizes cows and overgrazing, condemns astronomical population growth and illegal immigration, and provides the transcript of his interview with Joseph Wood Krutch, one of the last Krutch gave. The theme of unhindered development defined as progress (first seen in *Desert Solitaire* and acted upon by the characters in *The Monkey Wrench Gang*) is addressed in a 1984 article written for Tucson's *Arizona Daily Star,* "Arizona's Future: How Big Is Big Enough?," in which Abbey characterizes Arizona as a case study of what could happen when leaders are allowed to indulge their growth addiction.[56]

Abbey's portrayal of that addiction appeared first in 1968's *Desert Solitaire*, when he wrote, "There is no lack of water here, unless you try to establish a city where no city should be." But hydroelectric dams, power lines, and canals were necessary, in the words of the water project promoters, "'in anticipation of future needs, in order to provide for the continued industrial and population growth of the Southwest.'" Abbey then asserted, "And in such an answer we see that it's only the old numbers game again, the monomania of small and very simple minds in the grip of an obsession. They cannot see that growth for the sake of growth is a cancerous madness, that Phoenix and Albuquerque will not be better cities to live in when their populations are doubled again and again."[57]

Abbey continued the theme in *The Monkey Wrench Gang*. He described his fictional character George Washington Hayduke returning "to the American Southwest he had been remembering, only to find it no longer what he remembered, no longer the clear and classical desert, the pellucid sky he roamed in dreams. . . . The open desert was being scraped bare of all vegetation, all life, by giant D-9 bulldozers reminding him of the Rome plows leveling Vietnam."[58]

And in "How Big Is Big Enough?" Abbey wrote, "Governor Bruce Babbitt tells us that by the year 2000, only sixteen years from now, Arizona will gain two million new residents. . . . Tucson Mayor Lew Murphy—unable to conceal his smirking glee—predicts Tucson will become, within twenty years, a 450-square mile urbanized area. . . . This, our leaders tell us, is good news. Growth is good, they say, reciting like an incantation the prime article of faith of the official American religion: bigger is better and best is biggest."[59] Echoing *Desert Solitaire* and reiterating an analogy he used often, Abbey stated, "The one disease to which the growth mania bears an exact analogical resemblance is cancer. Growth for the sake of growth is the ideology of the cancer cell. Cancer has no purpose but growth; but it does have another result—the death of the host."[60] For Abbey, the cities of Arizona were consuming the state like a cancer; this was the Arizona his words constructed.

A surprise for many readers was Abbey's stance on immigration, though not to those who recognized a thread of arrogance running through his exhortations about growth and overcrowding. "Unless a way is found to stabilize the nation's population, the [national] parks cannot be saved. Or anything else worth a damn," he wrote in *Desert Solitaire*. He then proceeded to give his prescription for saving the parks and "Abbey's country."[61] His position was made clear, ominously so, in "Immigration and Liberal Taboos," a revised reprint of an article published in the *Phoenix New Times* in 1983 titled "The Closing Door Policy." Written at a time of increasing fervor over illegal immigration, when minority voices were being heard more loudly and in more venues (see the following sections), the article stoked the growing perception that American society was at risk of being inexorably changed, and not for the better. Abbey's article contributed to the cacophony of words surrounding issues of immigration, language, and race that eventually culminated in Arizona with Proposition 106 and the Official English amendment. The article was Abbey's favorite in the *One Life at a Time, Please* collection.[62]

Abbey's argument against immigration was primarily based on economics and environmental harm and could be set in the context of immigration discussions in the twenty-first century as well: "The United States remains burdened with mass unemployment, permanent poverty, an overloaded welfare system, violent crime . . . plus the ongoing destruction of what remains of our forests, fields, mountains, lakes, rivers, and seashores. . . . In which case it might be wise for us as American citizens to call a halt to the mass influx of even more millions of hungry, ignorant, unskilled, and culturally-morally-genetically impoverished people."[63]

He appealed to a xenophobia present in the discussions and railed against so-called anchor babies: "Can't break up families, can we? They came to stay and they stay to multiply." His words suggest that those brand-new little American citizens drew other family members across the border like iron filings to a magnet. He explained why this "alien mode of life," specifically Hispanic culture, did not appeal to the majority of Americans: "Because we prefer democratic government, for one thing; because we still hope for an open, spacious, uncrowded, and beautiful—yes beautiful—society, for another. The alternative, in the squalor, cruelty, and corruption of Latin America, is plain for all to see." Abbey was adamant that the United States could sustain no further population growth, and his was an equal-opportunity growth ban against both natural population growth and immigration, legal or not. "The United States has been fully settled, and more than full for at least a century," he declared.[64]

As naturalists, or environmentalists, Abbey and Zwinger appealed to different audiences, but both wrote of an Arizona (and of its and the nation's natural landscapes) in need of protecting. Abbey's position on immigration—while ostensibly invoking the environmental issue that more people equals more growth, which equals more environmental catastrophe—surprised many environmentalists who agreed with him on other issues. However, Abbey's was not a minority viewpoint in Arizona in the 1980s.

Ida Hunt Udall and Barbara Kingsolver: Biography, Fiction, and History

In 1987 filmmaker and director Bobbi Birleffi produced a documentary about Mormon missionaries. The film aired nationwide on PBS in May of that year and was met with "disappointment" by the church members and officials, who had cooperated with the director. "The Mormons: Missionaries to the World," chronicling the church's worldwide missionary program, focused on the two-year mission journeys that Mormon men undertake at age eighteen or nineteen.[65] Even as viewers learned about contemporary Mormon missionaries, readers could learn about Mormon missions of the past as the grandchildren of early Mormon settlers continued the practice of publishing their grandparents' diaries and letters. One such book, published shortly after Arizona celebrated its seventy-fifth year as a state, was *Mormon Odyssey: The Story of Ida Hunt Udall, Plural Wife* (1992), and it wrote into being the Mormon experience in Arizona from the women's perspective. Often the early frontier Arizona that readers discovered was a male-constructed Arizona, a place created from men's experiences and men's words. However, women were also pioneers and settlers, and they experienced the place differently from their male counterparts.

While sharing the same landscape as depicted in her husband's memoir (see chapter 3), Ida Hunt Udall's Arizona narrative was markedly different. As she worked to make a living for herself and her children in the Little Colorado River settlements, she endured unique hardships as the second of her husband's wives, spending the first years of her marriage in hiding as authorities sought to indict David K. Udall for polygamy and receiving less financial and emotional support than Ella, his first wife, throughout their marriage. Her story of life in Arizona Territory at the turn of the twentieth century became part of Arizona's written intellectual landscape one hundred years later.

Udall's biographer was her granddaughter Maria S. Ellsworth, daughter of Ida Hunt and David K. Udall's oldest child, Pauline. Ellsworth was born and raised in the Snowflake, Arizona, area where her grandparents had settled. A graduate of Arizona State Teachers College at Flagstaff (now Northern Arizona University), she taught in the primary grades and married S. George Ellsworth, who had earned a PhD in history at the University of California at Berkeley in 1951. The Ellsworths made their home in Logan, Utah, where George taught history at Utah State University (called Utah State Agricultural College when he began his career) and Maria became a specialist in Mormon history. Between 1971 and 1985 she authored seven book reviews for the *Journal of Arizona History*.[66] The biography of her grandmother, *Mormon Odyssey*, was awarded best biography of the year 1993 by the Mormon History Association.[67]

Ida Hunt Udall's journals and letters were given to Ellsworth by her mother, who had inherited them from her mother. Ellsworth explained that Pauline "bequeathed them all to me with the exhortation that I publish her mother's journal because her mother's story had never been told. These sources tell the family story. They also depict pioneer life in eastern Arizona and the struggle for existence in a harsh land." Ellsworth described her grandmother as a woman whom many people liked and admired: "My father, Asahel Henry Smith, had idolized his mother-in-law, and he and my mother told and retold stories about her." Ellsworth learned about Udall's influence on the people in her community—a man who had stopped smoking at Udall's urging and a woman who as a newborn was coaxed to breathe under Udall's care. "Hearing such stories increased my interest in Ida," Ellsworth wrote. "However it was not until I had spent years researching her life and reading and rereading her journal and letters that I came to know her. She has come alive to me."[68]

Ellsworth places her grandmother in context, explaining how Udall's experiences were different from her husband's: "That Ida did not get a fair deal in her marriage was the opinion of her Hunt family, friends, and especially her daughter. Though all of the Udalls suffered because of financial stress, Ida gave up more than the rest. . . . For most of her married life, she lived under primitive conditions . . . isolated from any social life and faced with never-ending hard work. It is little wonder that her health broke when she was still in her forties. Surely the last seven years of her life spent as a semi-invalid were tragic."[69] Ellsworth's and Udall's words created a different Arizona than did the male-centered narratives of settlement.

Important to understanding the place that drew forth pioneer stories is understanding the perception that the settlers had of the land they inhabited. While many came to love the landscape, most admitted theirs was a hard place requiring hard work. Often those descriptions of hardship were penned by men, detailing their struggles. Even when written by women—Sharlot Hall for example—the courageous individuals braving the hard land were inevitably men. David K. Udall extended the sphere of struggles to include the women in his community, writing patronizingly that while "of course the sisters did not take part" in decision-making meetings, nonetheless "they sustained and encouraged" the men without complaint.[70] But the women's experience was not the men's, and in Ellsworth's *Mormon Odyssey* their experiences became written into Arizona's narrative landscape.

Ellsworth's inclusion of just such a male-centered description in the front matter of her grandmother's biography does more than allow the inclusion of women in men's descriptions of their hard life; it claims those descriptions and hard lives as their own. Quoting from an 1908 address by Mormon church leader J. Golden Kimball in Salt Lake City,

Ellsworth provided the setting in which the story of her grandmother would unfold. "I would like to take you on a trip down to Arizona, in the St. Johns country," Kimball declared. "I preached faith there once, but I want to tell you I haven't got enough faith to stay in such an undesirable country. You talk about good people; you talk about righteous people; I tell you there are people in this city who are not worthy to unlatch their shoestrings. That hard country, and their obedience to the priesthood of God, has made those men great characters."[71] The president proclaims only men, but by including the address in her story, Ellsworth, and by extension all of the early women settlers, claimed its words for women as well.

The Hunt family was called to Snowflake, Arizona Territory, in 1878, where John Hunt, Ida's father, was to serve as bishop. Ida Hunt was twenty years old. A description of one of her journeys to Snowflake after a visit to Utah, written in her Grandma Pratt's journal and quoted by Ellsworth, creates 1880s Arizona anew one hundred years later. "Long and tedious has been her journey!" Grandma Pratt wrote. "Instead of performing it as she had hoped in two weeks the company were detained by high water [the Colorado River was ten feet deep] and sandy roads, scarcity of feed for their animals, till eight weeks labor would scarcely suffice to take them through."[72]

Ellsworth's biography also provides a narrative of the Mormon experience of polygamy from the point of view of a second wife in a plural union. "I spent a lonely, homesick day making preparations for my change of location," Udall wrote in 1885 from her husband's childhood home in Nephi, Utah Territory.[73] Although the words Udall wrote in her journal while "on the underground" (in hiding from authorities who sought to question her and indict her husband) were written in Utah, they are part of the Arizona story that was unfolding generally in Mormon communities all over the territory and specifically at St. Johns. These stories wrote into being the pioneer women's experience.

Life as a plural wife, especially when laws against polygamy began to be enforced, was isolating, and Udall spent most of her adult life working to support her family as a de facto single parent. Ellsworth writes of Udall's later years, "Ida's life on her homestead, which began in the spring of 1902, was one of monotonous hard work, long hours, and isolation from all church activities and all but a handful of scattered families. The years of hard work, medical neglect, and weariness began taking their toll on her health."[74] Udall suffered the first of three strokes in March 1906 and a second in December of that year. She succumbed to the third in 1915.

Unlike the words of Sharlot Hall—a contemporary of Udall's who spent her writing time composing poetry extolling the courage of the men and the beauty of the place, as well as penning articles describing the territory's wealth of natural resources—Udall's journals and letters reveal no penchant toward the natural landscape. Hers are words focused on family and church and on providing for the people of both. Udall's words are more akin to Helen Sekaquaptewa's descriptions of life and changing times on the Hopi reservation. Sharlot Hall's Arizona became part of the narrative landscape of the place as she was writing it into being, her work published in her lifetime. Ida Hunt Udall's Arizona became part of the narrative landscape nearly eighty years after her death. But both women's Arizona experiences and the stories about and brought forth from the place they lived exemplify the different Arizonas that readers encountered. Novelist and journalist Barbara Kingsolver added more layers to the written landscape with her books about women in Tucson and in Arizona's mining communities.

Kentucky native Barbara Kingsolver lived in Tucson for two decades, working as a science writer for the University of Arizona, where she earned her master's degree. As a freelance journalist, she wrote *Holding the Line* (1989), a history of the 1983 Phelps Dodge copper mine strike from the perspective of the women involved; as a novelist, she composed what *Business Insider* designated Arizona's most famous book, *The Bean Trees* (1988).[75] Kingsolver's main characters, in both novel and nonfiction, are women. She populated her work with the people society has overlooked or ignored—the abused, the homeless, orphans, and refugees. She gave equal space and value to Hispanics: those who have resided in the state longer than Anglo Americans have inhabited it and recent immigrants, both documented and not. Kingsolver's Arizona books of the 1980s bring dimension to an already varied landscape, adding stories of strong women inhabiting a southern Arizona cultural landscape that relegates people like them, and those for whom they advocate, to the edges of society. From Kingsolver's narratives readers learn about an Arizona different than the place found in the booster literature and in Edward Abbey's essays and fiction.

Both *Holding the Line* and *The Bean Trees* tell the stories of women making their way, and making a difference, in their communities and state. In her choice of topics and characters, Kingsolver contributed to the ongoing discussions about immigration, labor, ethnic interactions and racism, and women's part in changing longstanding narratives about Arizona. *The Bean Trees*, which "was published to an enthusiastic reception" in 1988, received an American Library Association award. A year later *Holding the Line* was released "to less universal praise."[76]

That *The Bean Trees* became the most famous book from Arizona (according to the *Business Insider* editors) indicates a wide readership, and thus it would have created for many people Kingsolver's version of Arizona. As J. B. Priestley used the Arizona desert to represent possibilities, Kingsolver also used the desert as a place for growth and beginnings. It is a place where Taylor Greer and her newly acquired child, Turtle, settle after being uprooted from Kentucky and Oklahoma. It is a place where Lou Ann Ruiz reinvents herself as a working single mom and a place where Central American refugees begin new lives, conducted to safe havens by immigration activist Mattie. The roots that all three women set down in the Arizona desert are symbolized by the wisteria tree, the "bean tree" of the title, with its interconnected, symbiotic root system.

As had Priestley in his memoir and Zane Grey in his novels, Kingsolver wove descriptions of Arizona's natural landscape into her story. "The whole Tucson Valley lay in front of us, resting in its cradle of mountains," Taylor says. "The sloped desert plain that lay between us and the city was like a palm stretched out for a fortuneteller to read, with its mounds and hillocks, its life lines and heart lines of dry stream beds." Taylor also describes an approaching storm, and with her words Kingsolver revealed how perceptions are formed:

> It looked something like a huge blue-gray shower curtain being drawn along by the hand of God. You could just barely see through it, enough to make out the silhouette of the mountains on the other side. From time to time nervous white ribbons of lightning jumped between the mountaintops and the clouds. A cool breeze came up behind us, sending shivers along the spines of the mesquite trees. . . . What still amazed me about the desert was all the life it had in it. Hillbilly that I was, I had come to Arizona expecting an endless sea of sand dunes. I'd learned of deserts from old Westerns and Quickdraw McGraw cartoons. But this desert was nothing like that. There were bushes and trees and weeds here, exactly the same as anywhere else, except that the colors were different, and everything alive had thorns."[77]

This is the desert that Krutch and Woodin wrote about and that Zwinger's and Abbey's readers knew.

The setting of the novel is the Arizona desert; the themes are those Arizonans were grappling with in the 1980s—race and immigration. Readers initially learn about an Arizona that is perhaps accepting of diversity through Lou Ann's experiences of Tucson's cultural landscape. Her mother disapproves of Lou Ann's husband, Angel Ruiz, because he is Mexican. Her husband's ethnicity does not matter to Lou Ann. "In Tucson, she tried to explain to her mother, there were so many Mexicans that people didn't think of them as a foreign race. They were doctors, bank clerks, TV personalities, and even owned hotels" (suggesting the 1930s *Arizona Guide* characterizations of wealthy Hispanics). Lou Ann's mother, "who lived in eastern Kentucky and had never seen a Mexican, thought Lou Ann was making this up." Lou Ann's grandmother does not like the husband either, calling him "a heathern [*sic*] Mexican."[78] Early in the novel, then, it is the outsiders who are racist.

However, at the time Kingsolver was writing the novel Arizonans were debating the merits of an English-only amendment to the state's constitution that would make English the official language of state and local governments and require all business done by any government entities to be conducted in English (see the next section). While the movement is never mentioned in *The Bean Trees*, the intolerance and fears that produced the Official English amendment are part of the story. In one scene Taylor and Lou Ann host a dinner party attended by a Guatemalan refugee couple. "I work with a very kind family who speak only Chinese. Only the five-year-old daughter speaks English. The father has her explain to me what I must do," Estevan says. Another neighbor, Mrs. Parsons, "muttered that she thought this was a disgrace. 'Before you know it the whole world will be here jibbering and jabbering till we won't know it's America. . . . They ought to stay put in their own dirt and not come here taking up jobs.'" Taylor is appalled. "I wanted to scream at her: This man you are looking at is an English teacher. . . . But Estevan didn't seem perturbed, and I realized he must hear this kind of thing every day of his life."[79] This fictional exchange illuminated the real lines each side drew in the debate and illustrated an Arizona citizenry struggling with the issues. The multicultural landscape, always present but until recently often silent and invisible, was now evident in the written words about the state, all sides embroiled in heated debates about multilingualism.

In *The Bean Trees* Kingsolver made the debate personal, showing the effects of immigration policy on her characters and entwining immigration and place. That connection, and the effect the first has on the idea of the second, is revealed in a conversation between Taylor and Estevan as they drive across the Southwest toward Oklahoma. "After a while Estevan said, 'What I really hate is not belonging in a place. To be unwanted everywhere.' I thought of my Cherokee great-grandfather, his people who believed God lived in trees, and that empty Oklahoma plain they were driven to like livestock. But then, even the Cherokee Nation was *someplace*."[80] *The Bean Trees* has a happy ending—Taylor adopts Turtle, and Estevan and his wife find sanctuary in Oklahoma. In Arizona, though, the debate over immigration continued, resulting in policy changes detrimental to immigrants and non-English speakers and creating an Arizona deemed by some to be Anglo-centric and intolerant.

Kingsolver's nonfiction *Holding the Line* tells the story of labor and the mining industry in Arizona in the 1980s. On July 1, 1983, miners belonging to thirteen different unions working at the Phelps Dodge copper mines at Clifton-Morenci, Douglas, and Ajo went on strike. The communities are separated by over three hundred desert miles (Clifton and Morenci are northeast of Safford; Ajo is west of Tucson, about halfway to the California border; and Douglas is over one hundred miles south of Tucson on Arizona's border with Mexico), but they were connected by their dependency on Phelps Dodge and by the striking miners' initial steadfast commitment to their position against the company. Most of the statewide and national publicity, and Kingsolver's book, focused on the Morenci and Ajo mines. The dispute centered on a cost-of-living allowance that the unions stated was necessary and that other mining companies in the state had accepted. Phelps Dodge refused to include the provision and also wanted to lower the base pay for beginning miners. The strike would ultimately last two and a half years and result in the decertification of the unions.[81] This book may have been readers' first introduction to Arizona mining or the only account they read from the strikers' perspective. Depending on which version of the strike was read—newspaper accounts and Phelps Dodge press releases, or Kingsolver's book—a different Arizona was portrayed.

As a freelance journalist Kingsolver covered the strike from its beginning and became acquainted with the strikers and picketers, especially the women, on her many visits to the towns. Her coverage of these strikers' stories earned her an Arizona Press Club award for feature writing in 1986. *Holding the Line* is the result of her interviews and research; focused on the women in these small mining towns, it provides a perspective different from the one portrayed in newspaper accounts.[82] Kingsolver witnessed things she had never seen before or had never heard of: "People were being jailed for simply calling a neighbor 'scab,' helicopters and squads of men with hefty-looking automatic weapons were coming in to break the strike, and strike supporters were answering back with extraordinary resistance. A fair number of the faces and hands on the strike's front lines belong to women." She continued, "I have left out much about the men. Their struggle was parallel to that of the women, equally difficult and often equally heroic, and their stories are not less deserving of an audience."[83]

Holding the Line, like *The Bean Trees*, tells the story of a place being acted upon by women. And like *Mormon Odyssey* it describes women's experiences that might be unfamiliar to readers. While the Associated Press's Arthur H. Rotstein reported that the police fired tear gas into a crowd of strikers "after carloads of copper workers were pelted with rocks"—and, the police stated, "somebody threw a Molotov cocktail"—Kingsolver wrote the story from the strikers' point of view: "When the National Guard and riot troops from Arizona's Department of Public Safety (DPS) were summoned to occupy Clifton and Morenci, no one expected the strike to last much longer. The women organized rallies, pickets, and more rallies. They were tear-gassed and arrested. They swore and screamed and sometimes threw rocks, and *always* they showed up for the picket." A DPS officer's comment illustrated the importance of the women's role, stating, "If we could just get rid of these broads, we'd have it made."[84]

Just as she wove description of the Arizona desert into her social commentary in *The Bean Trees*, Kingsolver also illustrated the story of the copper strike with description, creating a landscape both awful and strangely beautiful: "In the open-pit mine in Morenci, Arizona, the steady motion of mechanized shovels raises a yellow haze of fine dust. Yielding 290,000 tons of metal in a good year, it is the most productive copper mine in North America. The smokestacks of the copper smelter rise like a pair of giant horns out of the mountain's granite pate. Below the horned promontory, the earth's entrails are laid open in a pattern of circular, descending steps, exposing the strangely delicate colors of a mountain's insides: lavender, pink, and blue-grey."[85]

In addition to telling the women's story, Kingsolver explored the racism exhibited by the mining companies, a condition that had existed since the early days of statehood; this is a very different portrayal than those found in the *Arizona Guide* and the state's fiftieth-anniversary publications. Kingsolver discovered that "payroll records of the Jerome-Verde Copper Company show that in 1916, a better-paid Mexican laborer typically received about nineteen dollars for a six-day week, before hospital and store deductions. Employees with English surnames, listed as 'miners' rather than 'laborers,' were paid thirty-three dollars for the same week's work."[86] Readers learned about segregation that had lasted into the 1960s, which included housing, schools, and places of business. The racism did not end as the state matured. Carmina Garcia, whose "roots in the area are deeper even than P. D.'s copper veins," said, "Sometimes people will say, 'Go back to Mexico,' you know. What they don't understand is that we were always here, even before it was Arizona."[87] As in *The Bean Trees*, the themes in *Holding the Line* are injustice and intolerance told through the women's stories. Unlike *the Bean Trees*, the copper strike story had a less than happy ending.

While Kingsolver's portrayal of the miners was sympathetic to their cause, newspaper coverage made the miners' struggle a harder sell. Readers of the *Washington Post*, for example, learned that Phelps Dodge lost $74 million the year before the strike, "the worst year in its history," and the paper quoted Arizona's governor Bruce Babbitt saying the strikers "threatened to roll over the security guards like so many tenpins" when the company began hiring new workers.[88] The coverage changed somewhat after the riot of June 30, 1984, a conflict marking the strike's one-year anniversary that was blamed on the strikers and picketers but was actually initiated by the DPS riot troops.

Kingsolver described the events leading up to the melee, which began as a peaceful rally in the park attended by families with picnic lunches. After most of the strike supporters went home, about forty people remained on the picket line waving signs and shouting insults at the replacement workers during the shift change. A strong police presence was evident, but the picketers remained peaceful and allowed traffic to flow. However, one picketer "slapped the fender of a [DPS] sedan with his open hand," and at that moment the DPS teams descended on the group: "Down the hill, around the bend in the highway marched a full formation of two hundred riot troops with helmets, gas masks, and shields." People began to crowd the highway, and the police fired tear gas into the crowd and nearby buildings.[89]

Rotstein's AP article stated, "Riot-equipped police, saying they were assaulted with a Molotov cocktail, fired tear gas canisters into a crowd." Tucson's *Arizona Daily Star* pressed the DPS director, Ralph Milstead, about the presence of the riot troops when the strikers had done nothing illegal. "The riot did not start at 5:45 p.m., June 30 [1984]. It started July 1, 1983, when the strike first began," Milstead said. He believed DPS needed to act before dark, certain the strikers would have caused trouble if the police had not dispersed the group.[90] The confrontation was ostensibly preemptive, as the DPS acted before the strikers did. Most newspaper descriptions of the strike presented one side of the story; Kingsolver gave the other side. Readers of one or the other would have opposing views of both the strike and the state's reaction to it.

On the themes found in her books, Kingsolver said, "When I write a novel, I'm not thinking, 'Now how can I get the political themes into this?' I just write the novel. It grows out of the world I live in. And the world I live in happens to be full of sexism and racism and screwed up immigration policies and people who use power against other people in unjust ways. If I lived in another world I would write an entirely different kind of novel."[91] This was the Arizona Kingsolver portrayed, a more diverse representation of Arizona than many of the narratives depicted in the first seventy-five years of its existence as a state.

The Constitution of the State of Arizona: Article 28, Official English

In 1988 Arizona voters narrowly approved a citizens' initiative making English Arizona's official language, and the words of Proposition 106 became article 28 of the state's constitution.[92] Arizona was not the first state to pass an Official English measure. Ten states had designated English as their official language by 1988. Nor had the effort to make English the only language of the land been confined to the states. An English-language amendment to the U.S. Constitution was submitted to Congress several times during the decade of the 1980s. But Arizona's law was the most restrictive to date. Just as the words written in 1910 about the constitutional convention created an image of Arizona for readers, the words written about Proposition 106—on both sides of the issue—and the words of the amendment itself became part of the narrative landscape of the state and defined it in its seventy-fifth year. As minorities gained access to the means of communicating their own words and stories, including access to print media, other groups took steps to restrict, and in some cases deny, that access.[93]

Proponents of the Official English law argued their position using phrases that became talking points in the English-only movement—that English is the nation's "common bond" and the primacy of English was being eroded by a plethora of foreign-language media outlets accessible over the airways and at newsstands; and that federal and state governments were acquiescing to non-English speakers by providing multilingual information and ballots. These only slightly veiled racist justifications for the law were bolstered by a paternalistic, good-for-the-people reason: non-English speakers are left out of American society—economically and culturally. Allowing for multilingualism, supporters of the amendment believed, rendered the need to learn English unnecessary and resulted in foreign-language speakers refusing to learn it.

Opponents of the measure insisted an Official English amendment was unneeded, arguing that English was not in danger of being usurped as the language of government, commerce, or even of most of society. While the amendment's backers claimed to want more foreign-language speakers to speak English, the measure did nothing to encourage English-language learning. Even more dangerous, opponents argued, was the law's provision encouraging citizens to police each other, to assure only English was spoken or printed at every level of government, creating an environment of conflict, the opposite of Official English supporters' stated goals. According to the election publicity pamphlet explaining the proposal, Official English "could outlaw essential multilingual public service information such as pamphlets informing non-English speaking parents how to enroll their children in school."[94]

Titled "English as the Official Language," the text of Proposition 106 depicted Arizona as a place unfriendly to all who spoke other languages, even if that was not the law-crafters' intent. It addressed the role that the state government should play as the protector and enforcer of English as the written and spoken means of communication in and by the state. "The English language is the official Language of the State of Arizona," the first section stated. This rule applied to the ballot; public schools; the legislative, executive, and judicial branches; "all political subdivisions, departments, agencies, organizations, and instrumentalities of this State"; and all government officials and employees doing the state's business, including local and municipal governments.[95]

As if the English language was in danger of becoming a dead language, section two required that the state government "and all political subdivisions of the State shall take all reasonable steps to preserve, protect, and enhance the role of the English language as the official language of the State of Arizona."[96] Section three prohibited the use of any other language by the state except to comply with federal law (such as providing English as second language teachers in schools). Other exceptions included teaching foreign languages as part of an educational curriculum and the use of foreign language to protect public health and safety and to safeguard the rights of criminal defendants and crime victims.[97] The final section of the amendment gave the right to sue noncompliant Arizonans to anyone "who resides in or does business in the State."[98]

The Official English movement was a national effort to assert and codify the primacy of the English language in America. In Arizona the English-only measure was advocated and advanced by Arizonans for Official English; however, the Washington, D.C., lobby group U.S. English backed the Arizona group. The stated mission of U.S. English was to "maintain the blessing of a common language, and to reverse the spread of foreign language usage in the nation's official life." One of its objectives was the adoption of a constitutional amendment establishing English as the official language of the United States.[99] A primary talking point of the movement, one that was utilized in the Arizona campaign, asserted, "A common language is necessary to preserve the basic internal unity required for political stability and national cohesion."[100] The words drawn up by a national lobbying group and utilized by the local Arizona groups became part of Arizona's narrative landscape just as the words of the statehood fight had.

An English-language amendment (ELA) was introduced at the national level in several sessions of Congress during the 1980s.[101] One of the ELA's chief sponsors, California Senator S. I. Hayakawa, co-founded the group U.S. English with anti-immigration activist John H. Tanton when Hayakawa left Congress in 1983.[102] Arizona Senator John McCain testified against the ELA amendments in a hearing before the House Judiciary Committee and brought an Arizona perspective to the national debate. He stated that the amendments "fragmented and divided ethnic communities in my State. . . . They believe, many minorities in this country, not just Hispanic, but Indian—Native Americans as well, that this amendment is a direct assault on their ability to preserve their culture and heritage."[103] These arguments were also advanced within the state to protest Proposition 106.

U.S. English brought Official English to Arizona after its overwhelming 1986 victory in California. Senator Peter Kay introduced an Official English amendment in the Arizona state senate in 1987. Addressing Kay's position, the editors of the *Phoenix Gazette* wrote, "On this issue, Kay is wrong. On this issue, Gov. Evan Mecham, who opposes English-only as an unnecessary slap at Mexican Americans, is right."[104] Citing the controversy his proposal had created, Kay withdrew the amendment from consideration, thus prompting ELA supporters to begin a drive to place the amendment on the ballot by citizens' initiative.[105] Famous Arizonan Barry Goldwater agreed to serve as the honorary chairman of Arizonans for Official English. "Senator Goldwater is Mr. Arizona," said Robert D. Park, chairman of Arizona's Official English group. Goldwater explained, "You live in this country, you speak English, you live in Mexico, you speak Spanish, and if you live in France, you speak French."[106]

Responding to the several states considering Official English measures that year, the *Gazette* editors assured readers that while learning English is important, "There are plenty of incentives to learn the language. English needs no constitutional appendage to survive."[107] In response to the Official English drive in Arizona, State Representative Armando Ruiz announced the creation of the Arizona English Coalition and its plans "to ensure people with limited English proficiency are not barred from full participation in the economic and political processes of the state and union." The group proposed an initiative that would bar people from filing lawsuits to block bilingual education programs and other non-English services, in direct conflict with the wording in the

Official English initiative, which not only permitted but encouraged such actions in section four.[108]

Countering the assertion by Arizonans for Official English that the heritage of English as America's "common bond" was threatened or under attack, editors at the *Arizona Republic* wrote: "C'mon now, America's heritage is as strong as ever, and has always been based on cultural diversity. And don't believe it when they tell you that 'English in a fundamental sense is US' as in us, not U.S. They are wrong."[109] Words on both sides of the debate created opposing images of the state, liberal and un-American or conservative and racist; taken altogether, the narratives depicted a tumultuous place.

The role of the English language in Arizona had also been debated during the constitutional convention in 1910. A proposition requiring all underground workers (miners) to speak English, a proposal favored by the labor coalition, was debated. Delegates feared that its specific language ("aliens, who cannot speak the English language") was in conflict with the Fourteenth Amendment of the U.S. Constitution. The committee of the whole added the word "intelligently" to the end of the statement.[110] This proposal did not become part of the final document, and until 1988 the State of Arizona had no position on the nature of the English language. Unlike Arizona, when New Mexico drafted its constitution, it provided protection for the Spanish language rather than protecting the English language.

When Arizona voters received their information pamphlets for the 1988 general election, they read statements from prominent Arizonans and groups for and against the Official English amendment. Creating an Arizona for Arizonans in the "for" and "against" narratives, the pamphlet implicitly asked residents in which place they would like to live. The Legislative Council (a legislative committee that provides nonpartisan research and analysis) offered arguments favoring Proposition 106 by reiterating standard U.S. English and Arizonans for Official English rhetoric: "The State of Arizona is at a crossroads. It can move towards the fears and tensions of language rivalries and ethnic distrust, or it can reverse this trend and strengthen our common bond, the English language."[111] The council's argument opposing the proposition determined the measure would not preserve English: "Instead it will undermine the efforts of new citizens of our state to contribute to and enter the mainstream of American society. . . . English is now and will remain the language of Arizona. Ninety-eight percent of Americans are fluent in English." This opinion also countered the pro–Official English, patriotic-sounding words about "American heritage," stating, "This Proposition will not help or prompt anyone to learn English. It will not improve human relations. It will not lead to a better state. . . . It is unnecessary, counterproductive and, in the most fundamental sense, un-American."[112]

Arizonans for Official English chairman Robert Park presented that group's proapproval arguments, writing, "Official sanctioned multilingualism causes tension and division within a state." Park also provided an economic argument for the proposition, claiming that it would promote "a more efficient and cost-effective government."[113] In a joint statement, Carl J. Kunasek, president of the Arizona Senate, and Representative Dave Carson argued that English was recognized as the language of "unity and prosperity." They wrote, "Due to a trend toward official multilingualism, our great unifying force—the use of the English language—is eroding, and our nation is becoming a people separated by, instead of unified by, language."[114] The president of U.S. English, Linda Chavez, used scare tactics to push for approval: "Unless we become serious about protecting our heritage as a society of various cultures bound by a common language, we may lose a precious resource that has helped us forge a single people from so many diverse elements."[115] The misconceptions and lack of understanding in the Official English position are reflected in this statement; it fails to acknowledge the diverse cultures and experiences of minorities in its assertion that only an English-language heritage is worth protecting and that American society is "a single people." As for maintaining a common language, codifying an English-learner program and appropriating funds for it would accomplish much more than an English-only measure would.

Phoenix mayor Terry Goddard's and Arizona governor Rose Mofford's statements were included in the voter pamphlet section against approval of Proposition 106. Armando Ruiz, chairman of Arizonans against Constitutional Tampering and founder of the Arizona English Coalition, wrote a succinct and all-encompassing statement asserting on several grounds that the proposition was a lie: "It is a lie because it pretends that it will cause more people to learn English. Yet it contains *absolutely nothing* to provide that education. The key to English proficiency is education for youngsters in non-English speaking households and for adults who have never mastered the language."[116] Proposition 106 passed by a one percent margin. The Arizona now codified in its constitution, by words added to the state's foundational document in 1988, characterized a place fearful of its own multicultural citizenry and restrictive in its response.

In Summary

The Arizona reflected in written narratives in its seventy-fifth year was a more complicated place than the one portrayed at previous twenty-five-year anniversaries. The addition of Native American authors' and poets' works to the body of written words about and enabled by Arizona revealed relationships and stories that had always existed but had been invisible and unavailable to the majority of the reading public. The Arizona characterized in words in 1987 better represented the state's population with contributions by women and minority authors. Environmentalists and naturalists contributed works that contradicted booster and state leadership narratives; this Arizona was not a natural landscape with resources provided solely for humanity's use and extraction but rather a place that required responsible action for preserving those resources.

The diversity reflected in the intellectual landscape of the 1980s, particularly in the use of language, caused a strong reaction, resulting in the public approval of an English-language amendment to Arizona's constitution that made English the official language of the state. The permanence of diverse words and stories did not cause an eventual acceptance on the part of people who felt threatened, or believed somehow America was threatened, by such diversity. Though declared unconstitutional in 1998, the Official English measure was approved by voters once again in 2006.

The support for English-only laws and strict immigration policies would be reflected in Arizona's narratives over its next twenty-five years. Business and state leaders would have to contend with words depicting the state as intolerant and racist, even as they sought to promote continued growth and investment. The booster element, reflecting positions and themes ingrained for decades, was again prominent as the state prepared to celebrate its one-hundredth anniversary. Many of the words emanating from Arizona at its one-hundredth year reflected the place it had been, while minority and environmentalist voices strove to continue conversations focused on what the state could and should be.

OVERLOOK

A Twenty-First-Century State

"If the governor was smart," Barry Goldwater declared in 1987, "he'd quit and let Rose be governor." Rose Mofford, Arizona's secretary of state, was next in the line of succession if Evan Mecham, ten months new to the office, resigned or was removed from office. The *New York Times* informed readers throughout the nation what Arizona's recently retired senior U.S. senator thought about the Democrat from the mining town of Globe. Mofford, Goldwater believed, "was one of the greatest women that ever got into politics."[1] Mecham was impeached, indicted, and removed from office in April 1988, and Rose Mofford became Arizona's first female governor. In the last quarter of Arizona's first century, the state would have four women governors, the most of any state. The only man to hold the office in that time—Fife Symington, who served from January 1991 to September 1997—resigned less than halfway through his second term when he was indicted and convicted of fraud, extortion, and perjury.[2]

Though many readers knew Arizona as a Wild West state where descriptions of pioneers most often depicted men, or as the "Miraculous Growth" state where the drivers of that growth were portrayed as businessmen such as Valley National Bank president Walter Bimson and political leaders such as Goldwater, women had been active in leadership and politics since the state's inception. Arizona women claimed the right to vote in state and local elections in 1912, eight years before they received that right nationally with the passage of the Nineteenth Amendment. Recall that Sharlot Hall served as territorial historian in the years preceding statehood. A decade before Sandra Day O'Connor became the first woman appointed to the U.S. Supreme Court, she served as an Arizona state senator in the early 1970s and was elected majority leader of that body, the first woman in any state to hold that office. Margaret T. Hance was elected mayor of Phoenix in 1976, running as an independent when the Charter Government Committee, convinced a woman could not be elected, refused to support her. Hance won four two-year terms and was the first female mayor of a major U.S. city.[3]

In 1998 women were elected to the five highest offices in the state.[4] Governors Jane Dee Hull and Janet Napolitano oversaw another wave of growth as Arizona's population surged by 24 percent in the first decade of the twenty-first century. While the Phoenix metro area accounted for nearly 60 percent of that growth (the number included all of Maricopa County), Pinal County, bordering Maricopa on the southeast, grew by 110 percent and became the second-fastest-growing county in the nation.[5] Growth was fueled by a continually expanding high-tech industry, dominated at the turn of the twenty-first century by semiconductor companies such as Intel and MicroAge and by the inflow of skilled workers to staff the new fabrication plants.[6] These workers required schools, stores, restaurants, banks, and recreational facilities, and the area's service industries grew to sustain these needs. The construction industry grew apace, providing buildings for businesses and affordable single-family housing. Founded on the belief that the growth would always trend up, fed by the demand for inexpensive houses, and furthered by speculation in commercial real estate, central Arizona's housing market soared. Maricopa County issued over 48,000 building permits for single-family houses in 2005, and 43,300 in 2006.[7]

Continued massive growth proved to be unsustainable. The housing market plummeted in 2008; Maricopa County issued 33,000 fewer permits (10,300) in 2009 than it had just three years before.[8] What became known as the Great Recession hit Arizona hard, not only bursting the housing bubble but also reducing employment and investment opportunities. (Arizona's unemployment rate reached a high of 11.1 percent in early 2010.[9]) The passage of state laws aimed at restricting undocumented immigration (see the epilogue) curtailed even legal migrants and job seekers.[10]

On June 10, 2012, Rose Mofford celebrated her ninetieth birthday. Phoenix mayor Greg Stanton designated the day Rose Mofford Day and State Historian Marshall Trimble composed a song for her. "None can hold a candle to our Rose of Arizona / Heart bigger than the Grand

Canyon, everybody knows," Trimble sang.[11] Mofford had assumed the governorship following Evan Mecham's removal from office in 1988. The governor of Arizona in 2012, Jan Brewer, had voted against Mecham's impeachment as a newly minted state senator from Glendale. In the intervening twenty-five years Arizona flourished and regressed, becoming an example of what can occur when such growth goes unchecked and unregulated. The state's unemployment rate still averaged over 8 percent in 2012.[12] As Arizona citizens prepared for the centennial celebration and looked ahead to a new century, changing economic and demographic landscapes would be reflected in new stories.

EPILOGUE

Points of Departure, 2012

IN 1912 TWO HUNDRED THOUSAND PEOPLE lived in Arizona, clustered in a few population centers—Prescott, Flagstaff, Phoenix, Tucson—and scattered across its rugged landscape. At the state's centennial year, its population had grown to more than six and a half million, over fifty people per square mile if they were spread out evenly across deserts and mountains and forests. Nearly a third of those millions of people identified themselves as Hispanic or Latino, and over a quarter of Arizona's population spoke a language other than English at home.[1]

Arizona's narratives reflect this diversity. Early forms of literature—pioneer memoirs, cowboy stories, and booster tracts—were still being read a hundred years later; pioneers' descendants also wrote fondly of their grandparents' good old days, business leaders and politicians enthusiastically boosted their state, and Anglo advocates campaigned for Official English. Descriptions of Arizona's varied natural landscape still appeared in nearly every publication: the ubiquitous soliloquy to saguaro cactus; the insistence that Arizona is not all desert, with the largest yellow pine stand in the world to prove it; the theme of temporal extremes (oldest natural landscape, youngest state); and descriptions of thunderstorms, because in a land of little water an outpouring of the life-giving substance is cause for remark. But the landscape of written words had been transformed with narratives that better represented the population, with women, Native Americans, and Hispanics increasingly contributing to the body of literature about and enabled by the place. The complexity of the state's cultural landscape realized in the literature of the 1970s and 1980s continued to be reflected in the stories about and brought forth from the place in the first decade of the twenty-first century. The lens had been refocused to expose the words that had been neglected or invisible.

An Arizona that had been defined and created in words written by politicians, boosters, environmentalists, and poets and in forms as varied as essays, court documents, novels, and magazine articles was still being fashioned in 2012 from these same types of words and from similar sources. Groups and individuals still used words to emphasize their own perceptions of Arizona, what it was or should be, the diversity of the cultural landscape reflected in the variety of perceptions and the many genres that were used to move those viewpoints forward. The narratives that seem the strongest and the voices that sound the loudest now, standing as we are in the midst of them, may recede or become silent with the passing of time, may not be the words that stand out or endure when historians in 2037 look back at the intellectual landscape of the one-hundredth-anniversary year. But the narratives of the Arizona of 2012 will be the foundation on which the next stories are formed.

Viewing the Arizona narratives of 2012 at only a few years' remove does not provide a broad enough temporal span to select historically enduring works. But a 2012 body of literature is present and can be compared with the narratives of the past. At this moment, wherein these words cannot yet be considered history, additional representations of Arizona occur within a new medium for communicating the narratives. The Internet is now often the primary source of information about Arizona. The website TrueSnow.org, for example, contains a library's worth of material regarding the fight over the Arizona Snowbowl ski area and skiing on northern Arizona's San Francisco Peaks. TrueSnow.org's stance against snowmaking on the Peaks contrasts with the Snowbowl's promotional website ("In a high desert state at low latitude the art of snowmaking becomes a saving grace"[2]). As the Internet adds countless layers of information about Arizona, it seems to instantly create worlds of Arizonas and reveal Arizonas worlds apart.

In the first decade of the twenty-first century, Jeannette Walls, Arizona native and granddaughter of early pioneers, told her own and her grandmother's stories of life in Arizona, adding new narratives to the many already written about inhabiting the place. Author Luis Alberto Urrea recounted a different way of inhabiting the desert as he told the true and tragic story of Mexican migrants who perished in the Sonoran Desert. Arizona was created in words by the state government in another Official English amendment and in its Senate Bill 1070, a restrictive anti-immigration law. The Arizona centennial book *Arizona: 100 Years Grand* was a limited edition only available for purchase online, thus designating its readers, the consumers of its version of Arizona, as Internet users with credit cards. Many of the forms that the 2012 narratives take and the themes the words address are similar to, and consistent with, past stories. Yet new narratives emerge, revealing an Arizona many people are unaware of, a state unlike the one portrayed in official and promotional literature.

Naturalists, Environmentalists, and TrueSnow.org

Words about Arizona have often reflected and revealed residents' perceptions of and ideas about its natural landscape. From early booster tracts promoting the state's vast mineral resources to current e-mail blasts announcing protests against mineral extraction, the natural landscape and words about it have shaped perspectives. In the mid-twentieth century, conservationists' Arizona narratives influenced conversations about land use. In *Voice of the Desert* naturalist Joseph Wood Krutch declared an ethics of caring for the natural world beyond conservation, and Ann Woodin's Arizona desert home enabled a similar philosophy. "The land is something to be cherished, something to be admired as well as used, something to be passed on to the future," she wrote. "If we destroy it, whether a forest or a desert or a river, we destroy much of what makes life worth living. More than that, we destroy the source of our inspiration."[3]

Two decades later Ann Zwinger described the adverse effects of cattle grazing on desert landscapes and decried the loss of bosques due to groundwater depletion and arroyo cutting. As Arizona's leaders exuberantly pushed development, environmentalist Edward Abbey wrote about that attachment to unrestrained growth, comparing it to a cancer cell, declaring, "Cancer has no purpose but growth; but it does have another result—the death of the host."[4]

In the 1980s Native American writers' increased access to the mechanisms of publishing provided the means for presenting their words absent the Anglo filter. The growth of the Internet as a communications tool in the late twentieth and early twenty-first century provided previously inaccessible words to the world and offered a means by which any voice could be heard and any story could be told, including those of the environmentalists. In 2012 the website TrueSnow.org provided access to all manner of information relating to the controversial snow-making venture on Arizona's San Francisco Peaks, in forms as varied as PDFs of court documents and articles written by an anonymous author identified as Zen Pathfinder. At the time of Arizona's fiftieth anniversary in 1962, a debate about humanity's place in and use of the natural world was enjoined in the discussion surrounding Glen Canyon Dam and the flooding of a singular, remote landscape. In 2012 a similar question of use and misuse again pitted conservationists and environmentalists against private developers and their government allies. In this fight Native Americans and businesspeople also took prominent, and opposing, sides.

Rather than involving a canyon that relatively few people had visited or ever would visit, this controversy centered on the mountain that anchors the landscape of northern Arizona. Visible for hundreds of miles, the San Francisco Peaks are sacred to the American Indian tribes who live on the Colorado Plateau. Water was still the tool employed to destroy the landscape, but rather than the flooding of a canyon, the point of contention was the spraying of snow made from treated wastewater, effluent, over the slopes of Snowbowl, the ski area that has occupied the southwestern side of the mountain for decades. The intent of the various owners of the ski area to develop a profitable ski resort on national forestland outside Flagstaff had been an issue since the 1960s when the first extensive expansion was proposed. But the use of effluent to produce snow was an especially egregious act of desecration to those who honor the mountain as sacred and respect the natural world. Over the years numerous lawsuits have been filed, refiled, decided (alternately in favor of both sides), appealed, and settled. What began as a focus on tribal religious rights and the preservation of a fragile, high-mountain ecosystem evolved into a question about the properties of the manmade snow itself and the effects of effluent snow on human health.

TrueSnow.org is a doorway into the literature about the issue, a place to find information presented in both audiovisual and textual content. The site contains video documentaries about the effects on fish of effluent released into rivers, press releases from groups protesting the construction of pipelines and chairlifts, maps of the current ski area and the proposed expansion, and before-and-after photographs detailing the clear-cutting of trees along the pipeline route.[5] A virtual library, TrueSnow.org provides access to government and court documents, articles and calls for action posted directly on the website, and newspaper articles reposted or linked from other websites. With one click a reader is exposed to and can consume thousands of words about the Peaks controversy. The most persistent message on the TrueSnow website, ever-present even when a visitor selects a document to read (one must scroll down past the message), declares, "No to Poison Snow—Not on the Peaks—Not on the Mesa! Water Is Life."[6]

While the goal has not changed—an end to artificial snowmaking and Snowbowl expansion in the short term, and complete eradication of the ski resort from the mountain eventually—the focus has changed. The San Francisco Peaks are still revered as sacred and fragile; however, the stories now being told by ski-area opponents seek to draw new supporters with an emphasis on public health and are centered on the ramifications of the production of snow from wastewater. Arizona as an environmental battlefield—where the war against wanton extraction of resources, unrestrained population growth, and thoughtless encroachment of wild places has been waged for decades—is well documented in the narratives available at TrueSnow.org. The new material adds to the hallowed representations of the San Francisco Peaks the image of the mountain as a frozen toilet bowl.

For centuries Arizona's natural and culture landscapes have inspired words told and written in verse. The earliest inhabitants sang songs in their languages, songs that were eventually written down, translated into English, and interpreted by Anglo ethnographers and editors. In

1938 ethnographer Ruth Underhill described the saguaro fruit harvest and the ensuing ceremony and translated the Tohono O'odham songs to bring the rain. In the 1980s Native American singers published songs in their own languages, paired with English translations for English readers, demonstrating that English was not always singular or primary. Yaqui tribe member Felipe Molina interpreted and translated a book of Yaqui deer songs, and Wendy Rose (a Hopi woman who had never lived on the Hopi Mesas but whose blood flowed from that place) wrote of her connection to the Hopi land: "California moves my pen / but Hotevilla dashes / through my blood / like a great and / crazy dragonfly."[7] Rose's poetry differed markedly from the state's namesake poem, written in 1906, wherein Sharlot Hall proclaimed men's dominance over the land in an effort to prove the readiness of the citizens to become a state: "The men who from trackless forests and prairies lone and far / Hewed out the land where ye sit at east and grudge us our fair-won star."[8]

In 2012, among the government documents, journalistic articles, and calls to action posted on and linked to at TrueSnow.org, a prose poem by artist Shonto Begay gave voice to the San Francisco Peaks in "The View I Have from Here: A Prayer for the Desecrators."

> I have a view from here, "y'aa." What a view. My three sisters, they shine in the distance. "Sis na Jinni'" (Mt. Blanco to the east), "So Dzil'" (Mt. Taylor to the south), "Di be' N'tsaa" (Hesperus peak to the north). My view has clouds today, like cataracts outside of my eyes. Like clouds bearing no rain. It is hard to hold onto ice, onto "Ke'sh je'" songs. . . .
>
> I have a view.
>
> All about my footing, veins of pathways from the center, like pesky mosquitoes upon your shoulders. They fill their bladders with my potentials, their essentials. Empty patches upon my blanket, a measure of your wants. There is a tear, a loosening of fabrics upon my back. The cold and bitter wind that once begged in vain for shelter from itself, it invades the sanctity of warmth. . . .

> I have a view.
>
> I see, too, the folly of it all, for in the end, when mosquitoes lay waste their colonies; when monuments to Manifest Destiny are all reclaimed; when the last well-laid plans of empires fail . . . the last desperate clawing for a piece of my body. . . .
>
> I still see your tenuous blueprint in all its fallacies. I will still hear prayers of my children, upon the wind, upwards into the heavens, where twinkles really hold only darkness. My glittering crown, a beacon still, to distant and pregnant storm clouds. To coat my tears, scarrings upon my back; to lie down with me; to hold my Abalone Shell body; to hear my prayer, my enemy slayer; to hear my prayer, my gift of water.
>
> Yes. I have quite a view. . . .
>
> Impatience of the natural and seasonal cycles. Desperate dance at loss of songs and prayers frays my edge. My children's prayers, too, are drowned out in their disturbances. Your sense of justice prevails for now.
>
> Yes, I have this vision. Now clouded with tears, I pray for yours.[9]

The mountain, one of the four sacred mountains delineating Dinétah, the Navajo homeland, watched the clear-cutting on its slopes ("empty patches upon my blanket"), the making of wastewater snow ("impatience of the natural and seasonal cycles"), and the blatant disregard for Native American religious practices ("children's prayer drowned out"). The image of "pesky mosquitoes" filling their "bladders" emphasizes the mountain's frustration, a feeling anyone who has been plagued by the swarming insects can recognize. Yet rather than condemning outright, the author prays for increased vision for the desecrators, an opening of eyes to the wider picture, to a broader perspective. Each of these songs and poems about Arizona—the Tonoho O'odham rain songs, the Yaqui deer songs, Wendy Rose's poems, and Begay's verse prayer, all containing words about the same state and influenced by the same natural landscapes—write a different place into being.

Inhabiting Arizona: Jeannette Walls and Luis Alberto Urrea

Throughout Arizona's one-hundred-year history many writers have told stories about inhabiting the place. Written by women and men, by Anglo, Native American, and other minority groups, the words describe the natural landscapes and remark on the cultural landscapes. During the Great Depression, trader Hilda Faunce described the desert of the Navajo reservation she came to love. In that same decade English novelist and playwright J. B. Priestley observed the Arizonans around him, narrowly tailoring his perspective to describe only the Anglo communities he visited and only the people with whom he interacted.

In the mid-twentieth century, as Arizona celebrated its fiftieth anniversary, Joseph Wood Krutch and Ann Woodin described their inhabitation of the desert north of Tucson. At the same time, David K. Udall's memoir created the nineteenth-century Mormon settler experience. Hopi tribe member Helen Sekaquaptewa compared the way she and her family lived with that of her Hopi neighbors, belying the perception that because she and her husband were educated in Anglo boarding schools and sent their children to off-reservation schools, they were no longer traditional Hopi. And the 1980s author and poet N. Scott Momaday recounted living on the Navajo reservation and described a childhood memory of northern Arizona this way: "The little truck bounces over the dirt roads of the Navajo reservation, raises a great rooster tail of red dust. It is summer and there is a sharp glare on the sand, on the cottonwood leaves."[10]

At the turn of the twenty-first century, Jeannette Walls and Luis Alberto Urrea wrote about Arizona from their unique perspectives, from lives lived very differently than those explored in narrative thus far. Born in Phoenix in 1960, Walls spent her early childhood roaming the desert as her parents moved from place to place, often living out of their car or in abandoned buildings at mining camps and ghost towns as

Walls's father took odd jobs and mined for gold to finance his drinking habit and the glass castle he promised his daughter they would build. "We moved around like nomads," Walls wrote. "We lived in dusty little mining towns in Nevada, Arizona, and California. They were usually nothing but a tiny cluster of sad, sunken shacks, a gas station, a dry-goods store, and a bar or two. . . . The more desolated and isolated a place was, the better Mom and Dad liked it."[11] Luis Alberto Urrea—born in 1955 in Tijuana, Mexico, and a self-described son of the border, whose father is Mexican and mother is American—is "inspired by this cross-cultural upbringing and unique perspective of life on both sides of the border."[12] Both authors' stories reflect the diversity of Arizona's cultural landscape.

Walls's first memoir, *The Glass Castle*, was a *New York Times* best-seller; the editors of the *New York Times Book Review* named her second book, *Half Broke Horses*, a biography of her grandmother written as a memoir in the first person, one of the ten best books of 2009.[13] Though her childhood tales may have been different than others' stories of inhabiting the desert, Walls too describes the landscape graphically: "Mom had grown up in the desert. She loved the dry, crackling heat, the way the sky at sunset looked like a sheet of fire, and the overwhelming emptiness and severity of all that open land that had once been a huge ocean bed. Most people had trouble surviving in the desert, but Mom thrived there. . . . I loved the desert too."[14]

Readers of Walls's second book, the memoir-styled story of Lily Casey Smith, had met Grandma Smith, "a West Texas flapper who loved dancing and cussing and horses," in *The Glass Castle* when the Walls family stayed at her home in Phoenix.[15] Raised on a West Texas ranch, Grandma Smith lived alone in Chicago in the early 1920s, taught school in rural northern Arizona where she ran a ranch with her husband, and earned a teaching degree at Arizona State Teachers College in Flagstaff. Subtitled "A True-Life Novel," the book was written in the first person, in Grandma Smith's voice, using dialogue and details based on family stories Walls had heard (but not from Smith, who had died when Walls was a child). Unlike Maria Ellsworth's orthodox biography of her grandmother Ida Hunt Udall (wherein she added little that was not documented in diary, letters, or interviews and let her grandmother speak for herself from the pages of her journals and correspondence), Walls determined that the most compelling way to tell Grandma Smith's story was as a work of fiction (although the people were real, and the stories were ones she had heard all of her life). Momaday's memoir *The Names* similarly recounted conversations and events that had occurred before he was born; he called his account "an act of imagination."[16]

Many stories set in northern Arizona encompass the land north of Grand Canyon, the Arizona Strip. Lily Casey Smith was often assigned to teach at schools in this area; its remoteness is clear as Walls describes the drive from the ranch near Ash Fork, Arizona, to the Strip: first west through Arizona, then north through Nevada and Utah, then south to reach the Strip. Walls described the natural landscape of the region, as had Zane Grey and Edward Abbey. "The Arizona Strip was desolate but beautiful country," Grandma Smith explains. "There were grassland plateaus where distant mountain sparkled with mica, and sandstone hills and gullies that had been carved into wondrous shapes—hourglasses and spinning tops and teardrops—by wind and water. The sight of all that time-worn stone, shaped grain by grain over thousands and thousands of years, made it seem like the place had been created by a very patient God."[17]

Similar to Barbara Kingsolver, Walls wrote about women's experiences from the perspective of strong women affecting change in their communities and within their families. The women in Kingsolver's *The Bean Trees* raised children, worked full time as single mothers, rescued orphans, gave sanctuary to Guatemalan refugees, and fought against the racism and discrimination found in their southern Arizona community. In *Holding the Line*, Kingsolver described how the women organized rallies and pickets and were teargassed and arrested. Despite irregularly attending school during a childhood of wandering in the Arizona desert, Walls graduated from Barnard College and became a gossip columnist and reporter in New York City before retiring to write novels full time. Lily Casey Smith left her family's West Texas ranch as a young woman not yet graduated from high school and became a schoolteacher and rancher in northern Arizona. Walls translated her childhood experiences and the stories she had heard about Grandma Smith's life into contrasting Arizona narratives, with the state's natural and cultural landscapes serving as backdrops. Her nomadic, homeless existence in the desert stood at odds with Grandma Smith's hardworking, community-building life, yet both ended with the women's eventual personal success.

In the first decade of the twenty-first century, Arizona became known as a place inhospitable toward Hispanics, especially those suspected of crossing the border by other than legal means. Luis Alberto Urrea's nonfiction account of the May 2001 tragedy in which twenty-six Mexican immigrants were lost in the southern Arizona desert put a different perspective on inhabiting the desert. *The Devil's Highway* was a finalist for the 2005 Pulitzer Prize for nonfiction and a Kiriyama Prize winner.

"In the desert," Urrea wrote, "we are all illegal aliens."[18] This statement gives pause and requires reflection. The Tohono O'odham people (who centuries ago had learned to live with minimum rain and maximum heat) and the ancient Hohokam people (who dug canals to irrigate crops and built dwellings with feet-thick walls) perhaps belong to the desert. But most modern humans, who inhabit the desert in air-conditioned buildings and cars and draw more and more water out of aquifers and manmade catchments, are alien to the environment. As Urrea's story unfolds, the fate of the Mexicans abandoned by the men (called coyotes) whom they had paid to lead them safely across the border leaves readers ensconced in temperature-controlled living rooms less comfortable. This was an Arizona many people did not know.

Urrea described the desert as a nature writer might. "Dawn offered an astonishment of birds. In the scrub and mesquite hollows, there were more songbirds than could be heard in the Rocky Mountains," Urrea explained. Providing, as Momaday and Zwinger had, a setting that engages all of the readers senses, he described the men's early morning journey, before they discovered they were lost. "Crows, sparrows, mockingbirds. The cactus wren would have been making his small noises as he went about his business. . . . The almost cool air hugging the hardpan, not yet ignited by the white flames of the sun, felt blue. It moved slowly with the last stalling breezes of night."[19] These benign, pleasant images make even crueler what happened to the walkers as the days passed and the sun scorched and consumed the land and the men.

The coyotes had told the men nothing about the trip, and the walkers did not know what to expect. "They thought they were going to jump a big fence and hide in trees as helicopters bore down," Urrea wrote. Instead, they plowed through ankle-deep sand, ran down a dry wash and up the short three-foot bank on the other side, and "stepped over a dropped and rusted barbed wire fence. 'Los estados unidos, muchachos,'" the coyotes told them.[20] Urrea described what they encountered: "Cutting through this region, and lending its name to the terrible landscape, was the Devil's Highway, more death, another desert. They were in a vast trickery of sand."[21] The Devil's Highway, that legendary, barren track, took them north into Arizona, where "their feet crunched on the grit of the desert, and the plants began to tear at their arms and legs."[22] They were abandoned—and later found, some still alive—in the desert mountains of the Cabeza Prieta National Wildlife Refuge and the south end of the Barry Goldwater bombing range.

Urrea provided the backstory to this disastrous incident, his characterization contrasting with Edward Abbey's perspective. The desperation that motivated these men to get across the border is also part of the immigration story more generally. Economic and social conditions in Mexico at the turn of the twenty-first century offered little hope and facilitated a growing crisis. "Prices kept rising, and all families, mestizo and Indian, Mexican and illegal, Protestant, Catholic, or heathen, were able to afford less and less," Urrea explained. "Families continued to grow. The gringos and the missionaries and even the government representatives from Mexico City told them to stop procreating. It was simple: too many mouths caused hunger. But the Pope ordered them to continue being fertile—even condoms were wicked. And in the economy of hunger, which the fat men of the government did not understand, more mouths meant more chances to survive. . . . If one out of five died, that still left four to grow up and begin to work."[23]

The lure of money to feed families, clothe children, and repair houses was enough to draw waves of people into the desert, risking their own lives for the hope of providing better lives for those they left behind in Mexico. Men earned just over $2 a day in Mexico; employed in the agricultural fields or in the construction industry in California or Arizona, Mexican workers could earn $5 an hour, or $200 a week.[24] Urrea's book—in its depiction of Arizona's laws and governments, of Mexico, and of the people who do little to help the immigrants (before and after they cross the border)—is an indictment of humanity.

The Devil's Highway is a true story that reads like fiction, but one wholly unlike Zane Grey's stories, which are all about good men who overcome the wilderness and triumph over bad men in the end. In this narrative the walkers on the Devil's Highway overcame neither. Urrea's work is similar to Oliver La Farge's fiction in its unromanticized portrayal of tragedy, and like Kingsolver, Urrea provided the other side of the story, the story belonging to the powerless. Urrea's words about border crossings and the people who attempt them create a place many readers know little about, and what little they do know often reflects a viewpoint contrary to Urrea's.

Like Momaday, Urrea wrote about the importance of words, words that bring identity, place, and events into being. Words create home, he explained, "Home isn't just a place, I have learned. It is also a language. My words not only shape and define my home. Words—not only for writers—*are* home."[25] Urrea spoke directly to the English-only advocates, describing a sign he saw at a televised protest: "It said: America for Americans. A nearby man held up a sign exhorting the universe to speak English or go home. *The official language of the United States.*"[26] He followed with a list, several pages long, of "English" words of Spanish origin. The list included obvious words like "coyote" and "adobe," but also words like "alfalfa" and "beef jerky." "I don't know what we're going to do. Forget about purifying the American landscape, sending all those ethnic types packing back to their homeland," Ureah wrote. "The humanoids are pretty bad, but how will we get rid of all those pesky foreign *words* debilitating the United States?"[27]

Official Words: The Official English Amendment (2006) and Senate Bill 1070

Regardless of the non-English words populating the English language, and despite the state's first English-only measure being struck down by the Arizona Supreme Court in 1998, Official English proponents forged ahead with another amendment in 2006, placing Proposition 103 on the ballot that year. The Arizona Supreme Court had ruled in a unanimous decision that the 1988 measure violated both the First Amendment and the Equal Protection Clause of the Fourteenth Amendment to the U.S. Constitution, stating that it "adversely affects non-English speaking persons with regard to their obtaining access to their government and limits the political speech of elected public employees." In addition, the 1988 measure denied non-English speakers "the right to participate equally in the political process . . . a right which is one of the fundamental principle[s] of a representative government in this country."[28] Those words in the Arizona Supreme Court decision became part of the narrative landscape of Arizona, but the proponents of English-only sought to erase them.

The 2006 version of the Official English amendment contained many of the same provisions as the 1988 version, stating that "the Official Language of the State of Arizona is English," and that the role of government is to "preserve, protect, and enhance the role of English." The text of the amendment mirrored the rationale of the old measure—that English was "the common thread binding individuals of differing backgrounds"—and added the charge that governments promoted division in acquiescing to multilingualism. "In recent years," the measure stated, "the role of the English language as a common language has been threatened by governmental actions that either ignore or harm the role of English or that promote the use of languages other than English in official governmental actions, and these government actions promote division, confusion, error, and inappropriate use of resources."[29] Once again amendment writers based their words on the mistaken ideas that the English language was threatened and that using other languages created disunity.

The Legislative Council analysis, provided to voters in the voters guide, determined that in addition to its similarities with the original law, the new measure "would prohibit discrimination against a person because the person uses English in any public or private communication," an offense (persecution for speaking English) with no historical basis in reality. State Representative Russell Pearce argued for the measure, writing, "Had our government catered to each new group of immigrants by using their language instead of English, there would never have been any incentive to truly become American."[30] The "groups" in Arizona to which he referred had been residents of Arizona longer than English speakers. In response to the overturning of the first English-only amendment, Akimel O'odham tribe member Chris Milda reminded citizens, "Legislators and popular media persist at overlooking . . . that English is not even the first, original language of the Southwest in the first place. O'odham, Hopi, Navajo, and Apache languages—just to name a few—are the original languages of this region."[31]

Writing against the law, State Representative Steve Gallardo made use of the same argument that opponents of the 1988 measure had voiced—that learning English is beneficial, but nothing in the new law advanced that goal. In fact, the opposite was true, and Gallardo highlighted the hypocrisy of the measure's advocates, pointing out, "At this same election, the legislature hypocritically also asks you to vote on another measure (Proposition 300), which restricts the ability of adults to take classes to learn English." Employing the same language that opponents of the measure had used nearly twenty years earlier, Michael J. Valder and Eric Ehst of Arizona Advocacy Network wrote, "The legislature [stated] that the government should encourage greater opportunities for individuals to learn the English language. . . . Unless and until we adequately fund classes for English language learners, this recommendation is hollow at best."[32]

The results of the 2006 election represented a resounding defeat for advocates of a multilingual society. All of the propositions aimed at restricting the rights of undocumented and non-English-speaking residents passed, each with over 70 percent of the vote. Proposition 100, which denied bail for people in the United States illegally who were charged with a serious felony offense (which the legislature defined to include actually being in the country illegally), passed with 78 percent; Proposition 102, stating that "illegal aliens" could not receive punitive damages in civil lawsuits, passed with 74 percent; Proposition 300, the above-referenced measure that denied public funding to undocumented immigrants, passed with 71 percent; and Proposition 103, the Official English amendment, passed with 74 percent of the vote, twenty-five points higher than in 1988.[33] All of these laws officially defined Arizona as against any language besides English, anti-immigration, and ostensibly anti-Hispanic.

Against this backdrop of restrictive measures, in 2006 the Arizona legislature passed Representative Pearce's bill to make being in the country without documentation a state crime and to permit law enforcement officers to question individuals' immigration status. Governor Janet Napolitano vetoed that bill.[34] Elected to the state senate in 2008, Pearce reintroduced the bill in January 2010. Known widely as Senate Bill (SB) 1070, this measure passed both houses of the state legislature and was signed into law by Governor Jan Brewer in April 2010. The words of the bill enhanced the already prevalent perception of Arizona as a place hostile to minority groups, particularly Hispanics; the words demonstrated that a hierarchy of narratives about Arizona still existed—despite stories about border crossers dying in the desert and families being separated because of members' legal status.

The intent of the law was made clear at the outset. The legislature determined the state's best interests would be served if local (state and county) law enforcement worked with federal immigration officials to enforce the law, and declared, "The provisions of this act are intended to work together to discourage and deter the unlawful entry and presence of aliens and economic activity by persons unlawfully present in the United States."[35] SB 1070 allowed law enforcement officers to arrest anyone suspected of "any public offense that makes the person removable from the United States" and made it illegal "to transport or move an alien in this state . . . if the person knows or recklessly disregards the fact that the alien has come to, has entered, or remains in the United States in violation of law."[36] This last caused some consternation among suburban carpool parents, who wondered whether they could be arrested for driving neighborhood children to school.

In May 2010, ten individuals and fourteen organizations (including labor, religious, and civil rights groups) filed a lawsuit challenging SB 1070. U.S. District Court Judge Susan Bolton issued an injunction preventing some of the law's provisions from going into effect; her injunction was upheld by the Ninth Circuit Court of Appeals in April 2011. On June 25, 2012, the U.S. Supreme Court struck down key portions of the law, including the provision that made it a state crime for immigrants to not have federal documentation; another that made it a state crime for undocumented immigrants to seek work; and a third that allowed warrantless arrests.[37] The court upheld the provision allowing law enforcement officers to check "immigration status in certain circumstances," the popularly termed "Papers-Please" section titled "Enforcement of Immigration Laws."[38]

Since 2012 the strident nature of Arizona's immigration laws has been softened in the courts. Judge Bolton ordered that two groups that helped Pearce craft SB 1070, the Federation for American Immigration Reform (FAIR, see chapter 4, note 102) and the Immigration Reform Law Institute (FAIR's affiliated legal organization), must provide to the law's challengers the e-mails, letters, and memos sent to the lawmakers during the bill-drafting process. The ruling covered communications beyond those about SB 1070 and included e-mails and other documents regarding many of the previous years' measures against undocumented immigrants. Judge Bolton called these communications "'part of the historical background' of the enactment of SB 1070 and therefore relevant to determining whether that law violates constitutional rights of equal protection."[39] It will be for the historian of 2037 to determine if the words in Bolton's decision present a change in the overall tone in this matter and to decide if the hierarchy of narratives about and originating from this state has been reordered.

Boosting Arizona: *Arizona: 100 Years Grand* and Other Centennial Publications

At the same time SB 1070 was being debated and passed, the Arizona Centennial Commission was working on a plan to celebrate the state's one-hundredth anniversary of statehood. In a letter to "Fellow Arizonans" from the commission, the Arizona Centennial 2012 Foundation, and the Arizona Historical Advisory Commission, the groups declared that the centennial is a time for "the new Five Cs": commemoration, celebration, collaboration, community, and cooperation.[40] In the midst of a decade of legislative English-only and anti-immigration priorities, the top item on the centennial groups' "values" list was "inclusiveness." The letter stated, "The Centennial will embrace all citizens for the vital contributions they have made to our state over the last 100 years and the critical role they must continue to play for a successful future."[41] The organizers of the centennial celebration seemed totally divorced from what was occurring on a policy level. Each portion of government operated in separate spheres as if unaware of what the other was doing—the state legislature enacted discriminatory and divisive measures while state commissions charged with planning the centennial celebration proclaimed inclusiveness and community.

The centennial plan's "Why Celebrate" page mirrors words from past anniversary publications, especially the *Arizona Days and Ways* magazine's fiftieth-anniversary book. Recall the words of Governor Paul Fannin in that 1962 publication: "Arizonans have been men and women of rugged adventurous spirit, befitting their 'frontier spirit'"[42] In the 2012 centennial plan, the centennial commission declared, "Arizona was founded on rugged individualism matched with hard work and vision. It was this indomitable spirit that shaped and molded our state into the place we now call home."[43] Once again, the words of an anniversary publication reflected only one version of the forming of the place.

Arizona: 100 Years Grand was the official book of the Arizona centennial (according to its subtitle). Written by Lisa Schnebly Heidinger, the great-granddaughter of T. C. Schnebly (who named the town of Sedona after his wife), the coffee table book is an encyclopedia-like volume. Each of its one hundred entries (one chronicling each year of statehood) occupies a two-page spread complete with photographs. Entries include biographies of famous Arizonans; descriptions of well-known and lesser-known events; and stories about Arizona's natural landscapes, towns, and national monuments. Many of the entries contain quotes, none of which are cited, and the book contains no bibliography or reference section.

Unlike the 1962 *Arizona Days and Ways* anniversary edition, this book contains no advertising. Comments by the author indicate all time and services were volunteered; however, the book could be purchased through a dedicated website for $39.99, and "a portion of the price" went to underwriting the centennial celebration.[44] Like the 1962 anniversary publication, much of *100 Years Grand* promotes Arizona. For example, the entry for 1952 describes the Arizona-Sonora Desert Museum: "[It's] the desert, only better. It's what the desert would be like if the whole world were safe, comfortable, and interesting with little effort on our part. Which is kind of the point: to introduce people to the wonders, beauties, and mysteries of the arid landscape that may look desolate, but brims with life and growth."[45] This was not how Ann Woodin would have chosen to experience the Sonoran Desert, but it might reflect Joseph Wood Krutch's eventual conclusion that although living in the desert was preferable and would lead to an appreciation of the natural world, settlement would destroy the landscape, so visiting was better than no experience at all.

Descriptions in *100 Years Grand* of Arizona's natural landscapes evoke words that others have written. The Grand Canyon entry, for example, contains elements that bring to mind John Wesley Powell's geologic descriptions of Grand Canyon and Eliot Porter's descriptions of Glen Canyon: "One of the true wonders of the world, the Grand Canyon is alone in its geographic splendor. Some of Nature's finest work is on display here, created by her artists: water, wind, and time. . . . Going down the river, the canyon's geology falls open like an easily read book. It shows a thousand faces, from wide expanses with sandstone cliffs near Marble Canyon, to black glistening walls that loom high and close along the Inner Gorge."[46]

Heidinger missed opportunities to reveal the layers of Arizona's cultural landscape in the same way she did with the natural landscape of Grand Canyon. An entry for Saguaro National Monument provides nothing about O'odham songs or ceremonies celebrating harvesting saguaro fruit. Instead, a two-sentence paragraph makes any such use a thing of the past: "Saguaro *offered* much to indigenous people. For centuries they *harvested* the seeds to eat and feed animals and the fruit to make preserves or wine [emphasis added]."[47] The Tohono O'odham people still mark the seasons with song, and saguaro fruit harvesting continues.

The *Arizona Highways* "100-Page Centennial Issue" represented the state at one hundred for national and international readers. The magazine described an ideal Arizona (according to its editors and the Arizona Department of Transportation) as opposed to the Arizona found in Urrea's work or created by SB 1070 and the English-only amendments. Similar in content and layout to the past anniversary editions, the issue held nothing new, offered no twenty-first-century take on the state's one-hundred-year history. Instead, the issue contained reminiscences by Sandra Day O'Connor and Hugh Downs, a timeline and 1912 map, "100 Years in Pictures," and an article by Arizona native Marshall Trimble, folksinger, humorist, and official state historian.

"Arizona: 100 Years and Counting" is pure Trimble, reflecting his love of Arizona and his trademark wit. In one paragraph he employed many of the familiar boosters' phrases and clichés, including the standard humor about the state's heat: "The state is blessed with a moderate climate, open spaces, a lower cost of living, natural beauty, an abundance of natural resources, respected institutions of higher learning, and lower risk of natural disasters. Topographically, Arizona ranges from alpine mountains to lush deserts with every life zone in between. And despite the heat, even the desert can boast of having four seasons: 1) almost summer, 2) summer, 3) still summer, 4) Christmas Day. Yes, it does get a little warm in the Sonoran Desert, but remember: It's a dry heat."[48] This article could have been written and published in any of the last one hundred years. It is vintage Arizona boosterism.

Conclusion: Whither Arizona?

All of the words about Arizona, all of the narratives in its one-hundred-year history as a state, came from the words that preceded them, from the stories told before. They have created Arizona at each moment in time, and they continue to re-create Arizona as they are read and reread. Arizona's narratives and its natural and cultural landscapes entwine, each affecting and changing the other; the relationship is not static. The words discussed in this study from each twenty-five-year anniversary are connected to words previously written about Arizona, and they too become the next layer, the foundational words that the next stories will come from. The 2012 narratives may be the final words at the time of this writing, but they are only linking words in a long chain of narratives that continues on—words creating stories creating Arizona daily.

Employing the written intellectual landscape as the lens through which to study change over time reveals the same processes as those revealed when viewing change through political, economic, or more broadly focused cultural lenses. All of these aspects entwine to create an understanding of the past. This study is necessarily a synthesis, a survey. Studying change over time in Arizona through the lens of words requires examining a broad range of material produced over a long period of time. Exploring only tourist literature or newspaper articles, senate bills or novels, or studying words about Arizona only from 1937 or 1987 would not have provided the narrative arc necessary to see change occurring (or to see that no change occurred, in some cases). Exploring Arizona narratives involves examining where these words came from and how they provide a basis for understanding Arizona today.

Paradoxically, a writer cannot control what becomes of his or her story, the perceptions, places, and events the story creates and influences once it is written down. Narratives can be reproduced—copied, rewritten, retold—without affecting the original. But interpretation occurs the moment the words leave the storyteller's mouth, the instant a reader consumes the words on a page. Regardless of who or where the narrator is, listeners or readers bring their own ground with them. None of them (storyteller, writer, listener, or reader) stand in the same place. Arizona's stories demonstrate that many writers have discovered this truth. While strides have been made with respect to the diversity of stories, some modern narratives have changed little from those in the past. As Native American singers and poets continue translating their verses into English, and border residents continue publishing unvarnished narratives about the effects of immigration policy, and women continue writing their stories of strength and overcoming, Arizona's written landscape will continue to change and reflect that diversity.

Of course, all groups attempting to affect public policy employ words to move their agendas forward. Often they use misleading and hyperbolic words. Asserting in pamphlets that the English language is under attack to push for an Official English amendment, declaiming in press releases that undocumented border crossers are "illegal" people to justify restricting their civil rights, publishing articles decrying as governmental intrusion the setting aside of pieces of land to preserve the natural landscape, all of these policy-making words have created Arizona. Will these words change the place, and will the place change the words? Will the innumerable narratives from diverse voices change policy? Or, as the manifold components of the cultural landscape are indelibly written into narratives, will people who feel threatened by that diversity use their own words to silence those voices? With whom will the power of words rest in Arizona in 2037?

So, whither Arizona? What to make of a place that produces a rich body of literature written by a diverse citizenry but also restricts access to government to those who speak the English language? How does one describe Arizona: a rugged landscape that raises up strong men who overcome it, or a desolate wasteland that kills men who try to cross it? Is Arizona defined as a place where natural resources are readily available for extraction, or a place where humanity is quickly destroying the land that sustains us while seeking to restrict access to what is left untrammeled?

There cannot be one definition of a place-creating story. The Arizona of 2012, written into being over the previous one hundred years, may be the rugged desert hills covered with wildflowers described in the pages of the February issue of *Arizona Highways*. It can also be the undocumented border-crossers' desert death trap, the city planners' empty desert development opportunity, and the environmentalists' degraded and dying desert landscape, all words set down in other narratives and available to the same *Arizona Highways* readers. Anniversary publications that portray only one version of the state's creation story, with each installment a reproduction of the previous anniversary's words, insidiously write an unchanged Arizona into being. Framed by these writers, Arizona is the same place in that moment that it has always been, told in the voices of Anglo settlers and boosters. Each of these narratives creates an Arizona; the place that becomes real to readers depends on which stories they read and where they are standing when they read them.

Words Unending

I am still a student of Arizona stories. My understanding of Arizona's narrative landscape has developed in the same way the words have been laid down over time. I am astonished by the multitude of Arizonas that these stories reveal, that can be uncovered in exploring its written intellectual landscape. And I am mindful that this work too, my study of Arizona's narrative landscape, is now a part of that landscape and will create the place for others.

Like her great-granddad, my teenage daughter is a wonderful storyteller. As she tells stories about Arizona's past to the children with whom she crafts valentines while volunteering at Phoenix's Heritage Square, she is speaking into being the place for these kids. And as I listen to my daughter and her friends tell their own stories, multiracial, multilingual, multilayered narratives unencumbered by the notion that such diverse stories threaten order or unity, I am a witness to the next layer of Arizona's narratives forming. I see the words becoming double-helix chains, creating new Arizonas as my daughter chooses from and adds her own words to the vast array of stories laid out on, emanating from, and attached to the land. Her and her friends' words, entwined with the words of the past, create new perceptions of Arizona, words still bringing the place into being, and they influence my perceptions of the place. The future Arizona will be created from, built on, fashioned out of these narratives told about it and enabled by it today.

Prologue: Points of Entry

Epigraph. Momaday, *The Names*, 154 (1976 ed.)

1. I am paraphrasing Eudora Welty. See Welty, "Place in Fiction."

2. In *The Archaeology of Knowledge*, French philosopher Michel Foucault explored this idea of "documents" and wrote that they exist in the past, present, and future. Louise M. Rosenblatt, a literary theorist and professor of English, explored the process of reading in her seminal work, *The Reader, the Text, the Poem*. "Once the creative activity of the author has ended," she wrote, "what remains for others—for even the author himself—is a text" (15).

3. Momaday, *The Names*, 154; Momaday, "Man Made of Words," 167 (1979 ed.).

4. Stegner, "George R. Stewart and the American Land," 168.

5. See Stegner, "Sense of Place"; and Basso, *Wisdom Sits in Places*.

6. Weisiger, *Dreaming of Sheep in Navajo Country*, 54.

7. Stegner, "Sense of Place," 202.

8. Momaday, "Man Made of Words," 166.

9. Cronon, "A Place for Stories," 1349; Ingold, "Temporality of Landscapes," 153, emphasis in original. See also Ingold, "Bindings against Boundaries."

10. Cronon, "A Place for Stories," 1375.

11. Like Cronon, I will use the terms "story" and "narrative" interchangeably (see ibid., 1349, fn5). The proper name "Arizona" indicates the culturally constructed and politically bounded location that writers bring into being through words; the natural landscape—the place itself—becomes the raw material for those stories about Arizona and influences the character of the narratives.

12. Rosenblatt, "Transactional Theory of Reading and Writing," 1063, quoted in Latham, "Experiencing Documents," 545; Rosenblatt, *The Reader, the Text, the Poem*, 32. Rosenblatt is concerned with illuminating the entire process of reading, from the author, to the text, to the reader. Her emphasis is on the reader; mine is on the text.

13. My analysis of the narratives is affected by where I am standing. This became clearer to me as I read reviews of books about Arizona and realized the

words within the books had created an Arizona for me that did not always look like the Arizona the reviewers discovered in the stories. A next step proceeding from my study of place-creating words could be a study of individual reader's responses to specific stories—an analysis of correspondence regarding one of Zane Grey's bestselling novels set in Arizona, for example.

14. In many American Indian languages the words "people" and "land" are the same. For a discussion on this, see Hobson's introduction to *The Remembered Earth*, 11.

15. For a discussion about Hopi ancestral footprints, see Kuwanwisiwma and Ferguson, "*Hopitutswa* and *Ang Kuktota*."

16. See chapters 4 and 2, respectively.

17. The University of Arizona Press has published several volumes of Native American oral traditional knowledge in Sun Tracks: An American Indian Literary Series. See, for example, Evers, *South Corner of Time*; Hinton and Watahomigie, *Spirit Mountain*; and Rock Point Community School, *Between Sacred Mountains*. See also Basso, *Wisdom Sits in Places*.

18. Garcés, *Trail of a Spanish Pioneer*, 316, 319.

19. Ives, *Report upon the Colorado River of the West*, 5.

20. J. W. Powell, "The Scientific Explorer," 18; and J. W. Powell, *Canyons of the Colorado*, reprinted as *Exploration of the Colorado River* (1961 ed.).

21. Dutton, *Tertiary History of the Grand Canyon*, 139, 164 (2001 ed.). For more information on the creation of the idea of Grand Canyon, see Pyne, *How the Canyon Became Grand*.

22. Hamilton, *Resources of Arizona: Its Mineral, Farming and Grazing Lands, Towns, and Mining Camps*, 12 (1966 ed.).

23. Hamilton, *Resources of Arizona: Its Mineral, Farming, Grazing and Timber Lands*, quoted in introduction, n.p.

24. Higgins, *New Guide to the Pacific Coast*, 110, quoted in Hyde, *American Vision*, 224. Hyde explains that these words were not in general use until the last years of the nineteenth century.

25. Southern Pacific Company, *The New Arizona*, 6, 10.

26. Van Dyke, *The Desert*, 60, 61 (1918 ed.). For more information about Van Dyke and the trip he may not have made, see Wild and Carmony, "The Trip Not Taken"; Teague and Wild, *Secret Life of John C. Van Dyke*; and Wild, "Critical Introduction to the 1999 Edition," in *The Desert*.

Overlook. Arizona Territory: Prelude to a State

1. "Shut Out from Progress: The Isolated Conditions of the Territory of Arizona," *Washington Post*, Nov. 20, 1878 (hereafter cited as *WP*).

2. "The Great and Growing Territory of Arizona: Copper and Cattle," *Los Angeles Times*, Jan. 1, 1905 (hereafter cited as *LAT*).

3. U.S. Bureau of the Census, "Resident Population and Apportionment of the U.S. House of Representatives."

4. For information on railroad building in Arizona see Pry and Anderson, *Arizona Transportation History*, Report no. FHWA-AZ-11-660; and "Union Pacific in Arizona."

5. "Shut Out from Progress"; "Great and Growing Territory."

6. Fleming, *Charles F. Lummis*, 20.

7. Lummis, "Scouts and Liars," in Thrapp, *Dateline Fort Bowie*, 72.

8. Black, *Arizona: Land of Sunshine*, 7.

9. Ibid., 122, 123. Arizona's constitution would state that the instruction at all state educational institutions "shall be as nearly free as possible" (Constitution of the State of Arizona, art. 11, § 6).

10. Black, *Arizona: Land of Sunshine*, 126.

11. Smythe, *Conquest of Arid America*, 249, 328 (1969 ed.).

12. For information on the Salt River Valley Users' Association, Roosevelt Dam, and the Salt River Project, see K. Smith, "Campaign for Water in Central Arizona"; *The Magnificent Experiment*; and "Water, Water Everywhere." See also Billington and Jackson, "Early Multipurpose Dams."

13. Territorial Normal School at Tempe (today Arizona State University), 1885; Northern Arizona Normal School (today Northern Arizona University), 1899; and the University of Arizona, 1891.

14. For an organizational history of the Arizona Historical Society by a long-time member and leader of the society, see Sonnichsen, *Pioneer History*.

15. Casa Grande Ruins, 1878; Montezuma Castle and the Petrified Forest, 1906; Tonto, 1907; Grand Canyon and Tumacacori, 1908; Navajo, 1909. For more information on Arizona's national monuments and national parks see U.S. Dept. of the Interior, "National Park Service Archeology Program."

16. For more information see the websites for Lowell Observatory (lowell.edu) and the Merriam-Powell Center for Environmental Research (nau.edu/merriam-powell/Merriam).

17. Bancroft, *West American History*, x.

Chapter 1. Defining a New State, 1912

1. U.S. Bureau of the Census, "Resident Population."

2. Quoted in "Arizona Is Exploited: Railroad Magazine Circulated throughout Europe Devotes Entire Issue to Opportunities for Settlers and Tourists Here," *Arizona Republican*, Apr. 24, 1912.

3. Pry and Anderson, *Arizona Transportation History*, 3, 24–25.

4. Winchester, "'So Glad God Let Me Be an Outdoor Woman,'" 20. Early Arizona's written narratives not only portrayed a solely Anglo place, absent Native Americans, but when Native American stories were shared, they were written by Anglo authors for Anglo readers. This situation continued well into the second

half of the twentieth century (see chapter 4). For background on Sharlot Hall, see Maxwell, *A Passion for Freedom*; Weston, "Sharlot Hall"; Kauffman, "The Queen of Arizona," 48; and Winchester, "'So Glad,'" 18–25.

5. Hall, "Out West" (poem).

6. Hall, "Arizona" (poem), in *Cactus and Pine*, 106 (1924 ed.). While New Mexicans voted for joint statehood by a large margin (26,195 for, 14,735 against), Arizonans rejected the idea by nearly 70 percent (3,141 for, 16,265 against); see "Arizona's Vote on Joint Statehood," quoted in Spude, "Saving Arizona," 11. For a discussion of the different perspectives and issues regarding separate or joint Arizona and New Mexico statehood, see Noel, *Debating American Identity*.

7. Hall, "Arizona" (poem), 108.

8. "'Cactus and Pine' Markham's Approval: For Some Time the Poet Has Had His Eye on Miss Hall," *Arizona Republican*, Mar. 16, 1911.

9. Hall, *Cactus and Pine*, 1 (1924 ed.).

10. See, for example, Hamilton, *Resources of Arizona*, 2nd ed.; and Black, *Arizona: Land of Sunshine*.

11. Hall, "Arizona" (article), 73.

12. Ibid., 74, 75.

13. Hall, "His Place," in *Cactus and Pine*, 43. The poem is about the grave of Hall's friend, photographer Clarence H. Shaw. Shaw's photographs accompanied many of Hall's *Out West* articles. He died in 1905. His glass-plate negatives can be found at the Sharlot Hall Museum in Prescott. See www.sharlot.org/library-archives/days-past/glass-plage-negatives-show-photographers-genuis/June 4, 2007 (accessed Mar. 24, 2013).

14. Hall, "When Spring Comes to the Desert," 363.

15. Ibid., 368, 373.

16. Hall, "Spring in the Desert," in *Cactus and Pine*, 26.

17. Hall, "The Forests of Arizona," 474.

18. Hall, "Pines of the Mogollones," in *Cactus and Pine*, 48, 49.

19. Hall, "The Trail of Death," in *Cactus and Pine*, 45. Jornada del Muerto historically refers to the desert route between Las Cruces and Socorro, New Mexico. Information about Hall and the *New York Evening Post* is found in Weston, "Sharlot Hall," 543.

20. Hall, "Prescott, Arizona," 115.

21. Summerhayes, *Vanished Arizona*, 43, 66–67. See also the review of *Vanished Arizona* in the *New York Times* (hereafter cited as *NYT*): "For all who want to know about the past as it really was," the reviewer wrote. ("What 'Arizona' Used to Mean: Thrilling Days That an Army Officer's Wife Spent There in the Seventies," Aug. 27, 1911.)

22. Brininstool, "Back to Arizona," 37. The moderately sized first edition sold out in a short time, according to the author's preface to the second edition.

23. Ibid.

24. "The *Arizona Republican*: A Factor in the Development of Arizona," *Arizona Republican*, Nov. 6, 1911.

25. Ibid.

26. Christened the *Coconino Sun* in 1898 after several name changes, the newspaper was the primary publication in the town of Flagstaff. From 1908 to 1932 Fred S. Breen was its publisher and editor. The *Arizona Republican* was founded in 1890. Sims Ely became the editor around 1900 and owned the paper in partnership with S. W. Higley from 1909 to 1912, when Dwight B. Heard bought it. Ely continued to run the paper from 1912 to 1929. For more information about early Arizona newspapers, see the Library of Congress, Chronicling America, http://chroniclingamerica.loc.gov/lccn/sn87062055.

27. "The World's Great Wonder: Completely within Boundaries of Arizona—State Pride Should Keep It There," *Coconino Sun*, Sept. 16, 1910. See also "Wants Slice of Arizona: Utah again Asks for Strip," *LAT*, Feb. 17, 1910. The issue of Utah and the Arizona Strip arose several times in the first two decades of the twentieth century; Utah even proposed buying the Strip from Arizona in 1919.

28. "The No-Man's Land across the River," *Arizona Republican*, Nov. 5, 1911. See also "Incomparable Resources of the 'Arizona Strip,' Veritable Terra Incognito," *Arizona Republican*, Nov. 3, 1911. Hall's diary of the trip, *Sharlot Hall on the Arizona Strip*, was published by Northland Press in 1975.

29. Official website of the Havasupai Tribe, www.havasupai-nsn.gov. See also "Havasupai Reservation." In 1921 the Havasupai population in Cataract Canyon totaled about 175 people, a reduction attributable to the federal government's limiting their land to the canyon bottom, thus restricting the tribe's seasonal migration pattern between rim and canyon that had marked Havasupai life before Anglo encroachment. See Parezo, "The Havasupais," 104.

30. "Cataract Canyon Scenery: Wondrous Beauty of the Famous Canyon Well Worth the Trip and Hardships to Reach," *Coconino Sun*, June 10, 1910.

31. "Phoenix—The Capitol City," *Arizona Republican*, Nov. 6, 1911.

32. "Glendale—The Garden Spot," ibid.

33. "Mesa—18 Miles from Phoenix—The Chandler Ranch," ibid.

34. H. V. Failor, "Tucson: Pima County," ibid.

35. "Flagstaff, the Coming Northern Arizona Metropolis: The Town Which Has More Advantages," *Coconino Sun*, June 7, 1912.

36. "Such a Combination of Soil and Climate: A Traveled Resident of This Valley Has Found No Where Else," *Arizona Republican*, Jan. 6, 1910.

37. "Better Pleased with Arizona," *Arizona Republican*, Aug. 20, 1912.

38. "East Needs a New View of Arizona," *Arizona Republican*, Oct. 5, 1910.

39. Ibid.

40. See "Now to Arizona: Preparations for Chamber of Commerce Excursion the Middle of March Will Be Rushed," *LAT*, Feb. 24, 1910; and "The Arizona Excursion," *LAT*, Mar. 11, 1910.

41. John S. M'Groarty, "Devotion Proved: Arizona Seals Her Friendship," *LAT*, Mar. 19, 1910.

42. Ibid.

43. Ibid.

44. See Sheridan, "The Chiricahua Apaches," 70–71, and Sheridan, *Arizona: A History*, 86–97.

45. John S. M'Groarty, "Angelenos Fall in Love with Arizona," *LAT*, Mar. 20, 1910.

46. "What Arizona Brings Us," *LAT*, June 23, 1910.

47. E. D. Ewers, "Preparing for Statehood: Some Recent History in New Mexico and Arizona," *LAT*, Oct. 23, 1910.

48. Ibid.

49. "Arizona Today: The Land of Opportunity, Where Sol Reigns," *LAT*, Apr. 9, 1911.

50. Ibid.

51. For information on Native American water rights in Arizona, see Killoren, "American Indian Water Rights."

52. "An American Pompeii in Arizona's Desert: Science Is Restoring a Prehistoric City around the Casa Grande," *NYT*, Jan. 17, 1909. See also "Excavating a Buried City in Arizona: The Casa Grande Ruins," *NYT*, Feb. 3, 1907, and "Uncovers American Pompeii: Buried City at Casa Grande, Arizona," *NYT*, Dec. 21, 1908.

53. "American Pompey in Arizona's Desert."

54. "Prehistoric Arizona Ruins: Montezuma's Castle Five Stories High," *Washington (NJ) Star*, quoted in the *LAT*, June 3, 1911.

55. "Would Oust Navajo Indians: White Men in New States Reaching for Rich Lands of Proud Tribe," *NYT*, Apr. 18, 1912.

56. Limerick, *Legacy of Conquest*, 190.

57. Roosevelt, speech at Grand Canyon, May 6, 1903.

58. Helminger is quoted in "The World's Great Wonder: Completely within the Boundaries of Arizona," *Coconino Sun*, Sept. 16, 1910.

59. Murphy, *Three Wonderlands*, 113, 118.

60. "Grand in Its Solitude," *LAT*, Aug. 5, 1910.

61. Ibid.

62. Grey, *Last of the Plainsmen*, vi (1911 ed.). For background on Grey, see C. Jackson, *Zane Grey*; Kant, *Zane Grey's Arizona*; and Blake, "Zane Grey and the American West," 202–16.

63. "A Tale of the Desert: Mr. Zane Grey Finds a Novel Setting," *NYT*, Oct. 8, 1910.

64. Grey, *Heritage of the Desert*, 26, 43.

65. Ibid., 34, 47.

66. Ibid., 253, 254.

67. "Tale of the Desert."

68. Grey, *Riders of the Purple Sage*, 227.

69. "Western Tales and Biblical: Stories of Foreign Lands, Our Own City, with a Profane Episode by Hauptmann," *NYT*, Feb. 18, 1912; emphasis added. See also C. Jackson, *Zane Grey*, 56.

70. See Kant, *Zane Grey's Arizona*, 17; Blake, "Zane Grey and the American West," 208. Kant writes about Grey's visit to the Arizona Strip; the trip gave him the idea for setting a story there.

71. Grey, *Riders of the Purple Sage*, 82, 83, 86.

72. "Arizona Is the Scene of Zane Grey Film," *Arizona Republican*, Dec. 29, 1918.

73. Grey, *Desert Gold*, 4.

74. Ibid., 76.

75. Blake, "Zane Grey and the American West," 204.

76. Grey, *Last of the Plainsmen*, vi.

77. See Blake, "Zane Grey and the American West," 207, 209.

78. Constitution of the State of Arizona (Dec. 9, 1910), art. 8, Removal from Office, 1, Recall of Public Officers, § 1. This constitution was not the first for the region. Southern Arizona was covered by the constitutions of the Mexican states of Occidente and Sonora, adopted in 1824, 1831, and 1848. See Faulk, *Constitution of Occidente*; and Spicer, *Cycles of Conquest*. For information on the Arizona constitution, see McClory, *Understanding the Arizona Constitution*.

79. See Sheridan, *Arizona: A History*, 178 (1995 ed.).

80. Constitution of the State of Arizona (Dec. 9, 1910), art. 4, Legislative Dept., 1, Initiative and Referendum, § 1 (1). Recall is codified in article 8, Removal from Office, Recall of Public Officers, § 1. New Mexico's constitution, by contrast, included the referendum but not the initiative or recall provisions. Republicans, who were opposed to direct democracy provisions in any form, controlled that state's constitutional convention, also held in 1910. However, New Mexico's constitution codifies both English- and Spanish-language learning (Constitution of the State of New Mexico, art. 12, § 8) and protects the "Educational Rights of Children of Spanish Descent" (art. 12, § 10). Only one of the fifty two delegates to the Arizona constitutional convention was Hispanic; about a third of New Mexico's one hundred delegates were of Mexican heritage (see Martinez, "Hispanics in Arizona," 97). An analysis and comparison of the two states' conventions and resulting documents—and the newspaper articles chronicling the two events—would be a fascinating undertaking but is beyond the scope of study. For an analysis of how language played a role in creating each state, see Stull, "Language, Borders."

81. Constitution of the State of Arizona (Dec. 9, 1910), art. 20, Ordinance 4th and 12th. These provisions would be challenged with ballot initiatives a hundred years later.

82. Constitution of the State of Arizona (2008), art. 28. See also chapter 4 and the epilogue in this work.

83. See Sheridan, *Arizona: A History*, 175–76 (1995 ed.); Weiser, "History of Goldfield Ghost Town"; and Lost Dutchman Chapter 5917 Arizona, "Goldfield Mining District."

84. "Arizona Forewarned," *LAT*, Apr. 24, 1910.

85. Ibid.

86. "Arizona's Statehood," *NYT*, June 25, 1910.

87. "Keynote Sounded by Judge A. C. Baker," *Arizona Republican*, Aug. 21, 1910.

88. "A Grave Situation," *Arizona Republican*, Aug. 28, 1910.

89. "A Threat? Certainly," *Arizona Republican*, Sept. 2, 1910.

90. "The Mob Spirit," *Coconino Sun*, May 5, 1911; "Doings in Washington City," *Coconino Sun*, Aug. 23, 1911.

91. "Sloan Slams Constitution: Tells President It's Hodge Podge," *LAT*, Dec. 8, 1910.

92. Quoted in "The Full Text of the Nelson Amendment," *Arizona Republican*, July 20, 1911.

93. Wishing to avoid the experience of Oklahoma's admittance to statehood, wherein then-president Theodore Roosevelt disliked that state's constitution as written but believed he had no authority to require changes, Congress designed New Mexico and Arizona's enabling acts to require the approval of both Congress and the president.

94. "Message of Governor Geo. W. P. Hunt to the First Legislature of Arizona," *Arizona Republican*, Mar. 19, 1912; see also "The Message," *Arizona Republican*, Mar. 19, 1912.

Overlook. Booms, Busts, and Borders: World War I and the Great Depression

1. "Deputies and Armed Citizens Load 'Reds' onto Cattle Cars," *LAT*, July 13, 1917. The fact that most of the striking miners were also "citizens" went unreported. For information on the Bisbee Deportation, see "Bisbee Deportation of 1917," and Byrkit, *Forging the Copper Collar*.

2. "Traitors at Home, Enemies Abroad," *LAT*, July 15, 1917.

3. President's Mediation Commission, *Report on the Bisbee Deportations*, 6. About three hundred deportees brought civil suits against the mining companies and railroad; these were settled out of court. All but one of the suits against the vigilantes were dismissed, and that one ended in a not-guilty verdict. See "Bisbee Deportation of 1917."

4. Information about Arizona's post–World War I economy is found in D. Martin, *Arizona Chronology*, specifically the years 1913–36 (no page numbers); and in editions of the *Arizona Republican* (1918–21) and the *Tucson Daily Citizen* (1918–21); see also Nash, "Reshaping Arizona's Economy."

5. For more information, see Meeks, *Border Citizens*; and Sadowski-Smith, *Border Fictions*.

6. U.S. Bureau of the Census, "Resident Population"; see also Martinez, "Hispanics in Arizona," 104–5.

7. See D. Martin, *Arizona Chronology*, specifically the years 1913–16 and 1926–28 (no page numbers); see also editions of the *Arizona Republican* (1913–28).

8. See D. Martin, *Arizona Chronology*, specifically the years 1922–29 (no page numbers); Reisner, *Cadillac Desert*; and Colby and Jacobs, *Arizona Water Policy*. In March 1929 Utah became the sixth state to sign the Colorado River Compact, completing the ratification of the Swing-Johnson Bill. Arizona did not ratify the compact until 1944.

9. "West Battles Grazing Bill," *LAT*, Apr. 29, 1934.

10. See "Cattle Industry in Good Shape, Survey Shows," *WP*, Nov. 15, 1937.

11. The livestock reduction tragedy had its roots in the federal government's broken promise to add more land to the reservation to keep pace with the increasing Navajo population; in the New Dealers' inability to recognize that the Navajos' economy and culture centered on their herds; and in the Navajos' certainty that the rains would come once balance (*hózhó*) was restored. See Weisiger, *Dreaming of Sheep*. Weisiger provides a three-dimensional history of the program and of the many facets of the Indian New Deal and its effects on the Navajo people, and she also explores the mental landscapes (how participants thought about the issues) of both New Dealers and Navajos. See also Parezo, "The Diné"; and Iverson, *Navajo Nation*, especially chapter 2. For the story of the stock reduction from the Navajo perspective, see McPherson, "Navajo Livestock Reduction."

12. "Cattle Industry in Good Shape"; "Collier Denies Indians Forced to Pawn Beads," *WP*, June 19, 1937.

Chapter 2. Creating Arizona, 1937

1. Pry and Anderson, *Arizona Transportation History*. The U.S. Census figures for 1930 and 1940 are quoted on page 41.

2. Sheridan, *Arizona: A History*, 254 (1995 ed.).

3. See Weisiger, *Dreaming of Sheep*; Parezo, "The Diné"; Iverson, *Navajo Nation*; and McPherson, "Navajo Livestock Reduction."

4. See Martinez, "Hispanics in Arizona," 109–10.

5. Davis-Monthan Airport was built in accordance with U.S. Army guidelines but remained a municipal airport until 1940, when it became Tucson Army Airfield. Renamed Davis-Monthan Army Airfield in December 1941, four days before the Japanese attack on Pearl Harbor, it became the home of Army Air Corps troops on April 1, 1941. The airfield was renamed Davis-Monthan Air Force Base in January 1948, when the U.S. Air Force became a separate military service. See "History: Davis-Monthan History," in *Davis Monthan Air Force Base, 2013 Base Guide*, 28.

6. Priestley, "Arizona Desert," 358. For background on J. B. Priestley, see Cook, *Priestley*; and Atkins, *J. B. Priestley*.

7. Priestley, "Arizona Desert," 360, 359.

8. Ibid. (Priestly mistakenly gives the year of statehood as 1910.)

9. Ibid., 363, 365.

10. Ibid., 359–61.

11. See, for example, Phelps, "American Best-Seller," *WP*, June 26, 1937.

12. Priestley, *Midnight on the Desert*, 91.

13. Ibid., 2–3.

14. Ibid., 102.

15. Ibid., 105. *Journey Down a Rainbow*, Priestley's follow-up philosophical travel book, was written with his wife Jacquetta Hawkes as a series of essays and letters between them as they journeyed separately—she to New Mexico and he to Texas. It does expand the commentary somewhat to include Native Americans and Hispanics, but it does not include Arizona.

16. *Midnight on the Desert*, 118, 119, 110–11.

17. Ibid., 119, 121, 123, 126.

18. Murphy, *Three Wonderlands*, 113; Priestley, *Midnight on the Desert*, 284–85.

19. Priestley, *Midnight on the Desert*, 285.

20. Ralph Thompson, "Books of the Times: Red Indians Plays and Professors Space and Time," *NYT*, Mar. 27, 1937.

21. Federal Writers' Project (hereafter FWP), *The Apache*, 4. For an analysis of the FWP representation of Native Americans in the bulletins, see Isernhagen, "Identity and Exchange."

22. For information on writing the state guides, see Penkower, *Federal Writers' Project*; Weisberger, *WPA Guide to America*; and L. C. Powell, *Arizona: Bicentennial History*.

23. FWP, *Arizona: A State Guide*, 3 (hereafter cited as *Arizona Guide*).

24. Ibid., 4.

25. Ibid., 3.

26. The *Arizona Guide* writers categorize Spanish and Italian people as white. See page 41.

27. Ibid., 5.

28. Ibid., 7.

29. FWP, *New Mexico: A Guide*, 3 (hereafter cited as *New Mexico Guide*.) Significantly, the *New Mexico Guide* uses the term Spanish-American, whereas the *Arizona Guide* defines all Hispanic people as "Mexican." An in-depth comparison of the Arizona and New Mexico guides, and other place-making texts in the two states during the Great Depression, would be a fascinating project but is beyond the scope of this study. For an analysis and comparison of western and midwestern states' guides, see Wrobel, *Global West*, specifically chapter 5.

30. FWP, *Arizona Guide*, 7, 8.

31. Ibid., 159.

32. FWP, *New Mexico Guide*, 4.

33. FWP, *Arizona Guide*, 8.

34. Oliver La Farge addressed these issues in his books and short-story fiction; see the next section in this chapter.

35. FWP, *The Hopi*, 5. Exploring how Indian people have been written into the intellectual landscape, the way words have defined and described Native Americans in Arizona over time, would be a worthy project, but it is beyond the scope of this study.

36. Biases against oral narratives and traditions are deep-seated. For more information on oral and written traditions, see the First Nations Studies Program, "Oral Traditions."

37. FWP, *The Hopi*, 7.

38. FWP, *Arizona Guide*, 167.

39. Ibid., 32.

40. FWP, *The Navaho*.

41. FWP, *Arizona Guide*, 29; FWP, *The Apache*, 6.

42. FWP, *The Papago*, 5.

43. Ibid., 6

44. Ibid., 14.

45. Squires, "Back to the Blanket," 171. For background on La Farge, see Caffey, *Yellow Sun*; and Hecht, *Oliver La Farge*.

46. Caffey, *Yellow Sun*, 4.

47. La Farge, *Raw Material*, 148, 164.

48. La Farge, *Enemy Gods*.

49. Ibid., 46.

50. Ibid. See also Parezo, "The Diné." The boarding-school system was criticized in the 1928 Meriam Report as expensive and detrimental to Indian children's wellbeing; see Meriam, *Problem of Indian Administration*. Opening day-schools on the reservations offered one solution; however, these schools came with their own problems, such as Anglo teachers, who did not speak the Navajo language and did not understand Navajo culture, feeling isolated. Moreover, the day-school program was initiated just as livestock reduction was decimating Navajo livelihoods; see Iverson, *Navajo Nation*, 19, 41.

51. La Farge, *Enemy Gods*, 126.

52. La Farge, "North Is Black."

53. La Farge, "Higher Education."

54. Faunce, *Desert Wife*, 58.

55. Ibid., 67.

56. Ibid., 92.

57. Ibid.

58. Jean West Maury, "Of Indians: *The Enemy Gods*," *WP*, Nov. 7, 1937.

59. Margaret Wallace, "*The Enemy Gods* and Other Recent Fiction," *NYT Book Review*, Oct. 17, 1937.

60. La Farge, *Enemy Gods*, 46.

61. See, for example, Linderman, *Plenty-Coups, Chief of the Crows* (1930) and *Pretty-Shield, Medicine Woman of the Crows* (1932); Neihardt, *Black Elk Speaks* (1932); and Paytiamo, *Flaming Arrow's People* (1932). For more information on Native American autobiography and ethnographies, see Strong's review essay, "New Approaches to American Indian Texts"; Sands, "Cooperation and Resistance"; and Kelsey, "Native American Autoethnography."

62. La Farge, *Raw Material*, 154.

63. Left Handed, *Son of Old Man Hat*, xi. The "Old Man Hat" of the title was Left Handed's father's older clan brother. For background about Walter Dyk, see Eggan and Silverstein, "Walter Dyk."

64. Left Handed, *Son of Old Man Hat*, 8.

65. Wyman, "Book Reviews, North and South America," 309.

66. Underhill, *Autobiography of a Papago Woman*. For information about Ruth Underhill, see Squires, "Back to the Blanket"; and Kaschube, "Ruth Murray Underhill."

67. Underhill, *Autobiography of a Papago Woman*, 3, 4.

68. Ibid., 4. Underhill did not elaborate on what type of surgery was required. According to Jill Leslie McKeever Furst, in the First Times, when I'itoi spat on the shaman's head, I'itoi's saliva formed stones, which "sank into the shaman's heart." Tohono O'odham people believe every shaman has four stones in his or her heart (Furst, *Natural History of the Soul in Mexico*, 55–56).

69. Underhill, *Autobiography of a Papago Woman*, 4.

70. Underhill, *Singing for Power*, 3.

71. Ibid., 5, 6.

72. Ibid., 14. The men mentioned in the song, the men who did I'itoi's fighting, were the Tohono O'odham people, whom he brought up from underground.

73. Ibid., 21–22.

74. Ibid., 43. The singing up the corn song is from *Singing for Power: The Song Magic of the Papago Indians of Southern Arizona* by Ruth Murray Underhill, © 1938, 1966 Ruth Murray Underhill, published by University of California Press. Used with permission.

75. Introduction to Nequatewa, *Truth of a Hopi*, 4 (1947 ed.). According to Kelsey, *Truth of a Hopi* "suffered a hostile reception" from the Hopi people (Kelsey, "Native American Autoethnography," 24).

76. Nequatewa, *Truth of a Hopi*, 3.

77. Ibid., 4.

78. "Hopi Decide to Seek a New Home. How Certain Clans Received Their Names," in Nequatewa, *Truth of a Hopi*, 34.

79. See Parezo, "The Hopis," 237, 242.

80. See, for example, "Many Visit Casa Ruins: March Travel to National Monument and Arizona Cities Sets Record," *LAT*, May 12, 1935. Tuzigoot was named a national monument in 1939, raising those numbers to nine of twelve.

81. Elliot, *Great Excavations*, 132.

82. See Doyel, "Short History of Hohokam Research." For information on the Roosevelt Lake excavation, see Haury, *Roosevelt 9:6*, in Reid and Doyel, *Emil W. Haury's Prehistory*, 211–94.

83. See Haury, "Ball Courts," in Gladwin, Haury, et al., *Excavations at Snaketown*, 36 (1965 ed.).

84. Ibid., 37, 38.

85. Ibid., 39.

86. Eunson, "Did the Ancients Know?," 8.

87. "Game Courts Are Dug Up," *NYT*, Nov. 24, 1935. Identifying Arizona's ancient structures with Aztec, Inca, and Maya cultures was not a novel occurrence. Montezuma Castle and Montezuma Well were named under the misconception that they must have been built by ancient Aztec immigrants.

88. "Views of Old Canals of Arizona Indians: Dr. Judd of Smithsonian Institution Studies Intakes of Prehistoric Waterways," *NYT*, Jan. 22, 1930.

89. Haury, "Snaketown Canal," in Gladwin, Haury, et al., *Excavations at Snaketown*, 50, 52.

90. Caywood and Spicer, *Tuzigoot*, 13; see also Spicer and Caywood, *Tuzigoot Ruins near Clarkdale.*

91. Caywood and Spicer, *Tuzigoot*, 38, 40.

92. Niehuis, "Tuzigoot Ruins," 5. Rosaline Svob was Niehuis's tour guide on her trip to Tuzigoot and perhaps her source for the information in the article. Svob is thanked in the introduction of Caywood and Spicer's excavation report for her lab work in taking "care of skeletal material" (see Caywood and Spicer, *Tuzigoot*, 2).

93. Niehuis, "Tuzigoot Ruins," 5.

94. For an examination of the ways archaeologists obscured Hopi narratives, see Ishii, "Western Science Comes to the Hopis."

95. Caywood and Spicer, *Tuzigoot*, 105–6.

96. Niehuis, "Tuzigoot Ruins," 41.

Overlook. Mid-century Growing Pains: World War II and Postwar Arizona

1. Carlson (uncredited), "Nothing'll Stop the Army Air Corps," 14, 17.

2. Telegram, Carl Hayden to Mesa Chamber of Commerce, July 28, 1941; quoted in Teille, *Historical Review of Williams Air Force Base*, 9.

3. "Man on the Cover: Del Webb." See Sun City Marketing Materials Collection, Del Webb Sun Cities Museum, 1960–2010. Much of the collection has been digitized and is accessible at www.delwebbsuncitiesmuseum.org. The phrase "Way-of-Life" was always set in headline style.

4. Williams Field was renamed Williams Air Force Base in 1948 when the U.S. Air Force became a separate military service. Del Webb Construction was also awarded the contract to construct the buildings for the Poston Japanese internment camp in southwestern Arizona during World War II. Two internment camps—the U.S. government's reprehensible solution to a nonexistent problem—were located in Arizona. Poston not only became the largest camp in the country, but between 1942 and 1945 it was also Arizona's third largest city (after Phoenix and Tucson). See Niiya, *Japanese American History*; and Japanese American Veteran's Association, "Poston, Arizona."

5. See, for example, WASP [Women Airforce Service Pilots] Home, wingsacrossamerica.us/wasp; and Henderson and Abbott, "Arizona Lumber Goes to War."

6. Bracero History Archive, Center for History and New Media, 2016.

7. Del Web Sun Cities Museum, "Interview of John Meeker, President, DEVCO," by Melanie Sturgeon, Mar. 6, 1996, transcribed by Belva McIntosh, Mar. 27, 2007.

8. U.S. Bureau of the Census, *Statistical Abstract of the United States, 1961*, 12, 18. For an overview of Arizona's post–World War II economy, see Nash, "Reshaping Arizona's Economy," in Luey and Stowe, *Arizona at Seventy-Five*, 123–47.

9. "History Channel Selects Goettl for Desert Technology Program." For more information on Arizona and the Phoenix area's post–World War II growth, see VanderMeer, *Desert Visions and the Making of Phoenix*; and Konig, "Phoenix in the 1950s."

10. Constitution of the State of Arizona, art. 25, Right to Work.

11. Shermer, *Sunbelt Capitalism*, 107; and Arizona Department of State, "Proposed Amendment to the Constitution—Opportunity to Work." Election results from State Library of Arizona, at *Ballotpedia, Encyclopedia of American Politics.*

12. Arizonans chose Dwight D. Eisenhower over Adlai Stevenson by a 58 to 42 percent margin ("1952 Presidential Election Results—Arizona,"), and voted for Barry Goldwater over Ernest McFarland 51 to 49 percent ("Arizona U.S. Senate Race—Nov. 4, 1952").

13. The Arizona Supreme Court ruled in 1948 that Native Americans have the right to vote in state elections. For a history of Native American voting rights in Arizona, see Ferguson-Bohnee, "History of Indian Voting Rights"; see also Iverson, *Navajo Nation*, 47.

14. The Alianza Hispano-Americana began in Tucson in 1894 as a mutual-aid society for Mexican Americans. For more information, see De La Trinidad, "Collective Outrage"; and Martinez, "Hispanics in Arizona."

15. Judicial Branch of Arizona, Maricopa County, "Law Library—*Phillips v. Phoenix Union High Schools.*" Hayzel B. Daniels was the first African American to pass the Arizona bar exam and one of the first two African Americans elected to the Arizona legislature. (Daniels and Carl Sims were elected in 1950.) Herbert B. Finn was a prominent Phoenix attorney.

16. "The Town That's Changed Retired Living," *Arizona Republic* special supplement, Jan. 29, 1961; ellipses in the original.

Chapter 3. Becoming Arizona, 1962

1. Ralph Mahoney, "Thousands See Reenactment of Arizona Statehood Day," *Arizona Republic*, Feb. 15, 1962.

2. Stegner, "Wilderness Letter"; see also Wilderness.net, "Wallace Stegner."

3. See Littlefield, "Dedication to the Memory of Joseph Wood Krutch," 101.

4. Limerick, *Desert Passages*, 127.

5. For background on Joseph Wood Krutch, see Margolis, *Joseph Wood Krutch*; "Joseph Wood Krutch," *WP*, May 26, 1970; "Joseph Wood Krutch," *NYT*, May 26, 1970; and Littlefield, "Dedication to the Memory of Joseph Wood Krutch," 101–4.

6. Krutch, *Desert Year*, 96 (1960 ed.); see also page 114.

7. Krutch, *More Lives Than One*, 310.

8. Krutch, *Desert Year*, 8, 11.

9. Ibid., 9.

10. Ibid., 27. Throughout this study, descriptions of Arizona's natural landscapes by writers whose eyes were trained elsewhere (Priestley in England, Krutch in New England, for example) raise the question, Do people of the Southwest and West write about other regions in similar ways when they move? One reviewer of *The Desert Year*, Charles Poore, asked this rhetorical question: if Krutch so disliked New York, why would he return after his sabbatical year? Poore then speculated that if enough people were motivated to move to the Arizona desert by Krutch's descriptions, "the Southwest would in turn become overcrowded, and a few authors could come back and write about life in the deserted streets of Manhattan for readers in the populous valleys of Arizona to enjoy" (Charles Poore, "Books of the Times," *NYT*, Mar. 1, 1952).

11. Krutch, *Desert Year*, 88.

12. Ibid., 184.

13. Ibid., 127.

14. Krutch, *Voice of the Desert*, 16.

15. Ibid., 22.

16. Krutch, "Mystique of the Desert," 47.

17. Krutch, *Voice of the Desert*, 191.

18. Ibid., 193, 194.

19. Krutch, *Grand Canyon: Today and All Its Yesterdays*, 162.

20. Krutch, "Man's Mark on the Desert"; quotations are from the article reprinted in Krutch, *If You Don't Mind My Saying So*, 361.

21. Ibid., 362.

22. Ibid., 365.

23. For example, two of Udall's sons, Levi S. and Jesse A., served as chief justices of the Arizona Supreme Court. Levi's sons Morris and Stewart served as U.S. congressmen for Arizona; Stewart also served as secretary of the interior. Morris's son Mark served as a U.S. congressman and U.S. senator for Colorado; Stewart's son Tom serves as a U.S. senator for New Mexico. Another great-grandson, Gordon H. Smith, served as a U.S. senator for Oregon.

24. See Jones, *Arizona Sonora Desert Museum*. Bill Woodin became the museum's director in 1954.

25. Woodin, *Home Is the Desert*, 3, 5, 194. See also "Miss Ann G. Snow, Prospective Bride," *NYT*, Aug. 27, 1947; and "Wedding in Lennox for Miss Ann Snow," *NYT*, July 11, 1948. Bill Woodin was a grandson of Franklin D. Roosevelt's first secretary of the treasury, William H. Woodin.

26. Woodin, *Home Is the Desert*, 5.

27. Ibid., 13.

28. Ibid., 17, 18.

29. Ibid., 233, 170.

30. Ibid., 4.

31. Ibid., 7.

32. Ibid., 166.

33. Ibid., 140. See the next section for an exploration of the Glen Canyon story.

34. Ibid., 164.

35. Ibid., 236.

36. Sekaquaptewa, *Me and Mine* (see page 247).

37. While Helen Sekaquaptewa is ostensibly the author of the book, an "author's note" at the end of "The Line" chapter (63–84) is signed by Louise Udall, not Sekaquaptewa. A review of the book in *American Anthropologist* names Udall as the author yet calls the book an "autobiographical account of a Hopi Indian woman" (Eggan, "Book Reviews," 411). This is another example of an Anglo process maintaining control of a Native American story. For background on Helen Sekaquaptewa and Native American autobiography, see Kelsey, "Native American Autoethnology." For an analysis on the relationship between Sekaquaptewa and Udall, and on the book as Native American literature, see Hafen, "'Trail in the Sand.'"

38. Sekaquaptewa, *Me and Mine*, front matter.

39. Ibid., 12.

40. Ibid., 188.

41. Ibid., 22.

42. Ibid., 38.

43. See ibid., 236.

44. Ibid., 235.

45. Ibid., 248.

46. Eggan, "Book Reviews," 411.

47. Ibid., 412.

48. For the history of Mormons in Arizona, see McClintock, *Mormon Settlement in Arizona*; and Peterson, *Take Up Your Mission*.

49. See, for example, "Apache Mormonism: How the Republicans Feel on the Question," *Arizona Republican*, Aug. 2, 1890; and "Apache Republicans . . . A Ringing Set of Resolutions Adopted Upon the Vexed Mormon Question," *Arizona Republican*, Aug. 26, 1890.

50. See McClintock, *Mormon Settlement in Arizona*, 177–82; Peterson, *Take Up Your Mission*, 32–37.

51. Udall, *Arizona Pioneer Mormon*, 69, 71.

52. Ibid., 84.

53. Ibid., 88.

54. Ibid., 115.

55. Woodin, *Home Is the Desert*, 241.

56. Sekaquaptewa, *Me and Mine*, 246.

57. Ibid., 247.

58. Udall, *Arizona Pioneer Mormon*, 236.

59. Duffy, "Page, Arizona," 14.

60. Porter, *Place No One Knew*. The full story of the intellectual landscape of Glen Canyon (including the written words of stories, poems, and songs; and images in films, photographs, and paint) is begging to be told—a massive project for another time.

61. For background on early Glen Canyon dam site applications, see, among others, these *Los Angeles Times* articles: "Report against High Line Canal," Aug. 18, 1924; "Arizona Files on Glen Canyon Dam Site," Oct. 22, 1925; "Aid in Move to Change Damsite Sought," Dec. 5, 1929; "Two More Dams on Colorado River Urgent to Meet Southland's Pressing Power Needs," Sept. 5, 1947. For background on Glen Canyon, the dam, and Lake Powell, see Martin, *Story That Stands Like a Dam*; Farmer, *Glen Canyon Dammed* and "Glen Canyon and the Persistence of Wilderness"; Nelson, "Voices of Glen Canyon"; and Abbey, "Down the River," in *Desert Solitaire*, 173–220.

62. Porter, *Place No One Knew*, 14 (1988 ed.)

63. Ibid., 8.

64. Lee Gallery, "Eliot Porter Photography."

65. Porter, *"In Wildness Is the Preservation of the World."*

66. See Porter, *Place No One Knew*, 6. He journeyed with Georgia O'Keeffe in 1961; he also visited the canyon twice in 1962, once each in 1963 and 1964, twice in 1965 after the lake began to fill, and again in 1968 and 1971.

67. Ibid., 9.

68. Ibid., 13, 160.

69. Ibid., 178.

70. Ibid., 34, 94.

71. Ibid., 40.

72. Brooks Atkinson, "Critic at Large: *Place No One Knew* Is Photographic Elegy on Demise of a Western Canyon," *NYT*, June 11, 1963.

73. Dominy, *Lake Powell*, 9. Many of the images are Joseph Muench photographs from the 1964 *Arizona Highways* Lake Powell issue.

74. Ibid., 15, n.p., 16.

75. Carlson, "The Colorado," 1; Carlson, "The Bridge," 5.

76. Muench, "Lake Powell," 37.

77. Towle, "Boat Trip to Rainbow Bridge," 4, 2, 11.

78. Jack Goodman, "Rainbow Country: U.S. Officials' Visit to Natural Bridge Highlights Park Problems in West," *NYT*, Apr. 23, 1961.

79. In 1974 the Navajo tribe sued the secretary of the interior, the commissioner of the Bureau of Reclamation, and the director of the National Park Service in an attempt to preserve religious sites in danger of being inundated by Lake Powell's rising water. The tribe lost the lawsuit and the appeal. Today the Park Service requests that visitors treat Rainbow Bridge "in a manner respectful of its significance to the people who have long held it sacred" (U.S. Department of the Interior, Rainbow Bridge National Monument, "History and Culture").

80. Merlo J. Pusey, "Artificial Lake Proves Man Can Enhance Nature," *WP*, July 17, 1966.

81. "Lake Powell: A Controversial Reservoir in Glen Canyon," *LAT*, Sept. 11, 1966.

82. See the Pulitzer Prizes (1960), "Journalism, Public Service, *Los Angeles Times*." For Sherman's World War II articles, see his "Pacific Echoes" column, *LAT*, Aug. 1944–June 1945. For his reports from the atomic bomb tests at Yucca Flats, Nevada, see, among others, "A-Bomb Dropped by B-29 in New Nevada Desert Test," *LAT*, Oct. 29, 1951, and "GIs Four Miles from Biggest A-Bomb Blast," *LAT*, Apr. 22, 1953.

83. "Gene Sherman to Tell Growth of Arizona," *LAT*, Feb. 9, 1962; see also "Series on Arizona to Begin Sunday," *LAT*, Feb. 9, 1962.

84. Sherman, "Arizona Booming as Mecca for Sun Seekers, Industry," *LAT*, Feb. 11, 1962.

85. Ibid.

86. U.S. Bureau of the Census, *Statistical Abstract of the U.S., 1961*, 17, 18.

87. Sherman, "Arizona Booming."

88. Ibid.

89. Sherman, "Visitors Spur New Arizona Industry," *LAT*, Feb. 12, 1962.

90. Sherman, "Reporter at Large: Arizona at 50," *LAT*, Feb. 12, 1962.

91. Sherman, "Far Right Label," *LAT*, Feb. 13, 1962.

92. Ibid.

93. Sherman, "Arizona Less Parched," *LAT*, Feb. 14, 1962.

94. Sherman, "Arizona's Money Tide," *LAT*, Feb. 15, 1962.

95. Sherman, "Reporter at Large: Arizona at 50."

96. Thomas E. Lesure, "Out on the Range: Booming Arizona Still Has a Place for the Old West Atmosphere," *NYT*, Jan. 22, 1961.

97. Ibid.

98. Morris, "Arizona: Air-Conditioned Desert," 31.

99. Ibid.

100. Ibid., 64.

101. Fannin, "This Is the Land We Love," 8; Pulliam, "Arizona—A Magic Word," 1.

102. Arizona Development Board, "Enjoy Life: You're in Arizona," n.p.

103. Pulliam, "Arizona—A Magic Word," 1.

104. Fannin, "This Is the Land We Love," 8, 9.

105. Kennedy, "Letter to the People of Arizona," 61.

106. S. Udall, "Arizona—Its Promise and Challenge," 354, 355.

107. Kelland, "It Was Love at First Sight," 282, 283.

108. Mahoney, "Arizona's Earlier Residents," 130.

109. Mahoney, "Story of Arizona," 57.

110. Chinese Chamber of Commerce Arizona, "About Us"; see also Luckingham, *Minorities in Phoenix*, 119.

111. Phoenix Chinese Chamber of Commerce, "Arizona, Fiftieth Anniversary Memorial Edition," 2.

112. Peplow and Peplow, "Indian Wars Bloody Chapter in U.S.," 7. Rochelle Peplow was editor of Arizona State University's alumni publication *Arizona Statesman* in the 1970s. Edward Peplow wrote the three-volume *History of Arizona* (1958).

113. Peplow and Peplow, *Arizona's Golden Era*, 8, 9, 18.

114. E. Peplow, "Arizona . . . Illustrious Chapter," 17. An entire book could be written about *Arizona Highways* as a creator of the place Arizona in words, and the topic awaits future investigation. For information about the magazine as a unique piece of Arizona history, see Topping, "History of *Arizona Highways*"; Topping, "*Arizona Highways*: Half-Century of Journalism"; Cooper, "*Arizona Highways*: Pamphlet to Magazine"; Farrell, "*Arizona Highways*: People Who Shaped a Magazine"; and Goldman-Rivera, "Touring *Arizona Highways*."

115. Leggett, "Arizona: Nation's Fastest Growing," 43, 57.

116. Pollock, *Pictorial America*, 1; emphasis in original.

Overlook. Water Rights, Civil Rights, and State's Rights: The 1970s and 1980s

1. Wood and Smith, *Barry Goldwater*, 12. In 1962 Jack Bell, chief political writer for the Associated Press, wrote *Mr. Conservative: Barry Goldwater* (as a "postmortem," according to Leo Weinstein; see Weinstein, "Bell, Jack. 'Mr. Conservative: Barry Goldwater' [Book Review"]). Bell perhaps meant to reintroduce Goldwater to the nation in preparation for the 1964 presidential election. For more information on Goldwater, see Iverson, *Barry Goldwater*; and Shermer, *Barry Goldwater Remaking the Political Landscape*.

2. Martin Luther King Jr., "Goldwater's Nomination," *New York Amsterdam News*, Aug. 1, 1964; "Dr. King Foresees 'Social Disruption' If Goldwater Wins," special to the *NYT*, Sept. 13, 1964. The *New York Amsterdam News* (founded in 1909) was an early black newspaper that in the 1960s was still providing the black viewpoint. See "About Us," *New York Amsterdam News*: The New Black View, at amsterdamnews.com. See also M. S. Handler, "Dr. King Demands Goldwater Rout," *NYT*, Oct. 12, 1964; and "Wilkins: Race Thirsty, But Not for Goldwater," *Baltimore Afro-American*, Sept. 21, 1963.

3. For Goldwater's objections to the Civil Rights Act of 1964, see the text of his speech to the Senate on June 18, a day before its passage, in Perry, *Barry Goldwater: New Look*, 148–49.

4. The annual flow average was estimated (after adjustments) to be about 15 million acre-feet per year. The actual annual flow between 1895 and 2003 averaged 12.4 million acre-feet per year; see U.S. Department of the Interior, U.S. Geologic Survey, "Climatic Fluctuations, Drought, and Flow in the Colorado River Basin."

5. For information about the development and allocation of Colorado River water, see Reisner, *Cadillac Desert*; Sheridan, *Arizona: A History* (2012 ed.);

K. Smith, "Water, Water Everywhere"; K. Smith, *The Magnificent Experiment*; Wiley and Gottlieb, *Empires in the Sun*; and Boepple, *Colorado River Basin*. The Dolores River Project—namely McPhee Dam, built downstream from Dolores, Colorado, and the resulting reservoir—was included in the Colorado River Basin Project, one of the five Colorado projects negotiated in the deal making.

6. See Iverson, *Navajo Nation*; and Sheridan, *Arizona: A History* (2012 ed.).

7. Iverson, *Navajo Nation*, 106.

8. Bracken, *Arizona Tomorrow*, 27. Arizona Tomorrow Inc. included representatives from Western Savings and Loan; Valley National Bank; Arizona Public Service; Salt River Project; the AFL-CIO; the Arizona Farm Bureau; Motorola; Sundt; the presidents of the University of Arizona and Arizona State University; members of Pima and Coconino County boards of supervisors; Burton Bar, majority leader of the Arizona House of Representatives; Alfredo Gutierrez, majority leader of the Arizona State Senate; and attorneys, judges, educators, and citizens.

9. Wiley and Gottlieb, *Empires in the Sun*, 165.

10. Phillip Shenon, "'Startling' Surge," *NYT*, Feb. 21, 1986, quoted in Limerick, *Legacy of Conquest*, 339.

11. See Martinez, "Hispanics in Arizona"; Limerick, *Legacy of Conquest*; and Immigration Control and Reform Act of 1986, 99th Congress, 2nd session.

12. In response to the Clinton administration's "Don't Ask, Don't Tell" policy, Goldwater famously said, "You don't need to be straight to fight and die for your country. You just need to shoot straight" ("Goldwater Backs Gay Troops," *NYT*, June 11, 1993).

13. "Goldwater Has Harsh Advice," *NYT*, Oct. 10, 1987.

14. For information on Arizona's Martin Luther King Jr. holiday travails, see State Library of Arizona, "MLK Day."

Chapter 4. Realizing Arizona, 1987

1. Arizona's population was 1,302,000 in 1960; 2,718,000 in 1980; and 3,665,000 in 1990. Figures at U.S. Bureau of the Census, "Characteristics of the Population: Arizona, 1980 Census Population"; and U.S Bureau of the Census, "Arizona: Population of Counties."

2. "Arizona Tops List of States Stimulating Growth," *LAT*, Sept. 27, 1988; Sheridan, *Arizona: A History*, 326 (1995 ed.).

3. Luey and Stowe, *Arizona at Seventy-Five*, 9.

4. Stanger and Nudelman, "Most Famous Book in Every State."

5. Anglo "discomfort" with minority cultures was observed by Marshall Inwerson, "Push for Official English on Ballot in Three States," *Christian Science Monitor*, Oct. 27, 1988, 5.

6. Deloria, "Foreword," in Danky and Hady, *Native American Periodicals*, xi. In 1970 several Native American newspaper editors formed the American Indian Press Association, a group of Native American journalists working out of Washington,

D.C., who wrote articles for distribution and publication in the many Native American newspapers and newsletters. The Native American Journalists Association was established in 1984. See Trimble, "American Indian Press Association; and see Native American Journalists Association, naja.com. See also Littlefield and Parins, "Native American Press."

7. See Diné College, "History"; Navajo Community College Press, Open Library, http://openlibrary.org/publishers/Navajo_Community_College-Press (accessed Nov. 14, 2013); and University of Arizona Press, "Sun Tracks," http://uapress.arizona.edu/series/series_detail.php?s=7 (accessed Sept. 5, 2013). Tsaile is located in the center of the Navajo reservation, nearly on the New Mexico border, north of Fort Defiance and southeast of Kayenta. The small press has published thirty-five works since its inception (see Navajo Community College Press, Open Library).

8. See Roessel, *Navajo Stories of the Long Walk*; and Johnson and Roessel, *Navajo Livestock Reduction.* Roessel also wrote *Women in Navajo Society*, published by the Navajo Resource Center at the Rough Rock Demonstration School in 1981. For information about the founding of Navajo Community College and NCC Press, see Iverson, *Navajo Nation*, 123, 149. Iverson's first teaching assignment out of graduate school was at the newly opened Navajo Community College in 1969. For information on Ruth Roessel, see George Hardeen, "Navajo Education Visionary, Author, Leader Ruth Roessel Dies," *Navajo-Hopi Observer*, Apr. 16, 2012.

9. Haskell, *Southern Athapaskan Migration*, 12.

10. McAllester, *Myth and Prayers of the Great Star Chant*, viii. Bostonian Mary Wheelwright worked with Navajo religious leader Hastiin Klah in the 1920s and 1930s. The original edition of the book was published in 1956 by the Museum of Navajo Ceremonial Art in Santa Fe, the repository for the oral interviews transcribed in the book.

11. Blue, *Witch Purge of 1878*, 1.

12. Ibid., 5 (ellipses in original), 7.

13. Ibid., 31.

14. University of Arizona Press, "Sun Tracks."

15. Evers, "Sun Tracks: Brief History." See also Evers, "Introduction," in *South Corner of Time.*

16. Evers, "Sun Tracks: Brief History." Wendy Rose discovered this issue as she wrote about American Indian literature in a dissertation that had to be housed in an anthropology department (see next section in this chapter).

17. See Sadowski-Smith, *Border Fictions*, 77. The U.S. government recognized the Yaqui tribe in 1978.

18. Evers and Molina, "*Yopo Nooki*," in *Yaqui Deer Songs*, 8. See also Molina, "*Maso Bwikam*," in Evers, *South Corner of Time.*

19. Evers and Molina, "*Yopo Nooki*," in *Yaqui Deer Songs*, 8, 9.

20. Molina, "*Maso Bwikam*," 193; Evers and Molina, "*Senu Tukaria Bwikami*, One Night of Songs," in *Yaqui Deer Songs*, 89, 88. Lines from *Yaqui Deer Songs* © 1987 The Arizona Board of Regents, reprinted by permission of the University of Arizona Press.

21. See comments by Joseph Bruchac (xii), Paula Gunn Allen (11), Elizabeth Cook-Lynn (65–66), and Wendy Rose (253) in Bruchac, *Survival This Way*. Bruchac, whose heritage includes Abenaki ancestry (a Native American tribe of the northeastern United States) as well as English and Slovak roots, founded the Greenfield Review Press, which provided direct access to Native American authors and Native American literature at a time when Anglo presses did not. See Greenfield Review Press, http://nativeauthors.com/index.php?ukey=auxpage_1 (accessed Nov. 23, 2013).

22. Bruchac, "Magic of Words: Interview with N. Scott Momaday," in *Survival This Way*, 179.

23. Ibid., 180, 182.

24. Bruchac, "Bones Are Alive: Interview with Wendy Rose," in *Survival This Way*, 257.

25. Ibid., 254.

26. Momaday, *The Names*, 92. For more information about Momaday, see Woodward, *Ancestral Voice*; and Steed, "Momaday, N. Scott," *Oklahoma Encyclopedia of History and Culture*.

27. Momaday, *The Names*, 61

28. Bruchac, "Magic of Words," in *Survival This Way*, 183.

29. Momaday, *The Names*, 41, 60, 59, 61, emphasis in the original.

30. Ibid., 67.

31. Ibid., 68–69.

32. Rose, "Neon Scars," in Swann and Krupat, *I Tell You Now*, 253. For more information about Wendy Rose, see Rose, "Introduction," in *Bone Dance*; Momaday, "Preface," in Rose, *Lost Copper*; and Cagle, "'Pushing from Their Hearts.'"

33. Rose, "Neon Scars," 258.

34. See Rose, "If I Am Too Brown or Too White for You," in *Halfbreed Chronicles*, 52–53.

35. Rose, "Vanishing point: Urban Indian," in *Lost Copper*, 12. Lines reprinted by permission of the Malki Museum.

36. Rose, "Builder Kachina," in *Lost Copper*, 126. Lines reprinted by permission of the Malki Museum.

37. Bruchac, "Bones Are Alive," in *Survival This Way*, 256.

38. Rose, "Just What's All This Fuss?"

39. Rose, "Introduction," in *Bone Dance*, xiv, emphasis in the original.

40. Rose, "Handprints," in *Lost Copper*, 36. Lines reprinted by permission of the Malki Museum.

41. Rose, "Just What's All This Fuss?," emphasis in the original.

42. Information about Russian immigrants and sugar beet farming per personal communication, Kathryn and Ben Pearson. See also U.S. Dept. of the Interior, Bureau of Reclamation, "Reclamation and Arizona."

43. U.S. Bureau of the Census, *Statistical Abstract of the United States: 1990*, 21; "Nevada Leads in Population Growth," *LAT*, Dec. 29, 1989; U.S. Bureau of the Census, Population Division, "Arizona: Population of Counties."

44. Ferrell, "Water and the Desert Dweller," 11; Barstad, "Range Management," 38–43. Barstad does admit that Native American herders have raised goats for centuries; the novelty of "goating" is an Anglo perception.

45. Quoted in Wild, *Ann Zwinger*, 26.

46. Ibid., 19. For more information on Zwinger, see her "Preface to 1988 Edition," in *Beyond the Aspen Grove.*

47. Zwinger, *Mysterious Desert Lands*, 41.

48. Ibid., 86.

49. Ibid., 92, 94. The deep arroyos were caused by, among other things, overgrazing and Anglo farmers' attempts to divert water for irrigating; the resulting deep washes and lack of water affected the Akimel O'odham farmers as well.

50. Ibid., 96.

51. Ibid., 163.

52. Ibid., 232.

53. Abbey, "My Forty Years as a Grand Canyoneer," reprinted as "Forty Years as a Canyoneer," in *One Life at a Time, Please*, 124. For more information on Abbey, see Cahalan, *Edward Abbey.*

54. Abbey, *Desert Solitaire* (1971 ed.).

55. Abbey, *Monkey Wrench Gang*; citations in this work are from the 1975 Avon Books paperback edition.

56. Abbey, "Arizona's Future," reprinted as "Arizona: How Big Is Big Enough?," in *One Life at a Time, Please*, 20.

57. Abbey, *Desert Solitaire*, 145.

58. Abbey, *Monkey Wrench Gang*, 15.

59. Abbey, "Arizona: How Big Is Big Enough?," 20.

60. Ibid., 21.

61. Abbey, "Polemic: Industrial Tourism and the National Parks," in *Desert Solitaire*, 39–59 (1968 ed.). He named Arches National Monument "the center of the world, God's navel, Abbey's country, the red wasteland" in the book's first chapter (4).

62. See Abbey, "Preliminary Remarks," in *One Life at a Time, Please*, 1–3.

63. Abbey, "Immigration and Liberal Taboos," in *One Life at a Time, Please*, 42–43.

64. Ibid., 41, 43.

65. Taylor, "PBS Documentary Mormons Upset over 'Missionaries,'" *LAT*, May 13, 1987.

66. For background on Maria S. Ellsworth, see Maria Ellsworth Papers, 1880–1999, Utah State University, Merrill-Crazier Library, Special Collections and Archives Division, Logan, Utah (USU_COLL_MSS229). For information on S. George Ellsworth, see "Historian-Author-Teacher S. George Ellsworth Dies," *Desert News*, Dec. 25, 1997, desertnews.com/article/602674/Historian-author-teacher-S-George-Ellsworth-dies-html?pg=all (accessed Nov. 5, 2015). For additional information on the Ellsworth family, see SNAC, "Biographical Notes." For Maria Ellsworth's *Journal of Arizona History* book reviews, see "Life and Times of Joseph

Fish" (Apr. 1971); "Erastus Snow" (July 1972); "Take Up Your Mission" (Oct. 1973); "Twelve Mormon Homes Visited" (Oct. 1975); "Spencer W. Kimball" (July 1978); "Roots of Modern Mormonism" (Apr. 1980); and "Blazing Crosses in Zion" (Oct. 1985).

67. See Archives West, Maria Ellsworth Papers, 1880–1999, "Historical Note."

68. Ellsworth, *Mormon Odyssey*, xii–xxiii. For background on Ida Hunt Udall, see Long, "Laboring in the Desert." For a history of Mormon women in Arizona, see Phillips, "'As Sisters in Zion.'"

69. Ellsworth, *Mormon Odyssey*, x.

70. Udall, *Arizona Pioneer Mormon*, 88.

71. Ellsworth, *Mormon Odyssey*, front matter.

72. Ibid., 39.

73. Ibid., 97. Congress passed the Edmunds Act against polygamy in 1882. In 1890 LDS Church president Wilford Woodruff issued his Manifesto, which ordered Mormons to submit to the laws enacted by Congress and upheld by the Supreme Court and abandon the practice of polygamy. See Woodruff, Official Declaration 1.

74. Ellsworth, *Mormon Odyssey*, 199.

75. Stanger and Nudelman, "Most Famous Book in Every State." For information on Barbara Kingsolver, see Demar, *Barbara Kingsolver*; Austenfeld, *Critical Insights*; and Kingsolver's website, kingsolver.com.

76. Demar, *Barbara Kingsolver*, 11.

77. Kingsolver, *The Bean Trees*, 161.

78. Ibid., 28, 58.

79. Ibid., 106–7.

80. Ibid., 195, emphasis in the original.

81. Arizona's strong labor provisions in article 8 of the 1912 constitution had been weakened considerably by the addition of article 25 in 1946, which made Arizona a right-to-work state, limiting union influence.

82. According to Demar reviewers disliked the book; she stated, "The major issue related to Kingsolver's admitted lack of objectivity and her focus on the women involved to the exclusion, some reviewers felt, of the men, the actual strikers" (*Barbara Kingsolver*, 12). However, by focusing on the women, Kingsolver did tell the story of "actual strikers"; women were also miners. For more information about the strike, see Rosenblum, *Copper Crucible*. For contemporary national coverage of the strike, see "Arizona Copper Strike in Third Week without Talks," *NYT*, July 17, 1983; "Around the Nation: Copper Mine Shut Down under Threat of Violence," *WP*, Aug. 10, 1983; Arthur H. Rotstein, "Guards to Allow Mine to Open Peacefully," *Hartford Courant*, Aug. 21, 1983; Paul Taylor, "Striking Copper Workers Find They Can't Go Home to 'Mother,'" *WP*, Dec. 14, 1983; Judith Cummings, "Violence in Copper Mine Strike Mars a New Bid for Attention," *NYT*, Jan. 22, 1984; Arthur H. Rotstein, "Tear Gas Fired in Ariz. Copper Strike," *Philadelphia Inquirer*, July 1, 1984; William F. Rawson, "Yearlong Strike Leaves Arizona Town Struggling for Its Survival," *LAT*, July 29, 1984.

83. Kingsolver, *Holding the Line*, ix–x, xi. Sadly, Kingsolver had to justify leaving out men, even though writers have rarely needed to justify leaving women out of their narratives.

84. Rotstein, "Tear Gas Fired"; Kingsolver, *Holding the Line*, 15.

85. Kingsolver, *Holding the Line*, 3.

86. Ibid., 7.

87. Ibid., 66. Just as the Mexican families had established San Juan before the Mormon settlers arrived and renamed it St. Johns.

88. "Around the Nation: Copper Mine Shut Down."

89. Kingsolver, *Holding the Line*, 158.

90. Rotstein, "Tear Gas Fired"; "The Anatomy of a Riot," *Arizona Daily Sun*, July 8, 1984, quoted in Kingsolver, *Holding the Line*, 159. The strike lasted over two years, culminating in union decertification and the closing of the Phelps Dodge Morenci smelter. Strikers filed three separate civil cases against the State of Arizona and Phelps Dodge, alleging not only that striking miners had done nothing wrong, but also asserting that the strikers themselves had been wronged. Unlike the results of the Bisbee Deportation cases seventy years earlier, all three suits resulted in judgments in favor of all the plaintiffs. See Kingsolver, *Holding the Line*, 193.

91. Quoted in Dunaway and Spurgeon, *Writing the Southwest*, 103–4.

92. The final results were 50.5 percent in favor of the amendment to 49.5 percent against; see Arizona Department of State, Office of the Secretary of State, "State of Arizona Official Canvass." The Arizona Supreme Court ruled the amendment unconstitutional ten years later in *Ruiz v. Hull* (1998); in 2006 voters in Arizona again approved an Official English measure (see the epilogue).

93. States where English had been designated as the official language by 1988 were Arkansas, California, Indiana, Kentucky, Mississippi, Nebraska, North Carolina, South Carolina, Tennessee, and Virginia. In 1988 Official English amendments were on the ballot in Arizona, Colorado, and Florida; the measure passed in all three states.

94. Arizona Department of State, Office of the Secretary of State, *Arizona Publicity Pamphlet: The Choice Is Yours.*

95. Constitution of the State of Arizona, art. 28, § 1. For information on the Arizona Constitution see McClory, *Understanding the Arizona Constitution.*

96. Constitution of the State of Arizona, art. 28, § 2.

97. Ibid., art. 28, § 3.

98. Ibid., art. 28, § 4.

99. "In Defense of Our Common Language," U.S. English brochure, quoted in Tarver, "Language and Politics in the 1980s." For more information on the Official English movement see Stalker, "Official English or English Only." "Official English" was the preferred designation used by the movement's supporters. Opponents used the term "English-only." I am using both terms: Official English was the phrase attached to the proposition and the amendment; English-only zones within governments would be its result.

100. "Fact Sheet: English Language Amendment," quoted in Tarver, "Language and Politics in the 1980s, "234.

101. The text of the English Language amendments was simple. Section 1 usually stated that the English language would be the official language of the United States, section 2 that Congress would have the power to enforce the article. For a discussion of ELA, see Leibowicz, "Proposed English Language Amendment."

102. Tanton also founded the Federation for American Immigration Reform (FAIR). FAIR's purpose is to lobby for stricter immigration laws, and Tanton's connection to both groups understandably makes immigration activists skeptical. FAIR has been designated a hate group by the Southern Poverty Law Center; see "Federation for American Immigration Reform." Complicating the U.S. English story was the fact that Senator Hayakawa and Linda Chavez (another of the movement's leaders and former president of U.S. English) are non-Anglo, thus making the case that their advocacy for English-only was not racially motivated.

103. McCain testimony, 78.

104. "English Is Numero Uno," *Phoenix Gazette*, Mar. 9, 1987. Recall that Governor Mecham did oppose the Martin Luther King Jr. holiday. In 1988 he would be indicted and impeached on grounds of financial improprieties.

105. "Goldwater Will Assist Bid in State to Make English Official Language," *Arizona Republic*, Aug. 6, 1987.

106. Ibid.

107. "English Is Numero Uno."

108. "Amendment to Encourage Proficiency in English Urged by State Lawmakers," *Phoenix Gazette*, Oct. 12, 1987. Armando Ruiz's papers pertaining to the Arizona English Coalition and the fight against English-only can be found at the Arizona State University Libraries, Armando Rios Papers 1987–1989, MSS-73, ASU Library Chicano Research Center.

109. "U.S. Doesn't Need an Official Language," *Arizona Republic*, Jan. 12, 1987.

110. "Educational Day in Convention," *Arizona Republican*, Nov. 23, 1910. See also "It's Down to Knitting, Convention's Busy Day," *Arizona Republican*, Nov. 22, 1910. The stark contrast between Arizona and New Mexico, two places that were once one entity, is fascinating. A comparison of the language of the states' constitutions—drafted at the same time to create two states out of what had initially been one territory—would be a interesting study. For background on language and the New Mexico constitution, see U.S. Commission on Civil Rights, "Language Rights and New Mexico Statehood."

111. *Arizona Publicity Pamphlet: The Choice Is Yours*, 26.

112. Ibid., 26–27.

113. Ibid., 27.

114. Ibid., 28.

115. Ibid.

116. Ibid., 32, emphasis in original.

Overlook. A Twenty-First-Century State

1. "Goldwater Has Harsh Advice."

2. Arizona also became the first state in which a woman succeeded a woman governor, when in 2003 Democrat Janet Napolitano was elected and replaced Republican Jane Dee Hull. See Center for American Women and Politics, "History of Women Governors." For short descriptions about specific governors, see the individual pages at the National Governors Association website, nga.org.

3. See Arizona Women's Hall of Fame, www.azwhf.org; see also Osselaer, *Winning Their Place.*

4. Jane Dee Hull, governor; Betsey Bayless, secretary of state; Janet Napolitano, attorney general; Carol Springer, treasurer; and Lisa Graham Keegan, superintendent of public instruction.

5. U.S. Bureau of the Census, "Population Distribution and Change," 2, 6, 9.

6. See Rex, "Development of Metropolitan Phoenix." Intel exemplified the new semiconductor and microchip industry's contribution to Arizona's growth, adding $450 million a year in research and development to the local economy between 1996 and 2010. See "Intel Arizona History Dates Back to 1979," *Phoenix Business Journal,* Oct. 19, 2010. www.bizjournal.com/phoenix/news/2010/10/19/intel-arizona-history-dates-back-to-1979.html (accessed July 1, 2016).

7. Figures quoted in Sheridan, *Arizona: A History* (2012 ed.), 283.

8. Ibid.

9. Arizona Department of Administration, "Local Area Unemployment Statistics Data." The national unemployment rate in 2010 was 9.6 percent; see U.S. Bureau of Labor Statistics, "State Unemployment Rates 2010."

10. See Michael Clancy and Casey Newton, "Phoenix May Be Losing People: Population Dip Would Further Strain Budget," *Arizona Republic,* Jan. 12, 2009.

11. Laurie Merrill, "Happy Birthday Sweet Rose," *Arizona Republic,* June 11, 2012.

12. Arizona Department of Administration, "Local Area Unemployment Statistics Data."

Epilogue: Points of Departure, 2012

1. U.S. Bureau of the Census, "State and County Quick Facts: Arizona." The Census Bureau estimates for Arizona in 2012: population, 6,626,624; Hispanic or Latino, 30.2 percent; language other than English spoken at home, 2008–12, 26.9 percent.

2. Arizona Snowbowl, "Snowmaking Information."

3. Woodin, *Home Is the Desert,* 236.

4. Abbey, "Arizona: How Big Is Big Enough?," in *One Life at a Time,* 20.

5. TrueSnow.org contains no information about who created or maintained the site, although an article posted on the website contains a reference to "Rudy Preston, founder of True Snow" (Zen Pathfinder, "Arizona Snowbowl Violates

City Permit"). Zen Pathfinder wrote many of the articles posted at TrueSnow, but again, no information about that person is available on the site. The most recent addition to the site is a film released in May 2013; most of the posts are dated at the end of December 2012. A visitor to the Save the Peaks Coalition website (savethepeaks.org), once the hub of online activity for the Save the Peaks effort, now finds a page of graphic art with a note at the bottom in very fine print: "Check TrueSnow.org for more." A Protect the Peaks website, unaffiliated with any particular group according to its "About" page, is a community website, a place "for people to post any and all news about the San Francisco Peaks and the destructive activities of Arizona Snowbowl Ski Resort" ("About," protectthepeaks.org). The Indigenous Action Media website provides a forum and support for issues that impact indigenous communities. The Save the Peaks effort is highlighted at indigenousaction.org. See also the website Unsettling America ("an emerging network of autonomous groups and individuals dedicated to mental and territorial decolonization"), "Protect the Sacred San Francisco Peaks!"

6. TrueSnow.org.

7. Rose, "Builder Kachina," in *Lost Copper*, 126.

8. Hall, "Arizona" (poem), in *Cactus and Pine*, 109.

9. Shonto Begay, "The View I Have from Here," Mar. 16, 2012, TrueSnow.org. Originally written for *Flagstaff Live!* magazine's Letters from Home column, Mar. 15, 2012. Used with permission.

10. Momaday, *The Names*, 67.

11. Walls, *The Glass Castle*, 19.

12. *Moyers and Company*, "Luis Alberto Urrea."

13. "Jeannette Walls, Official Publisher Page, Simon and Schuster," authors.simonandschuster.com/Jeannette-Walls/19723841 (accessed Jan. 13, 2014). See also Alex Witchel, "How Jeannette Walls Spins Good Stories out of Bad Memories," *NYT Magazine*, May 24, 2013, nytimes.com/2013/05/26/magazine/how-jeannette-walls-spins-good-stories-out-of-bad-memories.html?pagewanted=2&_r=0 (accessed Jan. 13, 2014).

14. Walls, *The Glass Castle*, 21.

15. Ibid., 99.

16. Momaday, *The Names*, front matter.

17. Walls, *Half Broke Horses*, 164.

18. Urrea, *The Devil's Highway*, 120.

19. Ibid., 116.

20. Ibid., 103.

21. Urrea, *The Devil's Highway*, 4.

22. Ibid., 105.

23. Ibid., 44–45.

24. William Stockton, "Rural Mexico See the U.S. as a Magnet," *NYT*, May 18, 1986.

25. Urrea, *Nobody's Son*, 58, 11–12, emphasis in original.

26. Ibid., 12–13, emphasis in original.

27. Ibid., 14–15, emphasis in original.

28. *Ruiz v. Hull*, § 2, 50 (1998), quoted in Schmid, *Politics of Language*, 163–64.

29. Arizona Department of State, 2006 Ballot Propositions.

30. Ibid.

31. Brenda Norrell, "Racist Law Struck Down," *Indian Country Today*, June 15, 1998.

32. Arizona Department of State, 2006 Ballot Propositions.

33. Arizona Department of State, "2006 General Election Results."

34. Alia Beard Rau, "Arizona to Defend Immigration Law," *Arizona Republic*, Apr. 22, 2012. See also ABC News, "Timeline: SB 1070," June 25, 2012.

35. Arizona State Senate, Senate Bill 1070, § 1, "Intent" (hereafter cited as SB 1070). For more information about SB 1070, see Santa Ana and González de Bustamante, *Arizona Firestorm*, especially part 3, "Mass Media Roles," for analysis of U.S., Mexican, and Spanish- and English-language media coverage.

36. Arizona State Senate, SB 1070.

37. Jeremy Duda, "U.S. Supreme Court, Feds Gut SB 1070 Enforcement," *Arizona Capitol Times*, June 29, 2012.

38. ABC News, "Timeline: SB 1070"; Arizona State Senate, SB 1070, § 2.

39. Howard Fischer, "Judge Orders Release of SB 1070 Emails," *Arizona Capitol Times*, Jan. 2, 2014.

40. Arizona Centennial Commission et al., *Centennial 2012*, 2. The original "Five Cs" were copper, citrus, cattle, cotton, and climate.

41. Ibid., 3.

42. Fannin, "This Is the Land We Love," 8.

43. Arizona Centennial Commission, *Centennial 2012*, 4.

44. When checked in November 2013, the *Arizona: 100 Years Grand* website, az100yearsgrand.com, had been commandeered by Highgate Cross, a graphic design company located in Illinois. The domain name expired in November 2015.

45. Heidinger, *Arizona: 100 Years Grand*, 98.

46. Ibid., 31.

47. Ibid., 59, emphasis mine. Heidinger promotes the "Centennial Review Board" in the acknowledgments. This was not an official board; rather, it was a group of volunteers she assembled to review her work. "She not only did extensive research but she created a review board to help her decide what would make it into the book. The review board was composed of eighteen people all from different walks of life" (Ghiz, "Arizona Native Writes Book"). Of the board's eighteen members, fifteen were Anglo and the youngest among them was middle-aged. Six were identified as historians. I could find no information about three of the members.

48. Trimble, "Arizona: 100 Years," 19.

BIBLIOGRAPHY

Abbey, Edward. "Arizona's Future: How Big Is Big Enough?" *Arizona Daily Star*, Jan. 29, 1984. Reprinted as "Arizona: How Big Is Big Enough?," in *One Life at a Time, Please*, 20–24.

———. "The Closing Door Policy." *Phoenix New Times*, June 19–July 5, 1983, 8–9. Reprinted as "Immigration and Liberal Taboos," in *One Life at a Time, Please*, 42–43.

———. *Desert Solitaire: A Season in the Wilderness*. New York: McGraw Hill, 1968. Reprinted by Ballantine, 1971.

———. *The Monkey Wrench Gang*. Philadelphia: Lippincott, 1975. Reprinted by Avon Books, 1975.

———. "My Forty Years as a Grand Canyoneer." *National Geographic Traveler* 1, no. 1 (Spring 1984): 19. Reprinted as "Forty Years a Canyoneer," in *One Life at a Time, Please*, 123–26.

———. *One Life at a Time, Please*. New York: Henry Holt, 1988.

ABC News. "Timeline: Story of Controversial SB 1070," June 25, 2012. Accessed Jan. 6, 2014. http://abc15.com/dpp/news/state/timline-story-of-controversial-sb-1070.

Adamson, Joni. *American Indian Literature, Environmental Justice and Ecocriticism: The Middle Place*. Tucson: University of Arizona Press, 2001.

Arizona Centennial Commission, Arizona Centennial 2012 Foundation, and Arizona Historical Advisory Commission. *Arizona Centennial 2012, The Centennial Plan*. Updated Mar. 16, 2012. Accessed Jan. 12, 2014. http://az100years.org/wp-content/uploads/2012/03/centennial-plan_3_16_12_STAFF_UPDATE.pdf.

Arizona Department of Administration, Office of Employment and Population Statistics. "Local Area Unemployment Statistics (LAUS) Data." laborstats.az.gov/local-area-unemployment-statistics.

Arizona Department of State, Office of the Secretary of State. *Arizona Publicity Pamphlet: The Choice Is Yours*. General Election, Nov. 8, 1988. Compiled by Jim Shumway. Arizona Memory Project. Accessed Nov. 4, 2013. http://azmemory.azlibrary.gov/cdm/compoundobject/collection/statepubs/id/10531/rec/1.

———. "Proposed Amendment to the Constitution of the State of Arizona Amending the Constitution by the Addition of a New Article Providing for and Protecting the Right of Non-Members of Labor Organizations to the Opportunity to Work." *State of Arizona Initiative and Referendum Publicity Pamphlet, 1946.* Arizona Memory Project. http://azmemory.azlibrary.gov/cdm/compoundobject/collection/statepubs/id/10531/rec/1.

———. "State of Arizona Official Canvass—General Election—November 8, 1988." http://azsos.gov/election/1988/General/Canvass1988GE.pdf.

———. 2006 Ballot Propositions: Proposition 103. In *Publicity Pamphlet: Ballot Propositions and Judicial Performance Review*, 24–29. Arizona Memory Project. Accessed Oct. 23, 2016. http://azmemory.azlibrary.gov/cdm/compoundobject/collection/statepubs/id/10531/rec/1.

———. "2006 General Election Results." htpp://azsos.gov/election/2006/general/2006_general_results_query.htm.

Arizona Development Board. "Enjoy Life: You're in Arizona." *Arizona Days and Ways Magazine*, Feb. 11, 1962.

Arizona Snowbowl. "Snowmaking Information." Accessed Mar. 10, 2014. arizonasnowbowl.com/resort/snowmaking.php

Arizona State Senate. 49th Legislature, Second Session, 2010. Senate Bill 1070. Accessed Oct. 23, 2016. www.azleg.gov/legtext/49leg/2r/bills/sb2010p.htm.

"Arizona U.S. Senate Race—November 4, 1952." *Our Campaigns*. ourcampaigns.com.

Arrington, Leonard. "The New Deal and the West: A Preliminary Statistical Inquiry." *Pacific Historical Review* 38, no. 3 (Aug. 1969): 311–16.

Athearn, Robert G. *The Mythic West in Twentieth-Century America*. Lawrence: University Press of Kansas, 1986.

Atkins, John. *J. B. Priestley: The Last of the Sages*. New York: Riverrun Press, 1981.

Austenfeld, Thomas, ed. *Critical Insights: Barbara Kingsolver*. Ipswich, Mass.: Salem Press, 2010. http://literature.salempress.com.

Ayers, Edward L., Patricia Nelson Limerick, Stephen Nissenbaum, and Peter S. Onuf. *All Over the Map: Rethinking American Regions*. Baltimore, Md.: Johns Hopkins University Press, 1996.

Bancroft, Hubert Howe. *History of Arizona and New Mexico, 1530–1888*. San Francisco: History Company, 1889.

———. *West American History*. New York: Bancroft Co., 1902.

Barnes, Trevor J., and James S. Duncan, eds. *Writing Worlds: Discourse, Text, and Metaphor in the Representation of Landscape*. New York: Routledge, 1992.

Barstad, Jan. "Range Management with a New Look." *Arizona Highways* 63, no. 3 (Mar. 1987): 38–43.

Basso, Keith H. *Wisdom Sits in Places: Landscape and Language among the Western Apache*. Albuquerque: University of New Mexico Press, 1996.

Bataille, Gretchen M., ed. *Native American Representations: First Encounters, Distorted Images, and Literary Appropriations*. Lincoln: University of Nebraska Press, 2001.

Baudrillard, Jean. *America*. Translated by Chris Turner. New York: Verso, 1988.

Begay, Shonto. "The View I Have from Here: A Prayer for the Desecrators." *Flagstaff Live! Letters from Home*, Mar. 15, 2012; TrueSnow.org, Mar. 16, 2012.

Bell, Jack. *Mr. Conservative: Barry Goldwater.* Garden City, N.Y.: Doubleday, 1962.

Beresford, Maurice. *History on the Ground.* Gloucestershire, UK: Sutton, 1957, 1984, 1998.

Beresford, M. W. *Time and Place: Collected Essays.* History Series 31. London: Hambledon Press, 1985.

Billington, David P., Donald C. Jackson, and Martin V. Melosi, eds. *The History of Large Federal Dams: Planning, Design, and Construction in the Era of Big Dams.* Denver, Colo.: U.S. Department of the Interior, Bureau of Reclamation, 2005.

"The Bisbee Deportation of 1917: A University of Arizona Web Exhibit." Accessed June 2, 2016. www.library.arizona.edu/exhibits/Bisbee/history/overview.html.

Black, John A. *Arizona: The Land of Sunshine and Silver, Health and Prosperity, the Place for Ideal Homes.* Tucson, Ariz.: Republican Book and Job Print, 1890.

Blake, Kevin S. "Zane Grey and Images of the American West." *Geographical Review* 85, no. 2 (Apr. 1995): 202–16.

Blue, Martha. *The Witch Purge of 1878: Oral and Documentary History in the Early Navajo Reservation Years.* Navajo Oral History Monograph Series No. 1. Tsaile, Ariz.: Navajo Community College Press, 1988.

Boepple, Brendan, and State of the Rockies Project, 2011–12 Research Team. *The Colorado River Basin: An Overview.* Colorado Springs: Colorado College, 2011. www.coloradocollege.edu/dotAsset/e57e7c73-2983-477b-a05d-de0ba0b87a00.pdf.

Bogart, Barbara Allen. *In Place: Stories of Landscape and Identity from the American West.* Glendo, Wyo.: High Plains Press, 1995.

Bowser, Brenda J., and Maria Nieves Zedeño. "The Archaeology of Meaningful Places." In Bowser and Zedeño, *The Archaeology of Meaningful Places*, 1–14. Salt Lake City: University of Utah Press, 2009.

Bracero History Archive. Center for History and New Media 2016. Accessed May 24, 2016. http://braceroarchive.org/about.

Bracken, Paul. *Arizona Tomorrow: A Precursor of Post-Industrial America.* Summary. Croton-on-Hudson, N.Y.: Hudson Institute, 1979.

Brininstool, E. A. "Back to Arizona." *Trail Dust of a Maverick: Verses of Cowboy Life, the Cattle Range, and Desert.* Los Angeles: Dodd, Mead, 1914. Reprinted by E. A. Brininstool, 1914, 1921.

Bruchac, Joseph. *Survival This Way: Interviews with American Indian Poets.* Sun Tracks: An American Indian Literary Series 15. Tucson: Sun Tracks and University of Arizona Press, 1987.

Bryant, Keith L., Jr. *Culture in the American Southwest: The Earth, the Sky, the People.* Tarleton State University, Southwestern Studies in the Humanities No. 12. College Station: Texas A&M Press, 2001.

Burtner, Marcus Alexander. "Crafting and Consuming an American Sonoran Desert: Global Visions, Regional Nature, and National Meaning." PhD diss., University of Arizona, 2012.

Byrkit, James. *Forging the Copper Collar: Arizona's Labor-Management War.* Tucson: University of Arizona Press, 1982.

Caffey, David L., ed. *Yellow Sun, Bright Sky: The Indian Country Stories of Oliver La Farge.* Albuquerque: University of New Mexico Press, 1988.

Cagle, Amanda Nicole Bass. "'Pushing from Their Hearts a New Song': The (re) Construction of the Feminine in American Indian Women's Poetry." PhD diss., University of Connecticut, 2006.

Cahalan, James M. *Edward Abbey: A Life.* Tucson: University of Arizona Press, 2001.

Carlson, Raymond. "The Bridge." *Arizona Highways* 35, no. 8 (Aug. 1959): 5.

———. "The Colorado: Muddy and Magnificent, Mighty and Majestic." *Arizona Highways* 34, no. 6 (June 1958): 1.

——— [uncredited]. ". . . Nothing'll Stop the Army Air Corps . . . At Williams Field They Learn to Fly the Bombers." *Arizona Highways* 18, no. 6 (June 1942): 14–17.

Cather, Willa. *The Song of the Lark.* London: Jonathan Cape, 1915, 1936.

Caywood, Louis R., and Edward H. Spicer. *Tuzigoot: The Excavation and Repair of a Ruin on the Verde River Near Clarkdale, Arizona.* Berkeley, Calif.: National Park Service Field Division of Education, 1935.

Center for American Women and Politics. "History of Women Governors." Accessed Oct. 22, 2016. cawp.rutgers.edu/history-women-governors.

Chinese Chamber of Commerce Arizona. "About Us." Accessed July 22, 2013. www.ccocoarizona.org/about

Colby, Bonnie G., and Katharine Jacobs, eds. *Arizona Water Policy: Management Innovations in an Urbanizing, Arid Region.* Washington, D.C.: Resources for the Future, 2007.

Constitution of the State of Arizona (2008). www.azleg.gov/const/Arizona_Constitution.pdf.

——— (Dec. 9, 1910). "Original Arizona State Constitution with Signatures." Arizona Memory Project. http://azmemory.azlibrary.gov/cdm/compoundobject/collection/archgov/id/218/show/149.

Constitution of the State of New Mexico (2011). www.sos.state.nm.us/Public_Records_And_Publications/2013nmconst.pdf.

Conzen, Michael P., ed. *The Making of the American Landscape.* New York: Routledge, 1990, 1994.

Cook, Judith. *Priestley.* London: Bloomsbury, 1997.

Cook-Lynn, Elizabeth. "Why I Can't Read Wallace Stegner." In *Why I Can't Read Wallace Stegner and Other Essays: A Tribal Voice.* Madison: University of Wisconsin Press, 1996.

Cooper, Thomas Charles. "*Arizona Highways*: From Engineering Pamphlet to Prestige Magazine." Master's thesis, University of Arizona, 1973.

Cronon, William. "A Place for Stories: Nature, History, and Narrative." *Journal of American History* 78, no. 4 (Mar. 1992): 1347–76.

De La Trinidad, Maritza. "Collective Outrage: Mexican American Activism and the Quest for Educational Equality and Reform, 1950–1990." PhD diss., University of Arizona, 2008.

Deloria, Vine, Jr. "Foreword." In *Native American Periodicals and Newspapers, 1828–1982: Bibliography, Publishing Record, and Holdings*, edited by James P. Danky and compiled by Maureen E. Hady, xi–xii. . Westport, Conn.: Greenwood Press, in association with the State Historical Society of Wisconsin, 1984.

Del Webb Sun Cities Museum. "Interview of John Meeker, President DEVCO." Interview by Melanie Sturgeon, Mar. 6, 1996, transcribed by Belva McIntosh, Mar. 27, 2007. www.delwebbsuncitiesmuseum.org.

———. Sun City Marketing Materials Collection. www.delwebbsuncitiesmuseum.org.

Demar, Mary Jane. *Barbara Kingsolver: A Critical Companion*. Westport, Conn.: Greenwood Press, 1999.

Diné College. "History." Accessed Nov. 23, 2013. www.dinecollege.edu/about/history.php.

Dominy, Floyd. *Lake Powell: Jewel of the Colorado*. Washington, D.C.: U.S. Government Printing Office, U.S. Department of the Interior, 1965.

Doyel, David E. "A Short History of Hohokam Research." In Reid and Doyel, *Emil W. Haury's Prehistory of the American Southwest*, 193–210.

Duffy, Jean. "Page, Arizona: The Town a Dam Built." *Arizona Highways* 40, no. 1 (Jan. 1964): 2–5, 14–15.

Dunaway, David King, and Sara L. Spurgeon. *Writing the Southwest*. Albuquerque: University of New Mexico Press, 2003.

Durrell, Lawrence. *Spirit of Place: Letters and Essays on Travel*. Edited by Alan G. Thomas. New York: Dutton, 1969.

Dutton, Clarence E. *Tertiary History of the Grand Canyon District*. Washington, D.C.: U.S. Geological Survey, 1882. Reprinted by University of Arizona Press, 2001.

Eggan, Fred. "Book Reviews." *American Anthropologist*, New Series 72, no. 2 (Apr. 1970): 411–12.

Eggan, Fred, and Michael Silverstein. "Walter Dyk, 1899–1972." *American Anthropologist*, New Series 76, no. 1 (Mar. 1974): 86–87.

Elliot, Melinda. *Great Excavations: Tales of Early Southwestern Archaeology, 1888–1939*. Santa Fe: School of American Research Press, 1995.

Ellsworth, Maria S. "Blazing Crosses in Zion: The Ku Klux Klan in Utah." *Journal of Arizona History* (Oct. 1985): 345–46.

———. "Erastus Snow, Missionary and Pioneer for the Early Mormon Church." *Journal of Arizona History* (July 1972): 138–39.

———. "The Life and Times of Joseph Fish, Mormon Pioneer." *Journal of Arizona History* (Apr. 1971): 68–69.

———, ed. *Mormon Odyssey: The Story of Ida Hunt Udall, Plural Wife*. Urbana and Chicago: University of Illinois Press, 1992.

———. "Roots of Modern Mormonism." *Journal of Arizona History* (Apr. 1980): 98–99.

———. "Spencer W. Kimball: Twelfth President of the Church of Jesus Christ of Latter-day Saints." *Journal of Arizona History* (July 1978): 215–16.

———. "Take Up Your Mission: Mormon Colonizing along the Little Colorado River 1870–1900." *Journal of Arizona History* (Oct. 1973): 261–62.

———. "Twelve Mormon Homes Visited in Succession on a Journey through Utah to Arizona." *Journal of Arizona History* (Oct. 1975): 308–9.

Engel, Leonard, ed. *The Big Empty: Essays on Western Landscapes as Narrative.* Albuquerque: University of New Mexico Press, 1994.

Etulain, Richard W. *Telling Western Stories: From Buffalo Bill to Larry McMurtry.* Albuquerque: University of New Mexico Press, 1999.

Eunson, Bob. "Did the Ancients Know? Recent Archaeological Find in Northern Arizona Turns Strange Light on Life Long Ago." *Arizona Highways* 12, no. 2 (Feb. 1936): 8, 19.

Evers, Larry, ed. *The South Corner of Time: Hopi, Navajo, Papago, Yaqui Tribal Literature.* Sun Tracks: An American Indian Literary Series 6. Tucson, Ariz.: Sun Tracks, 1980. http://parentseyes.arizona.edu/southcorner.

———. "Sun Tracks: A Brief History and Checklist." In *Home Places: Contemporary Native American Writing from Sun Tracks*, edited by Larry Evers and Ofelia Zepeda, n.p. Tucson: University of Arizona Press, 1995. Accessed Sept. 5, 2013. http://parentseyes.arizona.edu/definingsw/homeplaces.html.

Evers, Larry, and Felipe S. Molina. *Yaqui Deer Songs,* Maso Bwikam: *A Native American Poetry.* Sun Tracks: An American Indian Literary Series 14. Tucson: University of Arizona Press, 1987.

Fannin, Paul. "This Is the Land We Love." *Arizona Days and Ways Magazine*, Feb. 11, 1962.

Farmer, Jared. "Glen Canyon and the Persistence of Wilderness." *Western Historical Quarterly* 27 (Summer 1996): 211–22.

———. *Glen Canyon Dammed: Inventing Lake Powell and the Canyon Country.* Tucson: University of Arizona Press, 1999.

Farrell, Robert James. "*Arizona Highways*: The People Who Shaped a Southwestern Magazine, 1925–1990." Master's thesis, Prescott College, 1997.

Faulk, Odie B., trans. *Constitution of Occidente.* Tucson: University of Arizona Press, 1967.

Faunce, Hilda. *Desert Wife.* Boston: Little, Brown, 1934.

Federal Writers' Project. *The Apache.* Arizona State Teachers College Bulletin 20, no. 1 (Aug. 1939). Flagstaff: ASTC, 1939.

———. *Arizona: A State Guide.* Flagstaff: Arizona State Teachers College, 1940. Reprinted as *The WPA Guide to 1930s Arizona* by the University of Arizona Press, 1989.

———. *The Hopi.* Arizona State Teachers College Bulletin 18, no. 2 (Sept. 1937). Flagstaff: ASTC, 1937.

———. *The Navaho.* Arizona State Teachers College Bulletin 18, no. 4 (Nov. 1937). Flagstaff: ASTC, 1938.

———. *New Mexico: A Guide to the Colorful State.* New York: Hastings House; Albuquerque, N.Mex.: Coronado Cuarto Centennial Commission, 1940. Reprinted as *The WPA Guide to 1930s New Mexico* by the University of Arizona Press, 1989.

———. *The Papago.* Arizona State Teachers College Bulletin 20, no. 3 (Oct. 1939). Flagstaff: ASTC, 1939.

Feld, Steven, and Keith H. Basso. *Senses of Place.* Santa Fe: School of American Research Press, 1996.

Ferguson-Bohnee, Patty. "The History of Indian Voting Rights in Arizona: Overcoming Decades of Voter Suppression." *Arizona State Law Journal* 48, no. 4 (Winter 2015): 1099–144.

Ferrell, Dennis B. "Water and the Desert Dweller." *Arizona Highways* 63, no. 1 (Jan. 1987): 4–11.

First Nations Studies Program, University of British Columbia. "Oral Traditions." Accessed Mar. 25, 2014. indigenousfoundations.arts.ubc.ca/home/culture /oral-traditions.html.

Foucault, Michel. *The Archaeology of Knowledge.* Translated by A. M. Sheridan Smith. New York: Pantheon, 1972.

Francaviglia, Richard V., and David E. Narrett, eds. *Essays on the Changing Images of the Southwest.* College Station: Texas A&M University Press, 1994.

Friederici, Peter. *What Has Passed and What Remains: Oral Histories of Northern Arizona's Changing Landscapes.* Tucson: University of Arizona Press, 2010.

Furst, Jill Leslie McKeever. *The Natural History of the Soul in Mexico.* New Haven, Conn.: Yale University Press, 1997.

Garcés, Francisco. *On the Trail of a Spanish Pioneer; the Diary and Itinerary of Francisco Garcés (Missionary Priest) in His Travels through Sonora, Arizona, and California, 1775–1776.* Translated and annotated by Elliott Coues. 2 vols. New York: F. P. Harper, 1900.

Ghiz, Alexandra. "Arizona Native Writes Book on Arizona's Centennial." Arizona Sonora News Service. Feb. 8, 2012. Accessed Jan. 5, 2014. http: //arizonasonoranewsservice.com/stories/34-stories/178-woman-writes-book -on-arizonas-centennial.

Goble, Dale D., and Paul W. Hirt, eds. *Northwest Lands, Northwest Peoples. Readings in Environmental History.* Seattle: University of Washington Press, 1999.

Goldman-Rivera, Dorie S. "Touring *Arizona Highways*: The State's Best Known Magazine as Tourist Site." PhD diss., Arizona State University, 2003.

Grey, Zane. *Desert Gold.* Rosyln, N.Y.: Walter J. Black, by arrangement with Harper and Brothers, 1913.

———. *The Heritage of the Desert.* Roslyn, N.Y.: Walter J. Black, by arrangement with Harper and Brothers, 1910.

———. *The Last of the Plainsmen.* New York: Outing Publishing, 1908. Reprinted by Grosset and Dunlap, 1911.

———. *Riders of the Purple Sage.* Roslyn, N.Y.: Walter J. Black, by arrangement with Harper and Brothers, 1912.

Griffin, Dori. "Reading Maps, Writing Landscapes: Illustrated Cartography in Arizona, 1912–1962." PhD diss., Arizona State University, 2010.

Hafen, P. Jane. "'A Trail in the Sand': Helen Sekaquaptewa's Spiritual Frontier." *Literature and Belief* 21, nos. 1, 2 (2002): 149–62.

Hall, Sharlot. "Arizona" (article). *Out West* 24, no. 2 (Feb. 1906): 71–135.

———. "Arizona" (poem). In *Cactus and Pine: Songs of the Southwest*, 106–10.

———. *Cactus and Pine: Songs of the Southwest*. Boston: Sherman, French, 1911. Reprinted by Republican Print Shop, Phoenix, 1924.

———. "The Forests of Arizona." *Out West* 25, no. 6 (Dec. 1906), 473–509.

———. "Out West." *Out West* 16, no. 1 (Jan. 1902): 3–5.

———. "Prescott, Arizona." *Out West* 16, no. 1 (Jan. 1902): 101–15.

———. *Sharlot Hall on the Arizona Strip: A Diary of a Journey through Northern Arizona in 1911*. Edited by Gregory Crampton. Flagstaff, Ariz.: Northland Press, 1975.

———. "When Spring Comes to the Desert." *Out West* 22, no. 6 (June 1905): 363–78.

Hamilton, Patrick. *The Resources of Arizona: Its Mineral, Farming, Grazing and Timber Lands; Its History, Climate, Productions, Civil and Military Government, Pre-Historic Ruins, Early Missionaries, Indian Tribes, Pioneer Days, etc., etc.*, 4th ed. San Francisco: A. L. Bancroft and Co., 1884.

———. *The Resources of Arizona: Its Mineral, Farming and Grazing Lands, Towns, and Mining Camps; Its Rivers, Mountains, Plains, and Mesas; with a Brief Summary of Its Indian Tribes, Early History, Ancient Ruins, Climate, etc., etc. A Manual of Reliable Information Concerning the Territory*, 2nd ed. Prescott, Ariz.: n. p., 1881. Reprinted by Piñon Press of Arizona, 1966.

Haskell, J. Loring. *Southern Athapaskan Migration, A.D. 200–1750*. Tsaile, Ariz.: Navajo Community College Press, 1987.

Haury, Emil W. "Ball Courts." In *Excavations at Snaketown: Material Culture*. Medallion Paper 25. Harold S. Gladwin, Emil W. Haury, E. B. Sayles, and Nora Gladwin, 36–49. Globe, Ariz.: Gila Pueblo, 1938. Reprinted by the University of Arizona Press, 1965.

———. *Roosevelt 9:6—A Hohokam Site of the Colonial Period*. Medallion Paper 11. Globe, Ariz.: Gila Pueblo, 1932. Reprinted in *Prehistory, Personality, and Place: Emil W. Haury and the Mogollon Controversy*, by Reid and Whittlesey, 211–94.

———. "Snaketown Canal." In *Excavations at Snaketown: Material Culture*. Medallion Paper 25. Harold S. Gladwin, Emil W. Haury, E. B. Sayles, and Nora Gladwin, 50–58. Globe, Ariz.: Gila Pueblo, 1938. Reprinted by the University of Arizona Press, 1965.

"Havasupai Reservation." Nature, Culture, and History at the Grand Canyon. http://grandcanyonhistory.clas.asu.edu/sites_adjacentlands_havasupaireservation.html.

Hecht, Robert A. *Oliver La Farge and the American Indian: A Biography*. Native American Resources Series No. 2. Metuchen, N.J.: Scarecrow Press, 1991.

Heidinger, Lisa Schnebly. *Arizona: 100 Years Grand*. Phoenix: Arizona Historical Advisory Commission, 2011.

Henderson, Esther, and Chuck Abbott. "Arizona Lumber Goes to War." *Arizona Highways* 19, no. 1 (Jan. 1943): 1–2.

Higgins, Charles. *A New Guide to the Pacific Coast, Santa Fe Route*. Chicago: n.p., 1894.

Hinton, Leanne, and Lucille J. Watahomigie, eds. *Spirit Mountain: An Anthology of Yuman Story and Song.* Sun Tracks: An American Indian Literary Series 10. Tucson: Sun Tracks and University of Arizona Press, 1984.

"History Channel Selects Goettl for Desert Technology Program." *Phoenix Business Journal*, Jan. 2, 2005. Accessed June 9, 2016. www.bizjournals.com/phoenix/stories/2005/01/03/story7.html.

"History: Davis-Monthan History." In *Davis-Monthan Air Force Base, 2013 Base Guide.* Accessed Mar. 25, 2014. http://mybaseguide.com/Military-Relocation-Guide/1275/davis_monthan_afb.

Hobson, Geary, ed. *The Remembered Earth: An Anthology of Contemporary Native American Literature.* Albuquerque, N.Mex.: Red Earth Press, 1979.

Hyde, Anne Farrar. *American Vision: Far Western Landscape and National Culture, 1820–1920.* New York: New York University Press, 1990.

———. "Cultural Filters: The Significance of Perception in the History of the American West." *Western Historical Quarterly* 24, no. 3 (Aug. 1993): 351–74.

Immigration Control and Reform Act of 1986. 99th Congress, 2nd Session. Accessed Oct. 23, 2016. library.uwb.edu/static/usimmigration/100 stat 3359.pdf.

Ingold, Tim. "Bindings against Boundaries: Entanglements of Life in an Open World." *Environment and Planning* 40 (2008): 1796–810.

———. "The Temporality of Landscapes." *World Archaeology* 25, no. 2. Conceptions of Time and Ancient Society (Oct. 1993): 152–74.

"Intel Arizona History Dates Back to 1979." *Phoenix Business Journal*, Oct. 19, 2010. www.bizjournal.com/phoenix/news/2010/10/19/intel-arizona-history-dates-back-to-1979.html.

Isernhagen, Hartwig. "Identity and Exchange: The Representation of 'The Indian' in the Federal Writers Project and in Contemporary Native American Literature." In Bataille, *Native American Representations: First Encounters, Distorted Images, and Literary Appropriations*, 168–95.

Ishii, Lomayumtewa C. "Western Science Comes to the Hopis: Critically Deconstructing the Origins of an Imperialist Canon." *Wicazo Sa Review* 25, no. 2 (Fall 2010): 65–88.

Iverson, Peter. *Barry Goldwater: Native Arizonan.* Oklahoma Western Biography Series 15. Norman: University of Oklahoma Press, 1997.

———. *Navajo Nation.* Contributions in Ethnic Studies 3. Westport, Conn.: Greenwood Press, 1981.

Ives, Joseph C. *Report upon the Colorado River of the West, Explored in 1857 and 1858 by Lt. Joseph C. Ives, Corps of Topographical Engineers, under the Direction of the Office of Explorations and Surveys, A. A. Humphreys, Captain, Topographical Engineers, in Charge.* Senate, 36th Congress, 1st Session. Washington, D.C.: Government Printing Office, 1861.

Jackson, Carlton. *Zane Grey.* Boston: Twayne Publishers, 1973.

Jackson, J. B. *A Sense a Place, a Sense of Time.* New Haven, Conn.: Yale University Press, 1994.

Japanese American Veteran's Association. "Poston, Arizona." javadc.org/poston.htm.

Johnson, Broderick, and Ruth Roessel, eds. *Navajo Livestock Reduction: A National Disgrace*. Tsaile, Ariz.: Navajo Community College Press, 1974.

Jones, Stanley A. *Arizona Sonora Desert Museum*. Tucson, Ariz.: Sun Country Publication, Shandling Lithographing, 1962.

Judicial Branch of Arizona, Maricopa County. "Law Library—*Phillips v. Phoenix Union High Schools and Junior College District*, Superior Court of Arizona in Maricopa County, No. 72909." Accessed June 13, 2016. www.superiorcourt.maricopa.gov/LawLibrary/LegalResearch/ArizonaResearch/ArizonaCourts-Resources/phillips.asp.

Kant, Candace C. *Zane Grey's Arizona*. Flagstaff, Ariz.: Northland Press, 1984.

Kaschube, Dorothea V. "Ruth Murray Underhill." *Southwestern Lore* 31, no. 5 (Mar. 1966): 69–73.

Kauffman, Bill. "The Queen of Arizona." *American Enterprise* 15, no. 5 (Aug. 2004): 48.

Kelland, Clarence Buddington. "It Was Love at First Sight." *Arizona Days and Ways Magazine*. Feb. 11, 1962.

Kelsey, Penelope Myrtle. "Native American Autoethnography, Sovereignty, and Self: Tribal Knowledges in New Genres." PhD diss., University of Minnesota, 2002.

Kennedy, John F. "Letter to the People of Arizona." *Arizona Days and Ways Magazine*, Feb. 11, 1962, 61.

Killoren, Daniel. "American Indian Water Rights in Arizona: From Conflict to Settlement, 1950–2004." PhD diss., Arizona State University, 2011.

Kingsolver, Barbara. *Barbara Kingsolver Authorized Site*. http://kingsolver.com.

———. *The Bean Trees*. New York: Harper & Row, 1988.

———. *Holding the Line: Women in the Great Arizona Mine Strike of 1983*. New York: ILR Press, 1989.

Konig, Michael. "Phoenix in the 1950s: Urban Growth in the Sunbelt." *Arizona and the West* 24, no. 1 (1982): 19–38.

Krutch, Joseph Wood. *The Desert Year*. New York: Viking, by arrangement with William Sloan Associates, 1951, 1952, 1960, 1963.

———. *Grand Canyon*. Garden City, N.Y.: Anchor Books, 1962.

———. *Grand Canyon: Today and All Its Yesterdays*. New York: William Sloane Associates, 1958.

———. *If You Don't Mind My Saying So . . . Essays on Man and Nature*. New York: William Sloane Associates, 1964.

———. "Man's Mark on the Desert," *Desert Magazine of the Southwest*, July 1962. Reprinted in Krutch, *If You Don't Mind My Saying So*, 361–67.

———. *More Lives Than One*. New York: William Sloane Associates, 1962.

———. "The Mystique of the Desert." *Saturday Review*, Apr. 17, 1954, 46–47.

———. *The Voice of the Desert*. New York: William Sloane Associates, 1955.

Kuwanwisiwma, Leigh J., and T. J. Ferguson. "*Hopitutswa* and *Ang Kuktota*: The Role of Archaeological Sites in Defining Hopi Cultural Landscapes." In Bowser and Zedeño, *The Archaeology of Meaningful Places*, 90–106.

La Farge, Oliver. *The Enemy Gods*. Boston: Houghton Mifflin, 1937.

———. "Higher Education." *Saturday Evening Post*, Mar. 31, 1934. Reprinted in Caffey, *Yellow Sun, Bright Sky: The Indian Country Stories of Oliver La Farge*, 45–68.

———. "North Is Black," *Dial*, Jan. 1927. Reprinted in Caffey, *Yellow Sun, Bright Sky: The Indian Country Stories of Oliver La Farge*, 11–22.

———. *Raw Material*. Boston: Houghton Mifflin, 1945.

Latham, Kiersten F. "Experiencing Documents." *Journal of Documentation* 70, no. 4 (2014): 544–61.

Lee Gallery. "Eliot Porter Photography." Accessed June 2013. www.leegallery.com/eliot-porter/eliot-porter-biography.

Left Handed. *Son of Old Man Hat: A Navaho Autobiography Recorded by Walter Dyk*. New York: Harcourt, Brace, 1938.

Leggett, Herbert A. "Arizona: The Nation's Fastest Growing State." *Arizona Highways* 38, nos. 2–3, Arizona's Golden Anniversary edition (Feb.–Mar. 1962): 43–57.

Leibowicz, Jospeh. "The Proposed English Language Amendment: Shield or Sword?" *Yale Law and Policy Review* 3, no. 2 (Spring 1985): 519–50.

Lensink, Judy Nolte. *Old Southwest, New Southwest: Essays on a Region and Its Literature*. Tucson, Ariz.: Tucson Public Library, 1987.

Limerick, Patricia Nelson. *Desert Passages: Encounters with the American Deserts*. Albuquerque: University of New Mexico Press, 1985.

———. "Disorientation and Reorientation: The American Landscape Discovered from the West." *Journal of American History* 79, no. 3. Discovering America: A Special Issue (Dec. 1992): 1021–49.

———. *The Legacy of Conquest: The Unbroken Past of the American West*. New York: Norton, 1987.

Linderman, Frank B. *Plenty-Coups, Chief of the Crows*. New York: John Day, 1930.

———. *Pretty-Shield, Medicine Woman of the Crows*. New York: John Day, 1932.

Littlefield, Daniel, Jr. "A Dedication to the Memory of Joseph Wood Krutch, 1893–1970." *Journal of the Southwest* 24, no. 2 (Summer 1982): 101–4.

Littlefield, Daniel F., Jr., and James W. Parins. "Native American Press in Wisconsin and the Nation, 1982 to the Present." *Library Trends* 56, no. 3 (2008): 618–34.

Long, Genevieve Jane. "Laboring in the Desert: The Letters and Diaries of Narcissa Prentiss Whitman and Ida Hunt Udall." PhD diss., University of Oregon, 2002.

Lost Dutchman Chapter 5917 Arizona. "Goldfield Mining District." Mar. 2, 2010. Accessed Mar. 5, 2013. http://ecv5917.com/Articles/goldfield.htm.

Luckingham, Bradford. *Minorities in Phoenix: A Profile of Mexican American, Chinese American, and African American Communities, 1860–1992*. Tucson: University of Arizona Press, 1994.

Luey, Beth, and Noel J. Stowe, eds. *Arizona at Seventy-Five: The Next Twenty-Five Years*. Tempe: Arizona Board of Regents, Arizona State University Public History Program, and the Arizona Historical Society, 1987.

Mahoney, Ralph. "Arizona's Earlier Residents." *Arizona Days and Ways Magazine*, Feb. 11, 1962.

———. "The Story of Arizona Is a Story of People." *Arizona Days and Ways Magazine*, Feb. 11, 1962.

"Man on the Cover: Del Webb." *Time* 80, no. 5 (Aug. 3, 1962): 55.

Margolis, John D. *Joseph Wood Krutch: A Writer's Life*. Knoxville: University of Tennessee Press, 1980.

Maria Ellsworth Papers, 1880–1999. Utah State University, Merrill-Crazier Library, Special Collections and Archives Division, Logan, Utah. USU_COLL_MSS229.

———. "Historical Note." Archives West. Accessed Nov. 5, 2015. archiveswest.orbiscascade.org/ark:80444/xv05932.

Martin, Douglas D. *An Arizona Chronology: Statehood, 1913–1936*. Edited by Patricia Paylore. Tucson: University of Arizona Press, 1966.

———. *An Arizona Chronology: The Territorial Years, 1846–1912*. Tucson: University of Arizona Press, 1963.

Martin, Russell. *A Story That Stands Like a Dam: Glen Canyon and the Struggle for the Soul of the West*. New York: Henry Holt, 1989.

Martin, Russell, and Marc Barasch, eds. *Writers of the Purple Sage: An Anthology of Recent Western Writing*. New York: Penguin, 1984.

Martinez, Oscar J. "Hispanics in Arizona." In Luey and Stowe, *Arizona at Seventy-Five: The Next Twenty-Five Years*, 87–122.

Marx, Leo. *The Machine in the Garden: Technology and the Pastoral Ideal in America*. New York: Oxford University Press, 1964.

Maxwell, Margaret. *A Passion for Freedom: The Life of Sharlot Hall*. Tucson: University of Arizona Press, 1982.

McAllester, David P., ed., *The Myth and Prayers of the Great Star Chant and the Myth of the Coyote Chant*. Recorded by Mary C. Wheelwright. Tsaile, Ariz.: Navajo Community College Press, in arrangement with the Wheelwright Museum of the American Indian, 1988.

McCain, John. Testimony. House Subcommittee on Civil and Constitutional Rights of the Committee on the Judiciary Hearing. *Proposing an Amendment to the Constitution of the United States Establishing English as the Official Language of the United States, HJ Res. 13, HJ Res. 33, HJ Res. 60, and HF Res. 83*. 100th Congress, 2nd Session, May 11, 1988. Washington, D.C.: Government Printing Office, 1989.

McClintock, James H. *Mormon Settlement in Arizona: A Record of Peaceful Conquest of the Desert*. Phoenix, Ariz.: n.p., 1921. Reprinted by the University of Arizona Press, 1985.

McClory, Toni. *Understanding the Arizona Constitution*. Tucson: University of Arizona Press, 2001.

McNamee, Gregory, ed. *Named in Sky and Stone: An Arizona Anthology*. Tucson: University of Arizona Press, 1993.

McPherson, Robert S. "Navajo Livestock Reduction in Southeastern Utah, 1933–46: History Repeats Itself." *American Indian Quarterly* 22, no. 1/2 (Winter–Spring 1998): 1–18.

Meeks, Eric V. *Border Citizens: The Making of Indians, Mexicans, and Anglos in Arizona*. Austin: University of Texas Press, 2007.

Meinig, D. W. "The Beholding Eye: Ten Versions of the Same Scene." In *The Interpretation of Ordinary Landscapes: Geographical Essays*, edited by D. W. Meining, 33–48. New York: Oxford University Press, 1979.

Merrens, H. Roy. "The Physical Environment of Early America: Images and Image Makers in Colonial South Carolina." *Geographical Review* 50, no. 4 (Oct. 1969): 530–56.

Meriam, Lewis. *The Problem of Indian Administration. Report of a Survey Made at the Request of Honorable Hubert Work, Secretary of the Interior.* Washington, D.C.: Brookings Institute; Department of the Interior, 1928.

"MLK Day." *State Library of Arizona Virtual Reference Desk.* https://statelibraryofarizona.wordpress.com/martin-luther-king-day.

Molina, Felipe. "*Maso Bwikam*: Yaqui Deer Songs." In Evers, *The South Corner of Time: Hopi, Navajo, Papago, Yaqui Tribal Literature*, 193–202.

Momaday, N. Scott. "The Man Made of Words." In *Indian Voices: The First Convocation of American Indian Scholars.* San Francisco: Indian Historian Press, 1970. Reprinted in Hobson, *The Remembered Earth: An Anthology of Contemporary Native American Literature*, 162–73.

———. *The Names: A Memoir.* New York: Harper and Row, 1976. Reprinted as vol. 16 of Sun Tracks: An American Indian Literary Series by the University of Arizona Press, 1987.

———. "Preface." In Rose, *Lost Copper*, ix–x.

Morgan, Neil. *Westward Tilt: The American West Today.* New York: Random House, 1963.

Morris, Joe Alex. "Arizona: Air-Conditioned Desert." *Saturday Evening Post*, June 17, 1961, 30–31, 62–64.

Moyers and Company. "Luis Alberto Urrea, Author." Accessed Dec. 12, 2013. http://billmoyers.com/guests/luis-alberto-urrea.

Muench, Joyce Rockwood. "Lake Powell: America's Newest Playground." *Arizona Highways* 40, no. 1 (Jan. 1964): 16–37.

Murphy, Thomas Dowler. *Three Wonderlands of the American West; Being the Notes of a Traveler, Concerning the Yellowstone Park, the Yosemite National Park, and the Grand Canyon of the Colorado River, with a Chapter on Other Wonders of the Great American West.* Boston: L. C. Page, 1913.

Nash, Gerald D. "Reshaping Arizona's Economy: A Century of Change." In Luey and Stowe, *Arizona at Seventy-Five: The Next Twenty-Five Years*, 123–47.

Neihardt, John C. *Black Elk Speaks: Being the Life of a Holy Man of the Oglala Sioux.* Lincoln: University of Nebraska Press, 1932.

Nelson, Michaelann. "Voices of Glen Canyon: The Influence of Place on Imagination and Activism." PhD diss., University of New Mexico, 2009.

Nequatewa, Edmund. *Truth of a Hopi and Other Clan Stories of Shung-Opovi.* Museum of Northern Arizona Bulletin No. 8. Edited by Mary-Russell F. Colton. Flagstaff: Northern Arizona Society of Science and Art, 1936, 1947.

Niehuis, Gladys Thompson. "Tuzigoot Ruins: An Account of Arizona's Newest National Monument." *Arizona Highways* 15, no. 9 (Sept. 1939): 5, 41.

Niiya, Brian, ed. *Japanese American History: An A-to-Z Reference from 1868 to the Present.* Publication of the Japanese American National Museum. New York: Facts on File, 1993.

"1952 Presidential Election Results—Arizona." *Dave Leip's Atlas of U.S. Presidential Elections.* uselectionatlas.org.

Noel, Linda C. *Debating American Identity: Southwestern Statehood and Mexican Immigration.* Tucson: University of Arizona Press, 2014.

Osselaer, Heidi J. *Winning Their Place: Arizona Women in Politics.* Tucson: University of Arizona Press, 2011.

Parezo, Nancy J. "The Diné (Navajos): Sheep Is Life." In Sheridan and Parezo, eds., *Paths of Life: American Indians of the Southwest and Northern Mexico,* 3–33.

———. "The Havasupais, Hualapais, and Yavapais: The Great Creator Has Given Us This Country." In Sheridan and Parezo, *Paths of Life,* 91–114.

———. "The Hopis: Hopivotskwani, the Hopi Path of Life." In Sheridan and Parezo, *Paths of Life,* 237–67.

Paytiamo, James. *Flaming Arrow's People.* New York: Duffield and Green, 1932.

Pearce, T. M. *Oliver La Farge.* New York: Twayne Publishers, 1972.

Pearsall, Marc. "Railroads of Arizona (2002)." www.azrymuseum.org/Information/Arizona_Railroad_Map.pdf.

Penkower, Monty Noam. *The Federal Writers' Project: A Study in Government Patronage of the Arts.* Urbana: University of Illinois Press, 1977.

Peplow, Edward H., Jr. "Arizona . . . Illustrious Chapter in the Epic of America." *Arizona Highways* 38, nos. 2–3, Arizona's Golden Anniversary edition (Feb.–Mar. 1962): 12–35.

Peplow, Rochelle, and Edward Peplow Jr., eds. *Arizona's Golden Era: Arizona's 50th Anniversary,* special newspaper supplement, Jan. 19, 1962.

———. "Indian Wars Bloody Chapter in U.S." *Arizona's Golden Era: Arizona's 50th Anniversary,* special newspaper supplement, Jan. 19, 1962, 7, 20.

Peterson, Charles S. *Take Up Your Mission: Mormon Colonizing along the Little Colorado River* Tucson: University of Arizona Press, 1973.

Perry, James M. *Barry Goldwater: A New Look at a Presidential Candidate.* Silver Springs, Md.: National Observer, 1964.

Phillips, James Cleith. "'As Sisters in Zion': Mormon Women and the United Order in Arizona's Little Colorado Colonies." *Journal of Arizona History* 51, no. 2 (July 2010): 155–72.

Phoenix Chinese Chamber of Commerce. "Arizona, Fiftieth Anniversary Memorial Edition, Congratulations." *Arizona Days and Ways Magazine,* Feb. 11, 1962.

Pihlainen, Kalle. "History in the World: Hayden White and the Consumer of History." *Rethinking History* 12 no. 1 (2008): 23–39.

Pollock, Paul W. *Pictorial America: Arizona's 50th Anniversary Edition.* Phoenix, Ariz.: Paul W. Pollock, 1962.

Porter, Eliot. *"In Wildness Is the Preservation of the World."* San Francisco: Sierra Club, 1962.

———. *The Place No One Knew: Glen Canyon on the Colorado.* Edited by David Brower. San Francisco: Sierra Club, 1963. Reprinted by Peregrine Smith, 1988.

Powell, J. W. *Canyons of the Colorado.* Meadville, Pa.: Flood & Vincent, 1895.

———. *The Exploration of the Colorado River and Its Canyons.* New York: Dover, 1961.

———. "The Scientific Explorer." In *Titan of Chasms: The Grand Canyon of Arizona*, 11–22. Chicago: Passenger Department, Atchison, Topeka, and Santa Fe Railway Co., 1902.

Powell, Lawrence Clark. *Arizona: A Bicentennial History.* New York: Norton; Nashville: American Association for State and Local History, 1976.

President's Mediation Commission. *Report on the Bisbee Deportations.* Washington, D.C.: Department of Labor, 1917.

Priestley, J. B. "Arizona Desert: Reflections of a Winter Visitor." *Harper's Monthly Magazine* 174 (Dec. 1936–May 1937): 358–67.

———. *Margin Released: A Writer's Reminiscences and Reflections.* London: William Hinemann, 1962.

———. *Midnight on the Desert: Being an Excursion into Autobiography during a Winter in America, 1935–1936.* New York: Harper and Brothers, 1937.

Priestley, J. B., and Jacquetta Hawkes. *Journey down a Rainbow.* New York: Harper and Brothers, 1955.

Pry, Mark E., and Fred Anderson. *Arizona Transportation History.* Report no. FHWA-Ariz.-11-660. Phoenix: Arizona Department of Transportation, Dec. 2011. Accessed Aug. 17, 2013. www.azrymuseum.org/Information/Arizona_Railroad_Map.pdf.

Pulitzer Prizes (1960). "Journalism, Public Service, *Los Angeles Times.*" Accessed June 22, 2013. www.pulitzer.org/awards/1960.

Pulliam, Eugene C. "Arizona—A Magic Word." *Arizona Days and Ways Magazine*, Feb. 11, 1962.

Pyne, Stephen J. *How the Canyon Became Grand: A Short History.* New York: Viking, 1998.

Reid, Jefferson, and David E. Doyel, eds. *Emil W. Haury's Prehistory of the American Southwest.* Tucson: University of Arizona Press, 1986.

Reid, Jefferson, and Stephanie Whittlesey. *Prehistory, Personality, and Place: Emil W. Haury and the Mogollon Controversy.* Tucson: University of Arizona Press, 2010.

Reisner, Mark. *Cadillac Desert: The American West and Its Disappearing Water.* New York: Penguin, 1986, 1993.

Rex, Tom T. "Development of Metropolitan Phoenix: Historical, Current, and Future Trends." Morrison Institute for Public Policy and Brookings Growth Case Study. Tempe: Arizona State University, 2000.

Rock Point Community School. *Between Sacred Mountains: Navajo Stories and Lessons from the Land.* Sun Tracks: An American Indian Literary Series 11. Rock Point, Ariz.: Rock Point Community School, 1982. Reprinted by Sun Tracks and University of Arizona Press, 1984.

Roessel, Ruth W., ed. *Navajo Stories of the Long Walk Period.* Tsaile, Ariz.: Navajo Community College Press, 1973.

———. *Women in Navajo Society.* Rough Rock, Ariz.: Navajo Resource Center, Rough Rock Demonstration School, 1981.

Roosevelt, Theodore. Speech at Grand Canyon, Arizona, May 6, 1903. "Complete Speeches and Addresses of Theodore Roosevelt." *Theodore Roosevelt, the 26th President of the United States of America.* Accessed Mar. 2013. www.theodore-roosevelt.com/images/research/textspeeches/62.txt.

Rose, Wendy. "Builder Kachina: Home-going, Third Mesa, Hopi Reservation, Arizona." In *Lost Copper*, 126–27.

———. "Handprints." In *Lost Copper*, 36–37.

———. "If I Am Too Brown or Two White for You." In *The Halfbreed Chronicles and Other Poems*, 52–53. Los Angeles: West End Press, 1985.

———. "Introduction." In *Bone Dance: New and Selected Poems, 1965–1993*, xi–xix. Sun Tracks: An American Indian Literary Series 17. Tucson: University of Arizona Press, 1994.

———. "Just What's All This Fuss about Whiteshamanism Anyway?" *Modern American Poetry.* "About Whiteshamanism." Accessed Sept. 9, 2013. http://english.illinois.edu/maps/poets/m_r/rose/whiteshamanism.htm. Reprinted from *Coyote Was Here: Essays on Contemporary Native American Literary and Political Mobilization*, edited by Bo Schöler, *The Dolphin*, no. 9 (Apr. 1984).

———. *Lost Copper: Poems.* Banning, Calif.: Malki Museum Press, 1980.

———. "Neon Scars." In *I Tell You Now: Autobiographical Essays by Native American Writers*, edited by Brian Swann and Arnold Krupat, 251–61. Lincoln: University of Nebraska Press, 1987.

———. "Vanishing point: Urban Indian." In *Lost Copper*, 12.

Rosenblatt, Louise M. *The Reader, the Text, the Poem: The Transactional Theory of the Literary Work.* Carbondale and Edwardsville: Southern Illinois University Press, 1978.

———. "The Transactional Theory of Reading and Writing." In *Theoretical Models and Processes of Reading*, 4th ed., edited by R. B. Ruddell, M. R. Ruddell, and H. Singer, 1057–92. Newark, Del.: International Reading Association, 1994.

Rosenblum, Jonathan D. *Copper Crucible: How the Arizona Miners' Strike of 1983 Recast Labor-Management Relations in America.* Ithaca, N.Y.: ILR Press, 1995, 1998.

Russell, Emily W. B. *People and the Land through Time: Linking Ecology and History.* New Haven, Conn.: Yale University Press, 1997.

Ryden, Kent. *Mapping the Invisible Landscape: Folklore, Writing, and the Sense of Place.* Iowa City: University of Iowa Press, 1993.

Sadowski-Smith, Claudia. *Border Fictions: Globalization, Empire, and Writing at the Boundaries of the United States.* Charlottesville: University of Virginia Press, 2008.

Sands, Kathleen M. "Cooperation and Resistance: Native American Collaborative Personal Narrative." In Bataille, *Native American Representations: First Encounters, Distorted Images, and Literary Appropriations*, 134–49.

Santa Ana, Otto, and Celeste González de Bustamante, eds. *Arizona Firestorm: Global Immigration Realities, National Media, and Provincial Politics*. Lanham, Md.: Rowman & Littlefield, 2012.

Santee, Ross. *Apache Lands*. New York: Charles Scribner's Sons, 1947.

Savoy, Maggie. "Arizona Originals Go Anywhere." *Arizona Days and Ways Magazine*, Feb. 11, 1962.

Schmid, Carol L. *The Politics of Language: Conflict, Identity, and Cultural Pluralism in Comparative Perspective*. Oxford and New York: Oxford University Press, 2001.

Schmieding, Sam. "Visions of a Sculpted Paradise: The Colorado Plateau as American Sacred Space." PhD diss., Arizona State University, 2002.

Sekaquaptewa, Helen. *Me and Mine: The Life Story of Helen Sekaquaptewa*. As told to Louise Udall. Tucson: University of Arizona Press, 1969.

Sheridan, Thomas E. *Arizona: A History*. Tucson: University of Arizona Press, 1995; rev. ed., 2012.

———. "The Chiricahua Apaches." In Sheridan and Parezo, *Paths of Life*, 70–71.

Sheridan, Thomas E., and Nancy J. Parezo, eds. *Paths of Life: American Indians of the Southwest and Northern Mexico*. Tucson: University of Arizona Press, 1996.

Sherman, Gene. "A-Bomb Dropped by B-29 in New Nevada Desert Test." *Los Angeles Times*, Oct. 29, 1951.

———. "Arizona Booming as Mecca for Sun Seekers, Industry: State Marking Its 50th Birthday Progresses in Population, Prosperity." *Los Angeles Times*, Feb. 11, 1962.

———. "Arizona Less Parched Than Court Pleas Hint: State Has Enough Water for Now, Some Residents Admit, But They Look to the Future." *Los Angeles Times*, Feb. 14, 1962.

———. "Arizona's Money Tide Inundates Desert Lore: Mounting Bank Deposits, Payrolls Show Tourism Gives Way to Economic Growth." *Los Angeles Times*, Feb. 15, 1962.

———. "Far Right Label Burr under Arizona's Saddle: State Registers Democratic but Is Known Most Widely for Goldwater Conservatism." *Los Angeles Times*, Feb. 13, 1962.

———. "GIs Four Miles from Biggest A-Bomb Blast: Record Explosion for Continental U.S." *Los Angeles Times*, Apr. 22, 1953.

———. Pacific Echoes column. *Los Angeles Times*, Aug. 1944–June 1945.

———. "Reporter at Large: Arizona at 50 Is Racing Like 90." *Los Angeles Times*, Feb. 12, 1962.

———. "Visitors Spur New Arizona Industry: Vacationers Fall in Love with State, See Great Possibilities." *Los Angeles Times*, Feb. 12, 1962.

Shermer, Elizabeth Tandy, ed. *Barry Goldwater and the Remaking of the American Political Landscape*. Tucson: University of Arizona Press, 2013.

———. *Sunbelt Capitalism: Phoenix and the Transformation of American Politics*. Philadelphia: University of Pennsylvania Press, 2013.

Silko, Leslie Marmon. "Landscape, History, and the Pueblo Imagination." *Antaeus* 57 (Autumn 1986): 83–94.

Simpson, John Warfield. *Visions of Paradise: Glimpses of Our Landscape's Legacy.* Berkeley: University of California Press, 1999.

Sloan, Stephen. "Negotiating a Sense of Place in the Salt River Valley: Urbanites and the Desert." PhD diss., Arizona State University, 2003.

Smith, Henry Nash. *Virgin Land: The American West as Symbol and Myth.* New York: Vintage Books, 1957.

Smith, Karen. "The Campaign for Water in Central Arizona, 1890–1903." *Arizona and the West* 23 (Summer 1981): 127–48.

———. *The Magnificent Experiment: Building the Salt River Project, 1870–1917.* Tucson: University of Arizona Press, 1986.

———. "Water, Water Everywhere, Nor . . ." In Luey and Stowe, *Arizona at Seventy-Five: The Next Twenty-Five Years*, 149–72.

Smythe, William E. *The Conquest of Arid America.* Seattle: University of Washington Press, 1969. Originally published by Harper, 1899, 1905.

SNAC. "Biographical Notes." Charlottesville: Institute for the Advanced Technology in the Humanities; Rectors and Visitors of the University of Virginia, 2013. Accessed Oct. 22, 2016. http://socialarchive.iath.virginia.edu/ark:/99166/w6nq1dxd.

Sonnichsen, C. L. *Pioneer History: The First Century of the Arizona Historical Society.* Tucson: Arizona Historical Society, 1984.

Southern Pacific Company. *The New Arizona: A Brief Review of Its Resources, Development, Industries, Soil, Climate, and Especially Its Advantage for Homemaking.* San Francisco: Passenger Department, Southern Pacific Co., 1900.

Southern Poverty Law Center. "Federation for American Immigration Reform." Accessed Nov. 2013. splcenter.org/get-informed/intelligence-files/groups/federation-for-american-immigration-reform-fair.

Spicer, Edward H. *Cycles of Conquest.* Tucson: University of Arizona Press, 1962.

Spicer, Edward. H., and Louis R. Caywood. *Tuzigoot Ruins near Clarkdale, Arizona: Home of Early Arizonans.* Office of the Yavapai County Immigration Commissioner and the Yavapai County Chamber of Commerce, 1935.

Spude, Robert L. "Saving Arizona: The Defeat of Jointure." *Territorial Times* 5 no. 1, Back Issue no. 9 (Fall 2011): 1–13.

Squires, Nancy Elam. "Back to the Blanket: The Indian Fiction of Oliver La Farge, John Joseph Mathews, D'Arcy McNickle, Ruth Underhill, and Frank Waters, 1927–1944." PhD diss., Harvard University, 2004.

Stalker, James C. "Official English or English Only." *English Journal* 77, no. 3 (Mar. 1988): 18–23.

Stanger, Melissa, and Mike Nudelman. "The Most Famous Book in Every State." *Business Insider*, Oct. 11, 2013. www.businessinsider.com/most-famous-book-set-in-every-state-map-2013-10.

State Library of Arizona. "Election Results." *Ballotpedia: Encyclopedia of American Politics.* https://ballotpedia.org/Arizona_Abolishment_of_Union_Membership_for_Employment,_Proposition_4_(1946).

———. "MLK Day." *State Library of Arizona Virtual Reference Desk.* https://statelibraryofarizona.wordpress.com/martin-luther-king-day.

Steed, Patricia L. "Momaday, N. Scott." *Oklahoma Historical Society's Encyclopedia of Oklahoma History and Culture.* Accessed Sept. 5, 2013. http://digital.library.okstate.ed/encyclopedia/entries/M/MO007.html.

Stegner, Wallace. *Beyond the Hundredth Meridian: John Wesley Powell and the Second Opening of the West.* Boston: Houghton Mifflin, 1954.

———. "George R. Stewart and the American Land." In *Where the Bluebird Sings to the Lemonade Springs: Living and Writing in the West,* 155–71. New York: Random House, 1992.

———. "The Sense of Place." In *Where the Bluebird Sings to the Lemonade Springs: Living and Writing in the West,* 199–206. New York: Random House, 1992.

———. "Wilderness Letter." Dec. 3, 1960. The Wilderness Society. Accessed Nov. 8, 2013. wilderness.org/OurIssues/Wilderness/wildernessletter.cfm; wilderness.org/bios/former-council-members/wallace-stegner.

Steinbeck, John. *Travels with Charley: In Search of America.* New York: Viking, 1962.

Stewart, George R. *Names on the Land: A Historical Account of Place-Naming in the United States.* New York: Random House, 1945.

Strong, Pauline Turner. "New Approaches to American Indian Texts: The Personal Narrative." *Journal of American Ethnic History* 17, no. 3 (Spring 1998): 99–103.

Stull, Ginger C. "Language, Borders, and Education: Language Policy and the Making of New Mexico and Arizona." *Working Papers in Educational Linguistics* 27, no. 1 (2012): 19–27. www.gse.upenn.edu/wpel.

Summerhayes, Martha. *Vanished Arizona: Recollections of the Army Life of a New England Woman,* 2nd ed. Salem, Mass.: Salem Press, 1911. Reprinted by the University of Nebraska Press, 1979.

Tarver, Heidi. "Language and Politics in the 1980s: The Story of U.S. English." *Politics and Society* 17, no. 2 (June 1, 1989). Accessed Nov. 2, 2013. http://pas.sagepub.com/content/17/2/225.citation.

Teague, David W., and Peter Wild. *The Secret Life of John C. Van Dyke: Selected Letters.* Reno: University of Nevada Press, 1997.

Teille, Betty A. *Historical Review of Williams Air Force Base.* Mesa, Ariz.: Mesa Chamber of Commerce, 1993.

Thrapp, Don L., ed. *Dateline Fort Bowie: Charles F. Lummis Reports on the Apache War.* Norman: University of Oklahoma Press, 1979.

Titiev, Mischa. "Review, *Truth of a Hopi.*" *Journal of American Folklore* 50, no. 198 (Oct.–Dec., 1937): 415.

Topping, Gary. "*Arizona Highways*: A Half-Century of Southwestern Journalism." *Journal of the West* 19, no. 2 (Apr. 1980): 71–79.

———. "A History of *Arizona Highways* Magazine, 1925–1970." Master's thesis, Northern Arizona University, 1970.

Towle, Thelma Hall. "Boat Trip to Rainbow Bridge." *Arizona Highways* 41, no. 7 (July 1965): 2–11.

Trimble, Charles E. "The American Indian Press Association . . . A Look Back." Accessed Nov. 22, 2013. iktomisweb.com/Amer_Ind_Press_Assoc.pdf.

Trimble, Marshall. "Arizona: 100 Years and Counting." *Arizona Highways*, centennial issue 88, no. 2 (Feb. 2012): 14–19.

Tuan, Yi-Fu. *Space and Place: The Perspective of Experience*. Minneapolis: University of Minnesota Press, 1997.

———. *Topophilia: A Study of Environmental Perception, Attitudes, and Values*. New York: Columbia University Press, 1974.

Turner, Frederick. *Spirit of Place: The Making of an American Literary Landscape*. San Francisco: Sierra Club Books, 1989.

Udall, David K. *Arizona Pioneer Mormon: David King Udall, His Story and His Family, 1851–1938, written in collaboration with his daughter Pearl Udall Nelson*. Tucson: Arizona Silhouettes, 1959.

Udall, Stewart L. "Arizona—Its Promise and Challenge." *Arizona Days and Ways Magazine*, Feb. 11, 1962, 354.

Underhill, Ruth. *The Autobiography of a Papago Woman*. Memoirs of the American Anthropological Association 46. Menasha, Wis.: American Anthropological Association, 1936.

———. *Singing for Power: The Song Magic of the Papago Indians of Southern Arizona*. Berkeley: University of California Press, 1938.

Union Pacific. "Union Pacific in Arizona." Accessed Aug. 17, 2013. www.up.com/groups/public/documents/up_pdf_nativedocs/pdf_arizona_usguide.pdf.

U.S. Bureau of the Census. "Arizona: Population of Counties by Decennial Census, 1900–1990." Compiled and edited by Richard L. Forstall. www.census.gov/population/cencounts/az190090.txt.

———. "Characteristics of the Population: Number of Inhabitants, Arizona, 1980 Census of Population." www2.census.gov/prod2/decennial/documents/1980a_azABC-01.pdf.

———. "Population Distribution and Change: 2000 to 2010." *2010 Census Briefs*, Mar. 2011.

———. "Resident Population and Apportionment of the U.S. House of Representatives: Arizona." Accessed June 1, 2016. www.census.gov/dmd/www/resapport/states/arizona.pdf.

———. "State and County Quick Facts; Arizona." http://quickfacts.census.gov/qfd/states/04000.html.

———. *Statistical Abstract of the United States, 1961*. Washington, D.C.: Government Printing Office, 1961.

———. *Statistical Abstract of the United States: 1990*. Washington, D.C.: Government Printing Office, 1989.

U.S. Bureau of Labor Statistics. "State Unemployment Rates 2010: The Economics Daily." Mar. 1, 2011. bls.gov.

U.S. Commission on Civil Rights. "Language Rights and New Mexico Statehood." In *The Excluded Student: Educational Practices Affecting Mexican Americans in the Southwest*. Mexican American Education Study, Report III. Washington, D.C.: U.S. Government Printing Office, 1972: 76–82. Accessed Dec. 5, 2013. www.languagepolicy.net/archives/nm-con.htm.

U.S. Department of the Interior, Bureau of Reclamation. "Reclamation and Arizona: The Fruits of Their Labor." www.usbr.gov/lc/Phoenix/Ariz.100/1910/fruits_of_labor.html.

———, Geologic Survey. "Climatic Fluctuations, Drought, and Flow in the Colorado River Basin." USGS Fact Sheet 2004–3062, version 2. pubs.usgs.gov/fs/2004/3062/index.html.

———, National Park Service. "National Park Service Archeology Program: Antiquities Act Centennial." Accessed May 10, 2016. www.nps.gov/archeology/sitemap.htm.

———. Rainbow Bridge National Monument. "History and Culture." www.nps.gov/rabr/historyculture/index.htm.

Unsettling America. "Protect the Sacred San Francisco Peaks!" Accessed Jan. 19, 2014. http://unsettlingamerica.wordpress.com/solidarity-projects/protect-the-sacred-san-francisco-peaks.

Urrea, Luis Alberto. *The Devil's Highway: A True Story*. New York: Little, Brown, 2004.

———. *Nobody's Son: Notes from an American Life*. Tucson: University of Arizona Press, 1998.

VanderMeer, Phillip. *Desert Visions and the Making of Phoenix, 1860–2009*. Albuquerque: University of New Mexico Press, 2012.

Van Dyke, John C. *The Desert: Further Studies in Natural Appearances*. New York: Charles Scribner's Sons, 1901.

Van Dyke, Ruth M. *The Chaco Experience: Landscape and Ideology at the Center Place*. Santa Fe: School for Advanced Research Press, 2007.

"Wallace Stegner: A Word for Wilderness." Wilderness.net. Accessed Nov. 8, 2013. http://wilderness.net/NWPS/Stegner.

Walls, Jeannette. *The Glass Castle: A Memoir*. New York: Scribner, 2005.

———. *Half Broke Horses: A True-Life Novel*. New York: Scribner, 2009.

Walsh, Tom, compl. *1870–1920 Timeline*. Unpublished manuscript, 2015 (personal communication).

Weinstein, Leo. "Bell, Jack. 'Mr. Conservative: Berry Goldwater' (Book Review)." *Annals of the American Academy of Political and Social Science* 345 (Jan. 1, 1963): 152–53.

Weisberger, Bernard A. ed. *The WPA Guide to America: The Best of 1930s America as Seen by the Federal Writers' Project*. New York: Pantheon Books, 1985.

Weiser, Kathy. "History of Goldfield Ghost Town." *Legends of America* (Dec. 2007). Accessed Mar. 5, 2013. http://goldfieldghosttown.com/history.html.

Weisiger, Marsha. *Dreaming of Sheep in Navajo Country*. Seattle: University of Washington Press, 2009.

Welty, Eudora. "Place in Fiction" (1956). In *The Eye of the Story: Selected Essays and Reviews*, 116–33. New York: Random House, 1978.

Weston, James J. "Sharlot Hall: Arizona Pioneer Lady of Literature." *Journal of the West* 4, no. 4 (Oct. 1965): 539–52.

Wild, Peter. *Ann Zwinger*. Boise State University Western Writers Series 111. Boise, Idaho: Boise State University, 1993.

———. "Critical Introduction to the 1999 Edition." In *The Desert: Further Studies in Natural Appearances,* by John C. Van Dyke. Baltimore, Md.: Johns Hopkins University Press, 1999. Originally published by Charles Scribner's Sons, 1901.

———. *The Opal Desert: Explorations of Fantasy and Reality in the American Southwest*. Austin: University of Texas Press, 1999.

Wild, Peter, and Neil Carmony. "The Trip Not Taken: John C. Van Dyke, Heroic Doer or Armchair Seer?" *Journal of Arizona History* 34, no. 1 (Spring 1993): 65–80.

Wiley, Peter, and Robert Gottlieb. *Empires in the Sun: The Rise of the New American West*. New York: G. P. Putnam's Sons, 1982.

Winchester, Juti A. "'So Glad God Let Me be an Outdoor Woman': The Conservationist Writing of Sharlot Mabridth Hall." *Journal of the West* 44, no. 4 (Oct. 2005): 18–25.

Wood, Rob, and Dean Smith. *Barry Goldwater—The Biography of a Conservative*. New York: Hearst Corp., Avon Books, 1961.

Woodin, Ann. *Home Is the Desert*. New York: Macmillan, 1964.

Woodroof, Wilford. Official Declaration 1. Accessed July 6, 2016. www.lds.org/scriptures/dc-testament/od/1.

Woodward, Charles L. *Ancestral Voice: Conversations with N. Scott Momaday*. Lincoln: University of Nebraska Press, 1989.

Wrobel, David M. *Global West, American Frontier: Travel, Empire, and Exceptionalism from Manifest Destiny to the Great Depression*. Albuquerque: University of New Mexico Press, 2013.

———. *Promised Lands: Promotion, Memory, and the Creation of the American West*. Lawrence: University Press of Kansas, 2002.

Wrobel, David M., and Michael C. Steiner, eds. *Many Wests; Place, Culture, and Regional Identity*. Lawrence: University Press of Kansas, 1997.

Wycoff, William. *Creating Colorado: The Making of a Western American Landscape, 1860–1940*. New Haven, Conn.: Yale University Press, 1999.

Wyman, Leland C. "Book Reviews, North and South America." *American Anthropologist,* New Series 41, no. 2 (Apr.–June 1939): 309.

Zen Pathfinder. "Arizona Snowbowl Violates City Permit and State Law, Complaint Filed." Dec. 26, 2012. TrueSnow.org.

Zwinger, Ann. *Beyond the Aspen Grove*. New York: Random House, 1970. Reprinted by the University of Arizona Press, 1988.

———. *The Mysterious Desert Lands: A Naturalist Explores the Four Great Deserts of the Southwest*. New York: Truman Talley, 1989.

———. "Writers of the Purple Figwort." In *Old Southwest, New Southwest: Essays on a Region and Its Literature,* edited by Judy Nolte Lensink. Tucson, Ariz.: Tucson Public Library, 1987.

INDEX

CPSIA information can be obtained
at www.ICGtesting.com
Printed in the USA
FFOW05n2027310817

9 780806 157382